THE JUST WAR
AND JIHAD

THE JUST WAR AND JIHAD

VIOLENCE IN JUDAISM, CHRISTIANITY, AND ISLAM

EDITED BY R. JOSEPH HOFFMANN

Chair, Committee for the Scientific Evaluation
of Religion at the Center for Inquiry

 Prometheus Books

Published 2006 by Prometheus Books

Inquiries should be addressed to
Prometheus Books
59 John Glenn Drive
Amherst, New York 14228–2197
VOICE: 716–691–0133, ext. 207
FAX: 716–564–2711
WWW.PROMETHEUSBOOKS.COM

10 09 08 07 06   5 4 3 2 1

Library of Congress Cataloging-in-Publication Data

The just war and jihad : violence in Judaism, Christianity, and Islam / edited by R. Joseph Hoffmann.
    p. cm.
Includes bibliographical references.
ISBN 1–59102–371–8 (hardcover : alk. paper)
    1. Violence—Religious aspects. 2. War—Religious aspects. 3. Just war doctrine. 4. Jihad. I. Hoffmann, R. Joseph.

BL65.V55J87 2006
201'.7273—dc22

2005027864

Printed in the United States of America on acid-free paper

CONTENTS

INTRODUCTION

THE GOD OF HOSTS

R. Joseph Hoffmann

The papers collected in this volume represent the independent and considered thinking of scholars from a variety of disciplines concerning the relationship between religion and violence, with special reference to the theories of "just war" and "jihad," technical terms that arise in connection with the theology of early medieval Christianity and early Islam, respectively.

In the long history of the monotheistic tradition, violence—often-bloody violence and warfare—has been not an occasional abnormality but its defining activity. Leaving aside ancient conflicts, like the violent taking of Canaan by the Hebrew tribes, and focusing simply on reviewing how the two younger of the monotheistic traditions has treated the eldest, the pattern is well established before the Middle Ages and prior to the preaching of the First Crusade (1095): the following list does not deal specifically with the wars of religion, prompted by the Protestant Reformation, the deaths of heretics by the thousands during the Inquisition, or the loss of life in contemporary struggles between Islam and the other monotheistic traditions.

554, at Clermont, slaughter of Jews and forced baptism of 500

1032, Fez, Muslim troops kill 6,000 Jews in bid to reconquer Spain

1066, Grenada, 4,000 Jews killed

1096, Germany, from Mainz to Speyer, thousands of Jews slaughtered

1099, Christian slaughter of Jews and Muslims in Jerusalem

1148, Christians and Jews in Islamic Spain forced to accept Islam or die

1236, across France, 3,000 Jews killed in a failed attempt to organize a Crusade

1298, professional "Jew Killers" move across Germany, looting, burning, and killing as many as 4,000 Jews

1328, 5,000 Jews killed in Navarre

1209, Beziers, Christian forces kill 20,000 Albigensian heretics—fellow Christians—and hundreds of Jews

1614, Frankfurt, 2,000 Jews killed

1032, Fez, Muslim troops kill 6,000 Jews in bid to reconquer Spain

As religion has become more innocuous and less influential, and war ostensibly a secular and political matter in the modern era, it has become easier to forget that Judaism, Christianity, and Islam were the chief propagators of war in the ancient world, during the Middle Ages, and throughout the Reformation. Religious warfare and religiously inspired "terrorism" are nothing new. The right to domination of the land—especially the Holy Land of what was once Roman Palestine—has been central to this quarrel between religious siblings, a Book-condoned state of affairs thought to originate in commands given by God to his various chosen peoples. The calculus of religious violence can be traced from ancient Mesopotamia to the Crusades, from India and Pakistan to Northern Ireland, from the highlands of Papua New Guinea to train stations in Madrid—and even to the political arena of "mainstream" American religion's inconclusive encounter with a resurgent fundamentalist Christianity. The last of these—religious liberalism versus the Christian (including the Catholic) Right—is a sinister example of how liberal *ennui* can lead to the demise of both liberal religion and humanism without a shot being fired by a well-armed, organized, and determined religious opposition, one which still believes that the "God of the Mighty Battle Line" regards its cause as synonymous with patriotic wars around the globe: thus, violent not that they are armed, but violent in condoning a state of violence in the name of their God. The "just war" calculus of the Neoconservative-Evangelical alliance is sufficient to render a term like "state-sponsored terrorism," if thought only to apply to violent excursions against the West by Islamic militants, indefinable.

The struggle continues—not only in the Arab-Israeli conflict, that strange combination of secular logic and jihadist intent—but now on a worldwide scale, as if the God of Hosts had been wakened from a long winter nap, thirsty for blood and energized by the vulnerable state of human affairs. The Yahweh-god of Abraham, god-the-Trinity, the Father of Jesus Christ, and Allah-god, the Compassionate, the Merciful, who spoke through the Prophet Muhammad, if ever truly one and the same (as liberal religious writers and inclusivists like to insist) has now devolved into a triad of powers which threaten the world with their wrath for ignoring the threat Abraham's God once directed at Moses: "If you spurn me, and if your soul abhors my laws, . . . I will do this to you: I will appoint over you sudden terror, consumption, fever that wastes the eyes and causes life to slip away. . . . I will set my face against you and you shall be smitten before your enemies; those who hate you shall rule over you, and you shall flee when none pursues you" (Lev. 26:14–17). Given such dialogue, a believer can be excused for thinking that the current wave of religiously induced terror and violence is nothing more than the fulfillment of ancient promises.

Similarly, if progressive Jews, Christians, and Muslims find such outbreaks of divine wrath and punishing anger atavistic, embarrassing, and out of keeping with the times, they are frankly guilty of not knowing their family story: the God of Hosts—the poetic subterfuge for the word "armies"—has always been quick to ignite ("a jealous God am I, transferring the sins of a father down to the third and fourth generations of those who hate me" [Exod. 20:5]) and has always threatened vengeance of cosmic proportions for not keeping his laws. Those laws, abusive in themselves, have supported what we would today regard as the basest human institutions and sentiments: cultural arrogance, slavery, subjugation of women, indifference to the young, subservience to violent authority, and, not least, tolerance of war as a first resort to defend oneself against all "enemies of God." Lest this last phrase be thought particularly resonant with Western views of Muslim rhetoric, westerners should be reminded of the American president's Manichaen paradigm: equating freedom and democracy as the forces of Good, and all else—every sort of political aspiration in conflict with curiously framed and even more curiously explained "democratic values"—the forces of Evil. The pursuit of freedom and democracy globally has become a method of distracting a credulous public from the pursuit of the *Magnalia Dei Americana*—the mighty acts of God, wrought on behalf of America. If it seems overemphatic to state the religio-economic foundation for much of America's current involvement with the world, it is because that involvement seems lacking any recognition that it resembles its most noxious opponents, opponents thought to be driven to fanatical extremes by the "terror texts of their tradition," more closely than at any time in modern history. Guantanamo, Abu Ghraib, and Fallujah will live in memory as grim reminders that Pogo was right: "We have met the enemy and he is us."

Defining exactly who *is* an enemy of God has been the overarching theme of the monotheistic traditions since their vague beginnings some thirty-five hundred years ago. The reason for the inbred violence of the Abrahamic faiths has been guessed about for over a hundred years, but a general recognition is that these traditions are really the victims, not the benefactors, of what for many would seem to be their distinctive contribution to Western society: belief in only one God. The reduction of a complex polytheism to an efficient monotheism has often been seen as one of civilization's great moments, just as the Gnostic opposite (unity of being replaced by a multiplicity of beings) was seen as intolerable heresy by the early Christian church—which nonetheless found itself sufficiently Gnosticized to settle on three "gods" in one.

Contemporary social analysis of monotheism has not been theologically generous, however. The god who replaced the gods of ancient and Hellenistic worlds, the complacent, often otiose, sometimes frivolous, always querulous, or frankly appetitive gods, male and female, was a god of law, to be sure, and a god of vengeance. He stood, in the language of the psalm, like a bulwark against murder, fornication, and theft—actions that at a purely social level the ancient world deplored as crimes (not sins) against tribal harmony. But the greater part of the divine *persona* was wrath directed against "those who hate his laws": a blend of idolaters, foreigners, sorcerers, heretics, homosexuals, drunken sons, dismissed wives, disobedient slaves, and above all the catch-all remainder of "those who do not do his will." The Abrahamic god must be understood in terms of two words: exclusivity and judgment. Unlike the gods of Greek and Roman antiquity with whom he struggled for place, the Lord of Hosts reigns without temporizing influences, the pleas of daughters or chiding of wives.[1] His rule is not an exercise in fraternal power sharing, and the wars whose outcome he decides is not the result of a decision made in council. The leviathan god of monotheism is the source and model for concepts of sovereignty and absolute monarchy as these have developed in the cultures of the Middle East and Europe. As Rodney Stark has commented:

The image of God that is most potent in terms of social effects is [also] . . . the most dangerous. It is precisely God as a conscious, responsive, good, supreme being of infinite scope—the One True God as conceived by the great monotheisms—who prompts awareness of idolatry, false Gods, and heretical religions. Particularism, the belief that a given religion is the only true religion, is inherent in monotheism.[2]

So also is violence. What Stark bands "particularism" as applied to a religion's claim to possess an exclusive purchase on theological truth is the source of antagonism and violence between religious faiths equally committed to their particular tradition. It is the source of hostility between Christianity and classical civilization, Christian anti-Semitism, early Islamic reprobation of Judaism, contemporary Islamic disdain for the Crusader culture of the West, and contemporary Western contempt for Islam in general. The strife between the great monotheistic traditions, of course, does not exhaust the antagonisms that monotheism incurs: conflicts among factions—Sunnis, Shiites, Sufis; Protestants and Catholics; Chasidic, Orthodox, and Reform Jews—may appear more dysfunctional than potentially dangerous, but they point up the fact that particularist religions are characterized by both interfaith rivalry and intrafaith hostilities. "If monothesists believe there is only One True God," Stark suggests, "they have been unable to sustain One True Religion. . . . Internal and external conflict is inherent in particularist religion."[3]

*   *   *

A famous BBC comedy of the seventies, *Bless Me, Father*, presented a loveable Father Duddleswell engaging an Anglican vicar in theological discussion. "The problem with you Anglicans," says the priest, "is that you don't believe in hell." To which the vicar replies, "And I suppose you Catholics do?" "Oh yes," says the priest. "We just don't believe anyone actually goes there anymore." Our temptation is to smile, when one should ask the difference between religions that no longer believe what they preach and religions that no longer preach what they believe. To the extent that doctrines like hell, the judgment of God, the resurrection of the elect, and the associated dogmas of religious particularism are no longer believed, intellectual honesty would seem to require the removal of their textual sources to the fiction section of libraries. Religious moderation and religious liberalism would seem to be the confessional equivalent of keeping unloaded guns in the house with no ammunition, just in case. As Sam Harris observes in *The End of Faith*, there are dangers to this procedure, since what is often described as religious moderation is "the product of secular knowledge and scriptural ignorance."[4] The religious liberal—perhaps especially the liberal Christian—is able to maintain his theological position by ignoring the gun in the closet or simply being ignorant of the fact his father didn't throw it out. But from the standpoint of those seeking to live according to the letter of the text which is the foundation of religious particularism, "the religious moderate is nothing but a failed fundamentalist. . . . The benignity of most religious moderates does not suggest that faith is anything more sublime than a desperate marriage of hope and ignorance, nor does it guarantee that there is not a terrible price to be paid for limiting the scope of reason in our dealings with other human beings."[5]

Moreover, the God of Hosts is not an empty gun in an out of the way closet. Recent political activity shows that his thirst for blood is unslaked, on the streets of Tel Aviv, on the West Bank, in Beirut, in New York and Paris, Nigeria, Indonesia, Spain, Iraq, the Sudan. Although it sometimes seems to be the case that one form of particularism—Islam—is more often implicated in acts of religious violence than others, one must ask whether this is so not because Islam is the most violent of the monotheistic religions, but because it is the particularist religion most in touch with its textual and historical origins. Perhaps, as Stark points out, it should not be concluded that Islam and Christianity are the only monotheists ready "to go to extreme lengths in behalf of their true faith."[6] Although because of their numbers Jews were seldom in a position to attack unbelievers, their traditions, above all their sacred writings, make them very much a part of the tournament to claim the One True God as their own. Religions "become" violent when significant threats are posed to their identity, and in the monotheistic faiths, these threats are rooted in common history; imagery; shared ideas of prophecy, destiny, and finality; reward and punishment; the causes of God's wrath; and the human necessity for his mercy. Fundamentally, this is a conflict about how to read the "will" of God, a conversation in which those armed with the written word in its unequivocal clarity are far better off than interpreters and allegorists who presume—like an Origen or an Averroes—to know better than the common believer what the word really says.

The papers collected here offer a valuable introduction to a subject that is at once provocative and perplexing: how in an age defined by scientific inquiry the ancient conflicts over the will and purpose of Abraham's God still sap the energies of politicians, academics, and ordinary women and men in cities and villages around the world. This, needless to say, is not a book of answers but an anthology of ideas. The fellows of the Committee for the Scientific Examination of Religion offer it as a resource for further discussion, reflection, and action.

R. Joseph Hoffmann
Chair, Committee for the Scientific Evaluation of Religion

NOTES

1. Though some see the cult of Mary as repairing this deficiency in Christian monotheism.
2. Rodney Stark, *One True God: Historical Consequences of Monotheism* (Princeton, NJ: Princeton University Press, 2001), p. 116.
3. Ibid., p. 117.
4. Sam Harris, *The End of Faith: Religion Terror and the Future of Reason* (New York: W. W. Norton, 2004), p. 21.
5. Ibid., pp. 20, 21.
6. Stark, *One True God*, p. 171.

1

SOME CENTRAL PROBLEMS IN JUST WAR THEORY

Judith Lichtenberg

T hose who think seriously about the ethical dilemmas raised by instigating and participating in warfare find a ready-made framework for sorting out the issues in just war theory, a body of thought dating back to Augustine in the late fourth century. Although Augustine said less about war than his place as father of the just war tradition would suggest, Aquinas's teachings nine hundred years later vindicate the association of the theory with medieval Christianity. Thinkers such as Francisco de Vitoria, Francisco Suarez, Hugo Grotius, and Emerich de Vattel developed the just war tradition between the fifteenth and eighteenth centuries; later political philosophers like John Stuart Mill and Henry Sidgwick also made contributions.

For contemporary academics and military officers, the source most commonly taught and consulted in thinking about just war is no doubt Michael Walzer's *Just and Unjust Wars: A Moral Argument with Historical Illustrations.*[1] First published in 1977, shortly after the Vietnam War, the book wrestles with the dilemmas posed by real violence and political conflict, especially the bloody history of the twentieth century. Other articles and books published since the 1970s have contributed to a full-scale renaissance of just war theory.

In this essay I focus on three central questions debated within contemporary just war theory. The first concerns two problem cases in the justification for waging war: the continuum of preemptive-preventive war, and armed humanitarian intervention. The second has to do with the distinction between combatants and noncombatants and its relation to the principle of noncombatant immunity, one of the fundamental tenets of just war. The third concerns the viability of the distinction within just war theory between *jus ad bellum* and *jus in bello*. The second and third problems are related, in ways that will become clear.

JUSTIFYING *AD BELLUM*

Just war theory has traditionally been divided into two sharply separated parts. *Jus ad bellum* concerns the justifications for waging war, *jus in bello* the rules that govern warfare once fighting has begun. In Walzer's analysis, which undergirds post–World War II doctrine as set out in the United Nations Charter,[2] the justifications for waging war derive from the "legalist paradigm," a set of precepts governing international relations. The central premise of the legalist paradigm is that the international order consists of sovereign states, and that "use of force or imminent threat of force by one state against the political sovereignty or territorial integrity of another constitutes aggression and is a criminal act."[3] Aggression justifies self-defense by its victim, and (it is generally agreed) assistance by other states that may come to the victim state's defense. (The first Gulf war, in which the United States came to the aid of Kuwait, which had been invaded by Iraq, is an example.) But self-defense (and third-party assistance) is not easily distinguishable from two other kinds of violent response generally held to be legitimate: law enforcement and punishment.

In recent years just war theorists and others interested in the limits of legitimate war have focused especially on two questions within *jus ad bellum.*

Preemptive and Preventive War

The paradigm of justified self-defense occurs when an aggressor invades another state. But, as in individual cases, to wait to respond until after being attacked can be to wait too long. As Walzer argues, "Both individuals and states can rightfully defend themselves against violence that is imminent but not actual; they can fire the first shots if they know themselves about to be attacked."[4] The central questions, then, are when one "knows" that one is about to be attacked, and how far the aggressor state must go before preemptive action is warranted.

In 1842 then-secretary of state Daniel Webster offered a strict interpretation of preemptive action. It must be shown, he asserted, that there is "a necessity of self-defense . . . instant, overwhelming, leaving no choice of means, and no moment for deliberation."[5] As Walzer argues, Webster's view "would permit us to do little more than respond to an attack *once we had seen it coming* but before we had felt its impact,"[6] and for this reason many would defend a more permissive account of preemptive action. But as the threat becomes less imminent, preemptive attack shades into preventive war, which by definition responds to a more distant danger and is therefore more difficult to justify. The war against Iraq, sometimes described by administration officials and others as preemptive, was—at best—preventive.[7]

Although some defend preventive war, it does not fit easily within the legalist paradigm. Potential aggression is not aggression, and the possibility of force is not identical with the imminent threat of force. That matter aside, allowing preventive war seems to open the floodgates. Walzer denies that preventive war is justifiable, and Luban argues that "giving a green light to preventive war would

make wars too frequent and too routine."[8] Recently some philosophers have argued against the legitimacy of preventive war on
deontological grounds: that it is impermissible to attack someone
who hasn't harmed you.[9] An argument of this kind, however, would
seem to extend to preemptive strikes as well, and some will find
that conclusion troubling.

Humanitarian Intervention

The question whether a state is morally permitted, or even morally
obligated, to intervene militarily in the affairs of another state has
become pressing over the last decades as we have witnessed brutal
violence against members of ethnic groups in Bosnia, Kosovo,
Rwanda, Somalia, and elsewhere. Armed humanitarian intervention appears to run counter to the legalist paradigm, according to
which states possess sovereignty and sovereignty forbids interfer-
ence by outsiders in a state's internal affairs. Yet it defies belief that
the United States (or any other country) would have done wrong by
intervening to stop the Rwanda genocide of 1994. Indeed, many
believe that the countries of the world did wrong *not* to intervene.

Walzer permits armed humanitarian intervention when the acts
it responds to "shock the moral conscience of mankind."[10] But his
defense of intervention takes place within the framework of the
legalist paradigm; humanitarian intervention has the character of an
exception justified by the gravity of the offenses committed (or at
least not prevented) by the state in question. Others have concluded
that the awkwardness humanitarian intervention creates for the
legalist paradigm demonstrates the defectiveness of the paradigm,
and specifically its centerpiece, the supremacy of state sovereignty.
At the very least, on this view, we should say that only legitimate
states possess sovereignty, and that states engaging in significant
human rights violations of their own people lack legitimacy.[11] We
thus reject their claim that what they do within their own borders is
their business alone.

But thinking about humanitarian intervention may impel a more wholesale reconsideration of the legalist paradigm and the supremacy of state sovereignty. Is state sovereignty a fundamental right or a basic value? Some who believe the answer is yes rest that conclusion on the view that states embody values that cannot be reduced to the interests or goods of individuals. Such a collectivist or organic view has often been criticized as obcurantist, incompatible with liberal values, or both. But there is nothing problematic either metaphysically or politically with the belief that entities such as cultures and the natural environment can have intrinsic value. Even if cultures have intrinsic value, however, it's implausible to think that they can be identified with modern nation-states or that nation-states are necessarily their best protectors. Moreover, it may be argued that the value of cultures, even if intrinsic, must take second place to the interests of individuals.

Some would insist, however, that *only* individuals have intrinsic value: "all goods and value in human affairs derive ultimately from persons and the valuations they individually and collectively make."[12] On this view, the value of state sovereignty derives from its ability to advance the interests of individuals; put another way, sovereignty must be reducible ultimately to individual values. And the most we are likely to be able to say on this score is that sometimes sovereignty does protect individual interests and sometimes it doesn't.

Thus, whether we believe that nonindividual entities like cultures can have intrinsic value or not, there are a variety of reasons for thinking that state sovereignty is at best an instrumental value. States cannot be identified with cultures; the value of cultures, even if intrinsic, is probably secondary to that of individuals; and states often violate the human rights of individuals within and outside their borders. The protection of individual interests (embodied, for example, in human rights), then, should be the benchmark by which we judge when state sovereignty may be infringed.[13]

NONCOMBATANT IMMUNITY

The central problem of *jus in bello* concerns the principle of non-combatant immunity, a fundamental tenet of just war theory according to which it is never permissible to attack noncombatants.[14] The principle can be found in Jewish, Christian, and Islamic writings and is enshrined in the Geneva Conventions.[15]

It's obvious that to interpret the principle we need a definition of "noncombatant" and a way to distinguish combatants from non-combatants. Sometimes the terms "civilians" and "soldiers" are used as if they were synonyms for "noncombatant" and "combatant" respectively, although whether the groups are coextensive remains to be seen (and I will argue that they are not). The underlying purpose is to distinguish between the class of people who are legitimate targets and the class of people who are not.

Assuming that at least some wars are just and therefore that lethal attacks on some of the enemy's people are legitimate, the question is whether certain classes of people in enemy territory or under the enemy state's sovereignty should be immune from attack. If the answer is yes, we need to sort people into the relevant categories, distinguishing the immune from the not immune.

It is natural to think of the moral principle underlying noncombatant immunity in terms of the idea of innocence. We speak of "innocent civilians" and "innocent women and children." As the Catholic philosopher Elizabeth Anscombe asserts, "It is one of the most vehement and repeated teachings of the Judaeo-Christian tradition that the shedding of innocent blood is forbidden by the divine law."[16] The inference is that it is sometimes permissible to attack those who are not innocent.

But what makes a person innocent? Two different factors, often confused, seem relevant and have played a part in analyses of legitimate violence. One has to do with a person's moral culpability, which depends on what she wills or what is in her control. In this sense the extreme opposite of innocence is *mens rea*, "guilty mind," which typically means that a person *intends* to commit a criminal act. People are sometimes culpable even when no evil intent occurs, however—for example, when they act recklessly or negligently. They can be culpable in such cases because their actions, or inactions, are within their control. And those who *desire* evil may possess a degree of moral culpability even if they do not carry out their wishes.

But moral culpability does not seem to track the distinction between combatants and noncombatants. Some noncombatants are culpable, and some combatants are not. As George Mavrodes argues,

> a person may be an enthusiastic supporter of a war . . . he may give it his voice and his vote, he may have done everything in his power to procure it when it was yet but a prospect, now that it is in progress he may contribute to it both his savings and the work which he knows best how to do, and he may avidly hope to share in the unjust gains which will follow if the war is successful.

And yet he is by the usual standards a noncombatant. "On the other hand," Mavrodes continues,

> a young man of limited mental ability and almost no education may be drafted, put into uniform, trained for a few weeks, and sent to the front. . . . He may have no understanding of what the war is about, and no heart for it. He might want nothing more than to go back to his town and the life he led before.[17]

The soldier may live under a dictatorship in which he has no real choice but to serve in the armed forces. Even if he lives in a democratic society without a draft, he may come from circumstances in which the army is the best of a bad set of options. Yet he is a combatant.

These observations suggest that the distinction between combatants and noncombatants does not necessarily track moral culpability. That leads us to the other theory, which draws the distinction in terms of the harm, or the threat of harm, that combatants pose to their enemies.[18] On this view, combatants are legitimate targets because they engage in harming and threatening harm; attacking them is therefore a form of self-defense (or the defense of third parties). Noncombatants do not harm or threaten harm and thus are immune from attack. We might call this the *causal account* of the distinction between combatants and noncombatants, to be contrasted with the *moral account* discussed earlier.

Taken in its pure form, the causal account of noncombatant immunity permits attacking so-called innocent threats, those who pose a threat without intending or being in any way responsible for the harm they threaten. Philosophers have dreamt up weird science-fiction examples of innocent threats, but we now have real ones ready to hand. Passengers on the planes heading to the World Trade Center were innocent threats; if time had permitted shooting down the planes before they crashed into the buildings the pure causal theory would justify doing so. Innocent threats pose a difficult case for morally conscientious action, and philosophers like Rodin and McMahan deny that innocent threats are legitimate targets.

Several points are worth noting in assessing and comparing the moral and causal accounts of legitimate violence.

1. On both theories, the distinction between combatants and noncombatants is vague, not black and white. People can be more or less culpable, and more or less threatening or dangerous. So on either account there can be borderline cases, and cases that contradict the identification of legitimate targets with soldiers and the immune class with civilians. The civilian leader of a government may be a legitimate target because he is morally responsible for aggression. The munitions worker may be a legitimate target because he is involved in the production of lethal weapons.

2. In many cases, the two theories may identify the same individuals. The morally culpable person typically does or threatens harm. This is true in the paradigm case of individual self-defense, which often provides the background for our thinking about justifying violence in war: the criminal harms or threatens harm, and does so intentionally.

3. Such cases, where moral and causal responsibility coexist, might lead some to say that *both* are necessary to justify attacking a person, or at least that this is the ideal case (if we can speak about ideal cases in these circumstances). And they may believe that ordinary soldiers fit this description—they harm or threaten harm, and are also morally culpable for what they do. But the moral and the causal do not always go together, and to require both would be to justify violence in fewer cases than we usually do.

4. I propose the following hypothesis: moral culpability tends to suggest causal responsibility, because moral culpability of any kind increases the chances of harm. This is clear in the case of the leader of an aggressive state: his actions and pronouncements are more than simply a small set of the myriad necessary conditions for war to occur. But it is also true to a lesser degree of supportive civilians, even if their support is only tacit: their behavior makes harm to the enemy more likely. The reverse, however, does not hold: being causally responsible for a harm—think of the innocent threat—does not imply being morally culpable.

Despite widespread commitment in principle to noncombatant immunity (cynical people might call it lip service), the principle is sometimes breached, even by those we believe have just cause on their side, and the breaches may even be defended. The Allied bombings of German and Japanese cities in World War II constitute the most telling case.[19] Some, whom we may call absolutists, refuse to allow breach of the principle no matter what the consequences. But few people adhere to such a pure view. Once we admit to exceptions, how do we define and cabin them? Walzer suggests two alternatives: the "sliding scale" and the "supreme emergency" view. According to the sliding-scale view, "the greater the justice of my cause, the more rules I can violate for the sake of the cause."[20] Walzer should also have added a necessity clause: the greater the justice of my cause and *the more violating a rule is necessary for my cause to prevail*, the greater my justification in violating the rule. By contrast, the supreme-emergency view allows a "sudden breach" of the rule, "but only after holding out for a long time against the process of erosion."[21] The difference between the two approaches has to do at least partly with the presumed psychological effects of departing from the principle. Walzer suggests that those who adopt the supreme emergency exception will be more reluctant to violate the principle of noncombatant immunity than adherents of the sliding scale and will bear a useful sense of guilt when they do violate it.

Two points are worth noting here. One is that even though the principle of noncombatant immunity is as sacred a rule of war as we will find, many thoughtful people allow exceptions to it. The other is the seeming disconnect between a theoretical willingness to allow exceptions on the one hand and a desire that practitioners "on the ground" treat the rule as sacred or nearly so. The disconnect arises from the fear that those who don't treat the rules as sacred will tumble down the slippery slope and fail to take them seriously at all. Whether this concern is warranted depends on facts about human psychology about which we need to learn more.

My own view is that the distinction between combatants and noncombatants cannot be made in a way that justifies the principle of noncombatant immunity as it is usually understood. The reason is that, as I have argued, neither the moral nor the causal account closely tracks the distinction between soldiers and civilians. Consider first the moral account. Some civilians are morally culpable— they give moral, intellectual, financial, or material support to the war. Some soldiers are morally innocent—either because they occupy noncombat roles and do not fight, or because they are not free *not* to fight, and it would be beyond the call of duty for them to resist the roles that have been thrust upon them. This last category is, I believe, the most telling. Consider soldiers fighting for Saddam Hussein or Adolf Hitler. Did they have a genuine choice about whether to fight or not? If not, they are not morally culpable, and a principle of noncombatant immunity rooted in culpability will not justify attacking them.[22]

If we may nevertheless attack such soldiers, another basis must be found. The basis generally offered is that they are harming us or threatening harm. What constitutes harming or threatening harm? In some cases it's clear: these soldiers are shooting guns at us or dropping bombs on us. But once we depart from the immediate production of harm, things get murky. Many soldiers are not engaged in causing or threatening harm—the cooks and medics, the photographers for the army newspaper. Yet they are nevertheless considered combatants, because they support those who directly cause harm. But many noncombatants also provide support, material or moral, essential to the war effort. Workers in munitions factories and employees of the Defense Department are the obvious cases, but there are many others. Even what we call moral support can become tangible and causally efficacious.

It may be argued that even if the standard distinction between soldiers and civilians is rough and crude, it's still useful, the best we've got, and that it undergirds the principle of noncombatant immunity. I agree that the principle and the distinction are useful, but they should be defended primarily on pragmatic grounds rather than in terms either of morality or causality. Following Mavrodes, I would say that the principle of noncombatant immunity is a useful convention designed to keep war contained within tolerable limits. Mavrodes imagines how a nation's leader, contemplating the "costliness of war . . . in human life and human suffering," might arrive at such a view:

> Under this convention, when two nations arrived at an impasse which would otherwise have resulted in war they would instead choose, each of them, a single champion (doubtless a volunteer). These two men would then meet in mortal combat, and whoever won, killing his opponent or driving him from the field, would win for his nation.[23]

Thus much bloodshed could be spared, to the same effect as all-out war.

On the one hand, soldiers are generally no more culpable than civilians; on the other, the participation and support of civilians is often essential for the war effort to succeed. Still, it's useful to declare some individuals legitimate targets and others off-limits. Wars would be even more ghastly if we didn't.

THE DISTINCTION BETWEEN
JUS AD BELLUM AND *JUS IN BELLO*

The distinction between *jus ad bellum* and *jus in bello* is deeply embedded in just war theory. According to this view, assessing the legitimacy of making war is one thing, assessing the conduct of the war another. We might call this view *the independence thesis*: a just war can be fought unjustly and an unjust war can be fought justly.[24]

But philosophers such as Jeff McMahan and David Rodin have recently called the independence thesis into question, emphasizing an oddness about the distinction and in the very idea that there can be rules governing the conduct of war. As Rodin puts it:

> If an aggressive war is fought within the bounds of *jus in bello*, then the Just War Theory is committed to the seemingly para-doxical position that the war taken as a whole is a crime, yet that each of the individual acts which together constitute the aggres-sive war are entirely lawful. Such a war, the Just War Theory seems to be saying, is both just and unjust at the same time.[25]

McMahan offers a detailed argument (simplified here) defending *the dependence thesis*. It aims to show that those who fight for an unjust cause will, almost inevitably, violate one of the fundamental rules of *jus in bello*, the requirement of proportionality. According to this requirement, "for an act of war to be permissible, its bad effects must not be out of proportion to the good."[26]

The bad effects of an act of war—killing and injuring people, harming property—are clear enough. What are the good effects?

Imagine an act of war contemplated by the Nazis during World War II. Increasing the chances of the Nazis' victory is *not* a good effect. The good effects—those that would justify violence—must take into account the interests of all affected, not simply those of the group contemplating the act. Indeed, it seems that no act of war by the Nazis could satisfy the proportionality requirement, because their aims are in no sense good. Thus McMahan argues for the general conclusion that "unjust combatants cannot participate in war without doing wrong."[27]

But the dependence thesis runs counter to traditional just war theory. Certainly we don't think of the typical soldier, even the "unjust combatant," as a criminal, even when he kills soldiers who (unlike him) have justice on their side. And both McMahan and Rodin agree that the unjust combatant who kills is not a murderer. So how do we reconcile this judgment with the claim that unjust combatants do wrong?

One way to reconcile them, explored by both Rodin and McMahan, is via the concept of excuse. The distinction between justification and excuse plays an important role in the criminal law. To *justify* an action is to show that although ordinarily it would be wrong, in the case at hand it is not; the wrongness is completely erased. When we *excuse* an action, by contrast, the wrongness remains but the agent's responsibility is diminished or denied.[28] To successfully plead self-defense to a charge of murder is to justify homicide, not to excuse it. To successfully plead insanity to a charge of murder is to excuse the act, not to justify it.

If we believe unjust combatants do wrong but hesitate to condemn them as we would ordinary criminals, we might argue that they act under duress, a standard excuse in the criminal law that reduces culpability. Rodin notes, however, that "duress is not generally thought to provide a legal or moral excuse for wrongful killing," and that English law "holds that a man ought rather to die himself, than escape by performing a wrongful act of killing."[29]

McMahan distinguishes between responsibility and culpability, arguing that although unjust combatants are responsible for their actions they may not be culpable and their actions may be fully excused. He distinguishes between fault in the act and fault in the agent, arguing that the agent may lack fault even when the act is faulty; he also allows that "there can be responsibility even in the absence of fault in the act."[30] It's not easy to sort out the meaning or implications of these claims, and it would take us too far afield to attempt to do so here. Whatever we make of them, McMahan believes that "it is true of most unjust combatants that their conduct is excused to varying degrees. . . ."[31]

On Rodin's view, however, the conduct of most unjust combatants is not *altogether* excused if, as seems plausible, the defense of their actions is some variant of duress. Thus they would still be culpable to some degree, a conclusion out of sync with traditional just war theory and, I believe, with popular thinking about the matter.[32] If instead we completely excuse the typical unjust combatant, the question is why we should then say his actions are wrong. Wholesale exoneration of a group's behavior seems to undermine the point of condemning its actions.

The dilemma arises in other cases as well. We condemn slavery in past societies yet we might hesitate to condemn slaveholders. If we hesitate, it's because we think the individuals in question weren't culpable. Why weren't they culpable? Not only because (we would say) they didn't believe slavery was wrong but because it would be unreasonable to expect them to have so believed. At the same time, we don't want to say that slavery "wasn't wrong for *them.*" It's not clear whether distinguishing between the evaluation of acts and the evaluation of agents solves the problem or simply avoids having to solve it.

This is the place to remind ourselves of the reasons to maintain a sharp line between *jus ad bellum* and *jus in bello*—to endorse the independence thesis—and the reasons to blur the line. The reasons for maintaining the sharp line seem to be rooted in pragmatic considerations. If unjust combatants inevitably do wrong—do wrong simply by fighting at all—then once having taken up arms, they have no incentive to fight with restraint: might as well be hung for a sheep as a lamb. We want to give soldiers incentives to limit the violence they do, and maintaining the distinction between *jus ad bellum* and *jus in bello* provides an incentive. The independence thesis assumes that expecting ordinary people to make reasonable judgments about the legitimacy of their nation's war is expecting too much.

On the other hand, while the independence thesis in one way provides soldiers incentives toward restraint, in another way it lets them off the hook, precisely because it permits them not to question the legitimacy of taking up arms. And we might think that it would be better if ordinary people *did* raise that question. What if soldiers believed that they might someday be held responsible for taking up arms? Might that reduce the total amount of pointless violence in the world?

It may seem that everything depends on how we answer these questions. But remember also that some who insist on the dependence thesis, like McMahan, at the same time absolve (most) unjust combatants of culpability for their actions. That seems to undermine the advantages of the dependence thesis. If we don't hold soldiers accountable for fighting for an unjust cause, what's the point in insisting that they do wrong?

McMahan concedes the oddness of this juxtaposition, and suggests that "the deep morality of war"—which on his view countenances the separation of *jus ad bellum* from *jus in bello*—"should not necessarily guide us in devising the laws of war."[33] This sounds perplexing, if not paradoxical. But the subject is perplexing, and McMahan's suggestion may be comparable to the view of noncombatant immunity articulated by Mavrodes that I defended in the last section. The rules of *jus in bello* must be justified pragmatically, and there is a sense in which they are conventional. But that isn't to say the moral stakes aren't very high.

NOTES

1. Michael Walzer, *Just and Unjust Wars: A Moral Argument with Historical Illustrations*, 3rd ed. (New York: Basic Books, 2000).

2. See David Luban, "Preventive War," *Philosophy & Public Affairs* 32, no. 3 (2004).

3. *Just and Unjust Wars*, pp. 61–62.

4. Ibid., p. 74.

5. Cited in *Just and Unjust Wars*, p. 74.

6. Ibid. Emphasis in original.

7. See William A. Galston, "The Perils of Preemptive War," *Philosophy & Public Policy Quarterly* 22 (Fall 2002): 10.

8. Ibid., p. 80, and Luban, "Preventive War," pp. 209, 218–32. But Luban allows preventive wars "again serious threats posed by rogue states" (p. 209).

9. See Jeff McMahan, "Preventive War and the Killing of the Innocent," unpublished paper, and David Rodin, "The Ethics of Preventive War," unpublished paper.

10. *Just and Unjust Wars*, p. 107.

11. For a view of this kind see Luban, "Just War and Human Rights," *Philosophy & Public Affairs* 9 (1980), reprinted in Charles Beitz et al., *International Ethics: A Philosophy & Public Affairs Reader* (Princeton, NJ: Princeton University Press, 1985).

12. David Rodin, *War and Self-Defense* (Oxford: Oxford University Press, 2002), p. 144. But: this statement is somewhat ambiguous and might be interpreted as compatible with the organic view described in the previous paragraph.

13. See Luban, "Just War and Human Rights," for a defense of this view.

14. See Walzer, *Just and Unjust Wars*, chaps. 9, 14, 16, and passim. Note that according to the principle, noncombatants may not be *attacked*. It is, however, deemed permissible to attack legitimate military targets while foreseeing that noncombatants will be killed in the process. If such actions were not permissible, war would not be either. The moral loophole is provided by the doctrine of double effect, originally devised by medieval Christian theologians to explain how war can be permissible

even though it inevitably kills noncombatants, innocent people. The doctrine allows one to perform actions with evil effects (such as the deaths of noncombatants) as long as these effects are not part of one's aim. Although to the naïve ear the doctrine may sound fishy, it cannot simply be dismissed. For discussion and criticism, see Walzer, pp. 151–59, and Judith Lichtenberg, "War, Innocence, and the Doctrine of Double Effect," *Philosophical Studies* 74 (1994).

15. See Article 48 of Protocol I of the 1977 Additional Protocols to the Geneva Conventions, at http://www.genevaconventions.org/ (accessed January 17, 2005).

16. "War and Murder," in *War and Morality*, ed. Richard Wasserstrom (Belmont, CA: Wadsworth, 1970), p. 52.

17. George Mavrodes, "Conventions and the Morality of War," *Philosophy & Public Affairs* 4 (1975), reprinted in *International Ethics*, pp. 80–81.

18. For a defense of this view see, e.g., Robert K. Fullinwider, "War and Innocence," *Philosophy & Public Affairs* 5 (1975), reprinted in *International Ethics*.

19. Walzer defends the bombings of German cities before 1942 as justified by the then-distinct possibility that the Nazis could win the war; he condemns the later bombings as not defensible on this "necessity" rationale. *Just and Unjust Wars*, chap. 16.

20. Ibid., p. 229.

21. Ibid., p. 231.

22. One question is whether the actions of such soldiers are *excused* rather than *justified*. The relevance of questions about justification versus excuse and their implications is explored by McMahan, "The Ethics of Killing in War," and Rodin, *War and Self-Defense*. I will return to it in the next section.

23. Mavrodes, "Conventions and the Morality of War," p. 82.

24. Walzer, *Just and Unjust Wars*, p. 21.

25. Rodin, *War and Self-Defense*, p. 167.

26. McMahan, "The Ethics of Killing in War," p. 709. The proportionality requirement is discussed in Walzer, *Just and Unjust Wars*, chap. 8; according to Walzer it was first articulated explicitly by Henry Sidgwick in *The Elements of Politics*.

27. Ibid., p. 714. McMahan allows occasional exceptions. In addi-

tion to the example he provides, we can conceive of one state invading another, violating the latter's sovereignty and thus waging an unjust war, but still producing benefits that outweigh the costs. But such cases, like the one he describes, will be highly unusual.

28. See, e.g., Rodin's discussion, *War and Self-Defense*, pp. 26–34.

29. Ibid., p. 171.

30. McMahan, "The Ethics of Killing in War," p. 723. McMahan acknowledges that his understanding of "responsibility" is "eccentric."

31. Ibid., p. 725.

32. Of course it's difficult to analyze popular thinking since most people probably think their own soldiers blameless, but also think their own side just. The test would be whether they believe enemy soldiers are blameless while at the same time thinking the enemy's war is unjust.

33. "The Ethics of Killing in War," p. 730.

2

THE OBSCENITY OF WAR AND THE IMPERATIVE OF THE LESSER EVIL

J. Harold Ellens

INTRODUCTION

"Just War is a medieval European concept that a ruler, by proper declaration and with proper motives, might employ armed force outside his normal jurisdiction to defend rights, rectify wrongs, and punish crimes. He could, that is, take up arms for a just cause (which in practice, of course, was interpreted according to one's own lights). The concept developed as early as Augustine in the fourth century and was still accepted by the Dutch jurist and writer on international law Hugo Grotius in the seventeenth. Its popularity thereafter declined though in the twentieth century it enjoyed a revival in somewhat new form, with the idea that a nation might resort to armed force in self-defense or in the execution of collective obligations toward international peace-keeping operations."[1] So begins the *Encyclopaedia Britannica*'s account of what Jews and Christians have styled historically as "holy war" and Muslims call a form of jihad.

I am a soldier. I have been for fifty years. I served in three wars and was wounded in two of them. I hate war. I am *for* the present

Iraq war. I do not have space here to give an account of why I am a soldier, why I hate war, or why I am for the present war. Rather, this essay sets forth a perplexing ambiguity in which every human being, in my judgment, should find himself or herself. It describes the importance of taking that ambiguity with the utmost seriousness as a central problem for human integrity. This essay is about sorting out that ambiguity. To do this I begin by reviewing briefly the history of Just War Theory and its motives, so as to describe the roots and purposes of the theory, and to demonstrate that Just War Theory is a tacit and obscene affirmation of massive violence, as well as a legitimation of its methods.

EXPOSITION

Just War, Jihad, and Holy War

Clement of Alexandria developed a theme taken from Philo's concept of the Logos. Philo understood the Logos to be a pervasive expression of the divine spirit throughout the universe, constituting the organizing principle in both the physical and moral universes. The Logos was both the template for the divine creation of both of those universes and also the expression of the structure, order, law, and word of God for humankind. Clement emphasized the role of the Logos as the divine law and the medium of God's authoritative word or self-expression on matters pertaining to human life in the world. He believed that Christians were called to obey both the word of God and the rule of the governmental authorities or laws. If a conflict arose between these two sources of authority, he was sure that Christians were to appeal to the higher law, namely the Logos. This moved Clement to articulate the notion that just cause might exist in such a case for open rebellion against an oppressive government.

The ancient Greeks had anticipated Clement in this perspective, and Augustine followed his line of thought two centuries after him, in developing the early Christian form of a Just War Theory. Roman law changed the Greek concept of peace as a peaceful era into a legal state of affairs in which specified regulations applied to the behavior of combatants. These notions were extrapolated for the formulation of regulations protecting noncombatants and personal property. In ancient Greece and Rome "a just war (*bellum justum*) meant not one that was just in nature, but one that complied with the formalities demanded by law and religion for engaging in war."[2] Augustine was clearly aware of the historic Roman legal theory and also of Clement's rather primitive hints at order, justice, and decency in war. Under Constantine, Christian ideals came to dominate the empire and so it became necessary to elaborate the rationale of various practical arguments Christians had been offering for a couple of centuries to justify their service in the Roman army.

In the fourth century CE Augustine, in *De Civitate Dei*, developed an intricate argument for the distinction between the secular state, The City of this World, and the state infused with Christian ideals, The City of God. The distinction was the foundation for a further argument regarding the reconciliation and integration of the ideas of these two cities, that is, of our mundane and transcendental worlds, politically and ethically. In that context he laid down the basic rubrics of Just War Theory, which have been in the back of the Western mind ever since, though today they are grounded in secular legal principles. Both Hugo Grotius, a Dutch legal philosopher of the late sixteenth and early seventeenth centuries, and Francisco de Vitoria, a Spanish theologian of the late fifteenth and early sixteenth centuries, fleshed out Augustine's construct.

Grotius wrote *De Jure Belli ac Pacis* (*On the Law of War and Peace*), which was published in 1625. The principles laid down were cogent and clear. First, war was unjustified except in defense or to set right some major international wrong. Second, war must have an adequate cause. Third, it must have a potentially constructive outcome: be able to do more good than harm. Fourth, it must be preceded by adequate attempts at alternative solutions and by a legal declaration of war. Fifth, there must be no excessive use of force or destruction. Sixth, noncombatants and POWs must be protected from harm or abuse. Seventh, there must be no wanton destruction of property. Eighth, war must not be waged for the acquisition of territory. Ninth, provision must be made for conscientious objection. Tenth, war must be conducted with adequate force to achieve the objective. Eleventh, there must be a constructive disengagement or exit strategy. Twelfth, the completion of the war must lead to reconciliation. Grotius and Vitoria both opposed the imperial acquisition of empires, such as those in South America and Africa, censuring the European nations for subjugation and abuse of native or primitive people; and they both opposed racism as justification for slavery.

These philosophical and legal efforts to introduce ethical structure into the practice of military violence were certainly an admirable effort to corral the moral turpitude that war always is, and resolve its inherent ambiguity and inevitable bestiality. However, it is reason for considerable pause to realize that these very efforts to structure war morally have a shadow side; and that is the implied justification of the resort to ultimate violence for the sake of achieving final solutions. Once that justification is established, the moral question of war, in and of itself, is removed from the ethical and political equation. This action creates a psychological ambience in which a host of evils are hatched, not the least of which is the provision of a rationale for almost any kind of field expedient that might seem urged on the spot by any developing combat situation. This puts humane constraints in jeopardy, makes ultimate violence for final solutions the order of the day, and places war as an objective phenomenon into a category outside of the domain of our normal censures upon violence. It makes war a legitimate form of violence.

So far as I know, no one has ever addressed this shadow side of Just War Theory with any significant depth or breadth. I contend that the very ethical system of a Just War Theory begs the original and ultimate question, "Is the bestializing obscenity of military violence ever permissible at all?" Moreover, the solutions offered by Just War Theory are merely semantic solutions. We solve the problem of the moral evil of violence by arbitrary definitions of terms.

The Obscenity of War

To certify the legitimacy and justify the moral validity of the violence and bestialization of war in this way is in itself an obscene act, just as war is under every circumstance obscene. War bestializes everything and everyone it touches. It bestializes soldiers to place these sensitive human beings in settings that soldiers endure in combat, among the broken remnants of their comrades; among the wrecked cities that once were burgeoning places of living, loving, and laughing children; among the smoking disaster of a battlefield strewn with shattered technology and artillery-shredded machinery; among the corpses and mass graves of innocent children and parents who are inadvertent collateral damage. It is not accidental that for two decades after a major military conflict, both winning and losing nations experience an enormous increase in violent crime in the streets of their cities.

It is obscene to traumatize the inner spirits, the souls and psyches of fine young men and women by subjecting them to the hardship, deprivation, loneliness, fear, and jeopardy to their hope and self-confidence which war, and particularly active combat, brings. By obscene I mean the performance of a behavior that is so far from the normal decorum of healthy psychosocial life that it is, and is experienced as, monstrous and inhuman. To subject enemy populations, combatant or noncombatant, to that same degradation and trauma is equally inhumane, bestializing, and obscene.

That is the reason that nobody hates war like a soldier hates war. It is an obscene fiction among the general naive population of those who have never served, that it is the military that makes war. Failed statesmen who have behaved as mere politicians make war.

Soldiers hate war, but serve for the sake of those they love. For a soldier, as it should be for a policeman, putting on the uniform is every day again a confession that he or she has agreed that if there is any wounding or killing, he or she will stand in the stead of the civilian. Real soldiers know that when they put on the uniform they have already given their lives. It remains only a question of how much fear, loneliness, and pain they will need to endure before the last moment comes. Soldiers hate war.

That is why I make the claim that it is no longer coherent or tenable to employ such terminology as *just* or *holy* for that kind of monstrous behavior which military operations inevitably are. Military operations are sometimes necessary, but they are even then obscene, bestializing, and monstrous. That there is something heroic about war is mainly the fiction of propagandizers and theater directors. There are heroic moments in war but they are never moments of consciously motivated heroism. They are, rather, moments of consummate expedience in which a very scared person puts his or her life at risk for some significant need.

When we speak of war as just, we are using legal terminology that insists that there is something about war that makes it legitimate on the basis of actions that the enemy has taken. We are thereby claiming that it is logically justified and, therefore, legally just. First of all, this implies an enormously illogical leap from logic to legality. Second, this line of thought implies a quid pro quo rationale. In all the wars during which I served we always employed this logic. It was never true. Sweeping categories of equivalence were constantly put before us as justification for the fight. But there is no justice or equivalence in the slaughter in an open field of five conscripts, or ten thousand, who have done nothing more than answer their nation's telegram to report for duty.

During all of my years of service the enemy was the USSR. We feared it and hated its threat to us, nationally and personally. One day in the 1980s I was at a conference in East Berlin. In midafternoon I took a walk through the forest near Potsdam. To my great surprise, in the middle of the forest, I came upon a very impressive structure with elaborately designed walls and massive decorative gates. I thought it was a palace, though it was obvious that it had been built in the mid-twentieth century. I was able to read the inscription in the Cyrillic alphabet over the gates and realized that it was a Soviet military cemetery. There, in well-kept silence, lay the honored Soviet dead. Row on row of tombs. It was massive. There were thousands. I found myself weeping profoundly. To say that they were the enemy was monstrous. They were no different than I, except that they were dead—and a long way from home. Called up by their country, serving for those they loved, dead from doing their duty. To say their uniform made them different from me is obscene. Words like justice do not apply. We will need other words if we must continue this business.

When we spoke of war as holy, which, of course, we seldom do in the West anymore, we always meant that it was sanctioned by God. That is the greatest obscenity of all. Does one really need to explicate that fact? We got that model, of course, from the Bible itself. Yahweh, the warrior, who stands in tension with Yahweh, the enticer, in much of the Bible, has fed his violent metaphors continuously into the unconscious archetypes of Western psychology and culture for four thousand years. "God's wars" became "good wars." Our wars, justified as "good wars," became "God's wars." That is monstrous and hence obscene. No wonder that Judaism and Christianity eventually gave that up. But the Islamic jihad is no different than the Jewish extermination of the Canaanites thirty-five hundred years ago and the Christian Crusades one thousand years ago, all of which were perpetrated as holy war.

Jihad originally meant and still mainly means the inner struggle in any human being against all forms of evil, that is, against everything within the person or within his or her cultural and social context that may in any way distract one away from an intense God-centeredness. That kind of jihad is no different than St. Paul's injunction and that of the Hebrew ethical prophets that we should have done with evil and triumph over it for the cause of God's Kingdom in, around, and through us. However, Mohammed betrayed his own cause in this regard when early in his leadership of the Islamic movement he resorted to military action to secure his domain in Mecca and Medina, calling this military process a jihad. Ever since that time there has lain at the core of Islam this fatal flaw, waiting to be exploited periodically by any militant who wishes to hijack Islam to justify his own violent purposes. All the monstrosities inherent to calling war holy or just are also inherent to this employment of the term "jihad."

The Imperative of the Lesser Evil

In the light of this line of thought, it is imperative, of course, to address the argument of war as the lesser evil. There are times when war is thrust upon us and we have no constructive alternative but to fight and to do it effectively. That fact of history and of life heightens the problem of the inherent ambiguity of war and gives that ambiguity specificity in concrete cases. It is, therefore, an almost inevitable imperative of simple logic to claim that such a war is better than a failure to conduct military operations. When we say it is better, we really do mean that it is pragmatically necessary for the protection or advancement of a desirable quality of life, freedom, decency, and civilization in our world, given whatever the threat is that we face. Therefore, we also mean to say that it is morally better than a failure to defend and enhance these ideals. From that position it is a short leap of logic, or illogic, to the claim that such military operations are a good thing. Another leap of illogic leads us to the meaning that such operations are good in and of themselves, not just existentially expedient. By this juncture in the equation we have arrived at the point of claiming that this lesser of two evils is a good evil, indeed, a better evil than some other evils. Are we, then, morons to have been seduced into believing such an oxymoron, and establishing costly national policy upon this stroke of illogic? What is logically justified we have made legally just and hence morally imperative or even sacred, a triple leap of illogic and erroneous ethics!

There can be no question about the fact that in some important cases war is necessary. To make this discussion more complicated, let me claim at least tentatively that I believe that the current war in Iraq is such a necessary war. What I am concerned about here, however, is that we recognize that the sequence of logical steps I have just unfolded above is a sequence of semantic procedures in which each step is true individually only by definition, that is, these steps are not, taken individually, answerable to reality in any specific given situation. This means that they may or may not be true and applicable in any real-life cases, and when combined they end us in an impossible oxymoron; nonetheless, we claim they are principial and we build our destiny out of them. Moreover, it is an established psychological principle that we feel about things the way we name them. Therefore, we must be intensely careful with what kinds of words we signify our claims and proclamations regarding this rationale for war, lest we trick ourselves into perspectives which are unreal, therefore untrue, and therefore destructive—at least psychologically, probably logically, and perhaps socioculturally and politically.

The logical or illogical sequence regarding which I am urging great caution is a casuistic notion, which lands us in the moral no-man's-land of semantic subterfuge that we impose upon ourselves by this line of thought. Can we really afford to hang the destiny of humanity and civilization on such a Jesuitical thread? Can we use language such as "lesser evil," "holy," or "just" to describe what is mere expedience in situations which have usually developed because of neglect and irresponsible failures to take more honorable and sensible actions in a timely way?

We must agree, I think, that there is such a thing out there that, for want of better languaging, we have called the lesser evil. We must speak of the imperative of something of that sort, but should we not stop calling it the lesser evil because that implies that it is a better evil, indeed, a good evil given the situation? Why not call it the Imperative of the Evil Expedient? That would be honest. That would be psychologically correct and healthy. That would be logical. It would constitute the basis for us all to agree that when we undertake war we are wading into the maelstrom of the moral and sociocultural underworld, so to speak. We could consciously know that we are deciding out of an unavoidable necessity to engage in barbarous evil. Let us call it what it is and then do it if we must! Let us admit the depravity and injustice of this business of war. Let us no longer invoke the honored principles of law and right with terms like "just" and "ethical" war. Let us no longer invoke God and the sacred with words like "holy" or "jihad."

In this way we could, in one fell semantic swoop, remove all of the self-imposed subterfuge by which we make ourselves comfortable with the violence, bestialization, and moral turpitude of war. We must take with utter seriousness the inherent ambiguity of war, especially when it is expedient, lest we play the psychological semantic tricks upon ourselves by which we decivilize ourselves: naming what is obscene as though it is a form of goodness or even godliness. The ancient prophets warned, "Woe to those who call evil good."

Nonetheless, we must find ways to handle the imperative of war in circumstances in which we are deprived of all alternatives and a resort to obscene violence is imposed upon us. What is the likelihood that our unconscious awareness that ultimate violence is always available to solve ultimate political, social, and religious impasses, and that it can be given false but consoling names, seduces societies to avoid less violent solutions earlier in the international equation, so as to prevent war?

The Divine Drivers of Our Obscenity and Ambiguity

Addressing these ambiguities of war with utter seriousness is an especially necessary course of action because humans are inherently violent under circumstances of threat. Our unconscious and conscious values as individuals and as a society are shaped and energized at the archetypal level by the central metaphors of Western civilization. The archetypal structures, as Jung made clear, are derived mainly from our primal urges toward survival and power, namely, control over our anxiety-inducing environment, from birth on. These archetypes are informed and empowered by the cultural metaphors of our Western tradition, most of which are religious. They derive from ancient Israelite traditions, conveyed to us in the Bible. Unfortunately, these foundational religious texts declare repeatedly that God's method for solving his ultimate problems is an early resort to ultimate violence: depopulation of Eden, drowning humankind in a flood, wiping out cities with fire and brimstone, genocide of the Egyptians, threatened genocide of the Israelites, genocide of the Canaanites, extermination of the ten tribes, exile of Judah, crucifixion of "his only begotten son."

Quite apart from the fact that these metaphoric narratives have no truth in them regarding God's disposition on the use of violence, the unconscious-level function of these traditions shapes us. The theology of grace is even stronger than these stories in the ancient scriptures of both the Old and New Testaments, but that grace perspective has never been able to rise up in a radical transcendence over and away from the conditioning barbarism of the violent metaphors. This is probably because the god of violence appeals more directly to our most primal instincts. Grace, as unconditional positive regard for the enemy, is inherently beyond human imagination.

A second source of destructive religious metaphors is the concept in ancient Israelite religion, mediated to us through the Bible, that we are up against a cosmic conflict; and God is up against it too. This is a dualism, resident in our unconscious worldview, imported into ancient Judaism from Zoroastrianism during the Babylonian exile, and which gives us a rule-of-thumb solution to the problem of suffering and evil. It is a lie, of course. There is no cosmic evil god out there operating in tension with the God of grace and creativity. There is only the God of grace and goodness. The evil in this world is only that which we do to ourselves. There is no empirical, historical, or literary evidence for cosmic evil forces, to say nothing about the absolutely crazy concept of ontic evil. That, in itself, should give us pause to reconsider this monstrous thing called war, expedient or inexpedient, and our unconscious inclination to justify it as a moral or sacred imperative.

CONCLUSION

Despite the illogic of just or holy war, nations continue to arm for the expediency and call it by idealizing names. Nobody hates war like a soldier hates war, yet the very existence of the well-prepared soldier or armed force may produce the neglect and irresponsible political process which fails to produce statesmen, and so causes us to allow things to deteriorate to the point at which we can and must employ armed forces for bestializing and obscene violence, justifying it as being in line with the nature and method of God. This barbarous equation regularly produces the Imperative of the Expedient Evil of military violence in the name of justice or the sacred. Is that not the most obscene of all obscenities? How truly obscene it is to "let loose the dogs of war"! Furthermore, regardless of the urgency of the Imperative of the Expedient Evil in any given situation, can there ever be a logical, legal, or moral justification for what has lately become honored with the estimable name of preemptive defense? To justify the bestiality of war on the ground of preemptive defense is not only to move the enterprise of war beyond any moral or ethical bounds by making it a matter of the private judgment of the warring nation or local commander. It was precisely that dangerous kind of out-of-bounds ethical end run that the entire history of Just War Theory development was most interested in preventing. Surely such a rationale for military action undercuts specifically the central supports for all efforts to establish some kind of humane constraints on warring nations and on war itself.

Such a new military philosophy, hatched by the Israelis in their current conflict with the PLO and adopted more recently by some voices in support of the current war in Iraq, is blatant violation of all human sense of justice.[3]

NOTES

1. *Encyclopaedia Britannica, Micropedia*, vol. 5, p. 646.
2. Ibid., *Macropedia*, vol. 19, p. 539.
3. Moreover, such rationale is unnecessary, and essentially inapplicable, particularly to the Iraq war. Those who have not yet noted the overwhelming evidence for Saddam Hussein's long-standing active "war" on his own people, his support of the suicide bombings by the PLO, his repeated activity or complicity in the various attacks upon the United States during recent years, and his support of al Qaeda, simply do not wish to know truth and deal with reality. It is my perception that war in Iraq, in that sense, particularly after the World Trade Center attack, was forced upon us as the imperative evil expedient.

REFERENCES

Cole, Juan. *Sacred Space and Holy War: The Politics, Culture and History of the Shi'ite Islam*. London: I. B. Tauras, 2002.

Ellens, J. Harold. "Fundamentalism, Violence, and War." In *Violence and War*, Chris Stout and Mary Fitzduff, Westport, CT: Praeger.

Ellens, J. Harold, ed. *The Destructive Power of Religion, Violence in Judaism, Christianity, and Islam*. Vol. 1, *Sacred Scriptures, Ideology, and Violence*; vol. 2, *Religion, Psychology, and Violence*; vol. 3, *Models and Cases of Violence in Religion*; vol. 4, *Contemporary Views on Spirituality and Violence*. Westport, CT: Praeger, 2004.

Stern, Jessica. *Terror in the Name of God: Why Religious Militants Kill*. New York: HarperCollins, 2003.

Talbott, Strobe, and Nyan Chanda, eds. *The Age of Terror: America and the World After September 11*. New York: Basic Books, 2001.

Tucker, Robert, and David Hendrickson. "Iraq and U.S. Legitimacy." *Foreign Affairs* 83, no. 6 (November–December 2004): 18–32.

3

JUST WAR AND JIHAD

POSITIONING THE QUESTION
OF RELIGIOUS VIOLENCE

R. Joseph Hoffmann

In their current simplification of world disorder and its causes, American leaders are fond of distinguishing between the essentially good and ethical core of a religious tradition and the perversion of its message and doctrines by unappointed apostles. According to the heuristics adopted since the events of September 11, 2001, a fundamentally peaceful religion was itself tyrannized by a relatively small band of theologically naive militants who are out of step with the religious mainstream of the Islamic world. In this essentially political formulation, the term "Islam" performs roughly the same function as the double-barreled term "Judaeo-Christian" performs, or used to perform, in prepluralistic America, when the locution seemed to suggest a way around using more specific names, such as biblical faith, *haggadah*, or Christian doctrine to describe particular ideas or moral commitments. And though theological correctness may cause us to prefer the idea of a refined essence, so designated, to the historical specifics of any tradition, we are all normally aware that the sentence "Islam is a peaceful religion" is no different from saying "The Judaeo-Christian tradition is about love and tolerance"—that is to say, an interpretative generalization not altogether supported by the weight of history and practice. In what follows, I want to look at the nature of interpretative generalizations and what they tell us about the nature of religion in general and religiously motivated violence in particular.

The origin of this generalization is relatively recent, or at least modern: it is traceable to late Enlightenment thinking, to Hegel's spiritual view of history, and that of his disciples Ludwig Feuerbach and D. F. Strauss, both of whom believed that if Christianity had outgrown the mythology of its sacred texts, the doctrinal formulations of its intellectual expounders—the church fathers, the medieval finery of the scholastics, and even the well-intentioned but incomplete housecleaning of the reformers, it nonetheless possessed in the teaching of the founder—so it was assumed by liberal Protestantism anyway—a pure ethical vision compatible with the enlightened morality of Kantian ethic. To read the theological work of Feuerbach or his early-twentieth-century heir Adolph von Harnack is to envision a triptych with Jesus Pedagogicus at the center flanked to his left by an inspired Kant, to his right by a self-satisfied Hegel, and a cloud surmounting the central figure emblazoned with the words "Love Truth, Observe the Zeitgeist, and Do Your Duty." It did not take much to destroy this image—though large sectors of the Christian community are unaware of its destruction—only the work of the Jesuit-turned-skeptic Alfred Loisy in a book directed against Harnack's *The Essence of Christianity*, a book about Christian ethicalism, in which he wrote, "Professor Harnack has looked long and deep into the well to find the historical Jesus, but has seen instead only the reflection of his liberal Protestant face."

I mention this lingering tendency of the late Enlightenment to reduce specific religion to general morality for a reason, not only because it remains a standard way of distinguishing between the religious ideal and temporal religious realities, but also because any attempt to understand any religion in this reductionistic way is subject to disconfirming facts, some historical, some intrinsic to the religion itself, that render the interpretive generalization absurd. To paraphrase Freud, we would not call someone a good or a peace-loving man and then go on to recite a history of his thefts and murders without assuming that the second statement had an effect on our original assertion. We would be stuck between asserting the first and keeping quiet about the second, which is deception, or reciting the list of crimes and being mistaken about the first, which is foolishness.

Religions of course are not thieves masquerading as saints, but for purposes of understanding the weakness of interpretative generalizations it is important to be aware of the vulnerability of "identifying," as Harnack tried to do, a pure and incorrupt kernel of Christianity, or any religious tradition—that of the founder—hidden by the husks of interpretation and doctrine. If postmodernism has done anything for the study of religion, it is in urging the end of the historicist project that locates truth—or perhaps accuracy—in the intention of the founder or the precise words of the sacred text.

But because many of the dilemmas we confront in understanding religion belong to historicism, it is significant to approach the problem in a way that acknowledges the long purchase historical thinking has had on theology. It is relevant, for example, that Jews, Christians, and Muslims are not the first to argue the principle that truth is old, and lies (false doctrines, heresy) are new, or that founders are good and interpreters and editors and unannointed readers are evil. It was a basic axiom of Rome and Hellenistic society in deciding which religions to legitimate: *quidquod veritas antiqua est*—truth is old, or more specifically "that which is true is old." The importance of this axiom is expressed in the grudging Roman tolerance of Judaism, as being older than the cults of Rome, and intolerance of Christianity—a "malevolent and unapproved superstition, recently arrived" to borrow from Tacitus. It explains the Christian appropriation of the Hebrew Bible as a foundational text—supporting pillars of the new covenant—as well as the disposition to distinguish the truth of the apostolic teaching from the novelty and corruptions of the heretics, and even why in the seventh century the legitimacy of the Prophet's revelations, though unique, final, and unrepeatable, were nonetheless thought to be validated by prior revelations, however unreliable, or ancient holy places such as the Kabbah, however abused by traditional Arab religious practices. We can find this line of argument used repeatedly from Josephus to Seneca to Tertullian and extending from the religious debates of late antiquity to modern efforts to excavate the sayings of Jesus from the traditions about him, or the various "hadith projects" designed to prioritize and catalogue the traditions about the Prophet's sayings, explanations, and rulings on legal matters.

The ancient projects and their modern and postmodern extensions, if they differ in motive, seem to find common ground in the ancient belief, replete with neo-Platonic tremors, that truth falling through time becomes enmeshed in error. And there is a logical price to pay for this belief: to rediscover, to defend, or to restore the truth is an act of supreme faith—as it was for the purifying and violent Maccabees of the second century BCE, the heresiologists of Irenaeus's day, the Muslim armies in their slaughter of the Quraithah Jews, the verbal attacks on the philosophers by al-Ghazali, the physical attacks of the Church on suspected heretics in the Inquisition, Baruch Goldstein's slaughter of Muslims at the Hebron mosque in 1994, the suicide attacks of militant Muslims against "crusader" targets in New York in 2001. It seems either deceptive or foolish, in the terms of Freud's parable, to argue that the last of these events—that is, the suicide attacks of 2001—is not related to other religious acts within and outside the Islamic tradition—that is, that it can be understood simply as the corruption of a uniformly recognized religious principle, closer in character to heresy than a defense of orthodoxy. *Not* to recognize the act as specifically religious is not to understand the event. Radical purifying movements, as distinct from the hermeneutics of cultic and schismatic groups, historically have remained closer to the textual traditions of their foundations and often guard a low hermeneutical tradition that discourages philosophical reformations and cultural adaptations of the received text. This tendency, it seems to me, explains pacifist-scribal apocalyptic traditions such as those at Khirbet Qumran (the Dead Sea commune) in opposition to the assumed perversion of the priesthood and interpretative traditions of the Jewish intelligentsia, and violent apocalyptic traditions such as Masada; it explains as well some, but not all, early Christian groups. The apocalyptic dimension of religious violence is another and broader subject and here we can only allude to its persistence in the book traditions as a powerful spur to action—but action that often residuates in suicide as the violent outcome rather than defensive wars. Apocalyptic after all—the belief that God will intervene violently in history to save a few and condemn the many—is both a form of hope and a form of hopelessness.

Let me repeat that expressions of religious violence are not understandable at all if they cannot be understood as expressions of the specific religious culture from which they emerge. Briefly said, they are expressions of particular histories. Lest this statement be appraised as only a Western view of the proudly and defiantly elusive Islamic religious and legal system, one should regard the 1998 fatwa issued by Osama bin Laden, a statement rich in allusion to the glory of the Arab past and the indefatigability of Arab culture and Islamic religious values. It is relatively late in this remarkable piece of literature that he prescribes violence as the only way to defend the truth:

> All these crimes and sins committed by the Americans are a clear declaration of war on God, his messenger, and Muslims. And ulema have throughout Islamic history unanimously agreed that the jihad is an individual duty if the enemy destroys the Muslim countries. This was revealed by Imam Bin-Qadamah in "Al- Mughni," Imam al-Kisa'i in "Al-Bada'i," al-Qurtubi in his interpretation, and the shaykh of al-Islam in his books, where he said, "As for the militant struggle, it is aimed at defending sanctity and religion, and it is a duty as agreed. Nothing is more sacred than belief except repulsing an enemy who is attacking religion and life."[1]

The lines are drawn with Manichean simplicity between powers of dark and light, in terms strikingly similar to the language used by the ancient Qumran or Dead Sea community and its discussion of the war between the sons of light and the sons of darkness. A similar strain can be seen in the liberal use of primary textual sources by the most famous of the 9/11 hijackers, Muhammed Atta, in the so-called Doomsday Document, found in his luggage, and a source of fascination for scholars since its release by the FBI in 2002. In the most learned of recent appraisals, Juan Cole has written in an article for the Yale Center for Genocide Studies[2] that the document was understood as a psychological prep sheet, by which "the hijackers misused various techniques of Islamic spirituality to achieve a psychological state of mind in which it was possible for them to commit mass murder and their own suicides." In fact, the document is a pastiche of quotations ranging from Qur'anic verses to the writings of the Sufi teacher al-Ghazali to hadith of prophet concerning the legitimacy of the raid as a way of pursuing political and religious victory. The more interesting portion of the document, however, is the section titled "The Last Night," designed to fortify the martyr in a time of doubt: Cole describes it in this way:

> The raiders are directed to "vow to accept death." The word for 'vowing to accept,' tabayu`, is related to the term bay`ah, which means "giving fealty to," used to describe giving allegiance to a caliph or leader of the Muslim community. It is a pledge of loyalty, but instead of being given to the leader of Islam, here it is proffered to death itself. Muslim Brotherhood founder Hasan al-Banna had written, "Always intend to go for Jihad and desire martyrdom. Prepare for it as much as you can." Then, the document advises, the hijacker must "renew admonition" (tajdid at-tanbih). The reference is to an admonition of the base self (an-nafs), which Muslim mystics saw as the primary impediment to undertaking selfless acts of worship. In this document, the carnal self is the enemy of the vow to die, selfishly seeking to hang on to life, and so must be vanquished. Admonishing the self is the way to contain it and remain true to the death vow.

The raider is then directed to shave the extra hair on his body, to perfume himself, and to ritually wash himself. Instruction 2 is merely practical, saying that the raider should know the plan well "from every angle." Instruction 3 reverts to mind-set. The raider must read two chapters of the Qur'an, "The Spoils" and "Repentance." He must meditate on their meaning and on the rewards God has promised in them to martyrs. This immersion in key sacred texts is important to attaining the mind-set of the martyr, to thinking of oneself as already dead and preparing to receive the delights of divine recompense. "The Spoils" was revealed after the battle of Uhud between the pagan Meccans and the Muslims of Medina in 625, in which a small Muslim force of 700 defeated a much larger attacking army. The general context is thus the Muslim raids on and wars against the Meccans (there were seventy raids and three major wars). Uhud came after the Battle of Badr. The Surah of Spoils thus situates—or equates—the Twin Towers and Pentagon raids in Islamic history for the al-Qaeda cult. It mapped the United States onto Pagan Mecca. Both had superior military force and both were extremely wealthy commercial centers.

In light of the traumatic events of September 2001, historical instruction does not seem especially cathartic, perhaps, but the crassness of well-intentioned pieties following the event has made it virtually impossible to understand the events through the lens of historical discernment, and whatever gains were achieved for civil obedience on the home front by the assertion that neither 9/11 nor the American response to it had anything to do with "Islam"; the targeting of Afghanistan, Iraq, Iran, Syria, and pari passu Saudi Arabia and Yemen left little room at home that at least certain political leaders saw the struggle in a context not completely different to the extremists, a battle between the children of light and the children of darkness: that is, a resurgent Islam had jogged the historical memory of post-Christian Europe and Crusader America, reminding them that secularism is not an irresistible force in the political world.

*   *   *

That historical memory includes the following oration: after a long invocation of biblical verses, a Roman bishop of the eleventh century wound up his sermon as follows:

> I, or rather the Lord, beseech you as Christ's heralds to publish this everywhere and to persuade all people of whatever rank everywhere, as their oath, foot-soldiers and knights, poor and rich, to carry aid promptly to those Christians and to destroy that vile race of Arabs, remove it from the lands of our friends and to destroy it utterly, abolishing it from the face of the earth. I say this to those who are present, it meant also for those who are absent. Moreover, Christ commands it. All who die by the way, whether by land or by sea, or in battle against the pagans, shall have immediate remission of sins. This I grant them through the power of God with which I am invested. O what a disgrace if such a despised and base race, which worships demons, should conquer a people which has the faith of omnipotent God and is made glorious with the name of Christ! With what reproaches will the Lord overwhelm us if you do not aid those who, with us, profess the Christian religion![3]

The voice of course is distant—Urban II in preaching the first crusade, and the motives like the modern thirst for oil, not altogether religious; but the intentionality seems clear enough—a sacred and exclusive text authorizes violence. "No, Christ commands it."

The rationale that religious truth is original to a religious community—chiefly through the revelation or instruction of its founder, prophet, and teacher and secondarily in the process of its earliest transmission has as its corollary the belief, variously expressed, that prophecy dies, heresy emerges, the enemies of God (literally, the apostates) stray from the truth and seek the ruin of souls. Given the persistent view in the book traditions—that corruption is the risk truth takes when faith encounters history, the obligation to save the faith by acts of martyrdom (self-directed violence), acts of aggression (outwardly directed violence), is persistent as well. The situation can be made more extreme when the religions in question are, as it were, cousins fighting over Grandfather's estate, when the sacred texts have the same general cast of characters, when the real estate to be passed down is essentially the same land parcel. Wills, estates, and patrimony are not, indeed, *analogies* but the basic *terms* of a legal framework from which three similar theological systems have emerged. And their attempts to identify truth, historically, have been—to use John Hick's imperfect nomenclature—exclusivistic (one should be careful in using that term to know that Hick and other comparativists using his categories do not believe that all the book traditions are equally "exclusivistic"). Christianity is often identified, at least in its liberal sectors, as a religion "formerly exclusivistic" that has now dropped its ancient claim to possess the way, the truth, and the life.

However, Hick and others often underestimate the role of memory in the book traditions. The push for inclusivism and interfaith understanding—however nobly intentioned—often misses the point that the generosity of Christian liberalism can be interpreted as slackness, infidelity, moral uncertainty, and even atheism by those whose memory has a longer historical purchase. In this respect at least, the significant liberalizing trends in philosophy which profoundly shaped the Christian theology of Europe were also successful in erasing much of the cultural memory that had guaranteed Christians a place at the table as a People of the Book. It is stunning to me that insofar as Christianity in its European and American variety is the subject of opprobrium in Islamic polemic, it is not that doctrines like the trinity versus the tawhid of the Godhead are at issue; it is rather the depressing view that Christians have no doctrines left to defend, or rather none they wish to defend energetically, and have left the table. It is almost impossible to imagine the pragmatic religious companionship of the twelfth cen-

tury, which permitted the Jewish physician-philosopher Maimonides to write, concerning his duties to a Muslim caliph,

> My duties to the Sultan are very heavy. I am obliged to visit him
> every day, early in the morning. Hence, as a rule, every day, in
> the morning I go to Cairo. Even if nothing unusual happens there,
> I do not return to Fostat until the afternoon. Then I am famished,
> but I find the antechambers filled with people, both Jews and
> Gentiles, nobles and common people, judges and policemen,
> friends and enemies—a mixed multitude who await the time of
> my return.[4]

*   *   *

It is an annoying weakness of many (of the many) recent books on
religion and violence that their authors seem to subscribe to a view
that the closest analogy to Islamic extremism, as one is prone to call
it, is the extremism of Waco, or the followers of the Reverend Jim
Jones in Guyana, whose violence was that of a suicide pact cobbled
together by desperate souls in the temporary sway of weirdly
charismatic leaders, or the random bombing of an abortion clinic or
the killing of a Christian missionary nurse in Lebanon. It seems to
me highly doubtful that the present state of religious violence globally can be understood by forcing inapposite events into apposition.
The sectarian violence of eccentric preachers should not be catego-
rized with a radical populist movement that has many more sym-
pathizers throughout the Islamic world than it has practitioners and
theorists. Nor is the question of "positioning" religious violence a
matter of creating a hierarchy of "violent religions" and then
finding in their doctrines and traditions the sources of human conduct and particular acts of violence.

Positioning the question requires the nonviolent to do something
that extremists are able to do far better than the generality of Muslims, Christians, and Jews: the task requires the believer to relearn the
significance of exclusivism and the mind-set that drives it.

Tertullian's famous dictum—often reiterated by Pope Pius IX, "Outside the church there is no salvation"—may have been innocuous enough in a time when Christians were forbidden to join the Roman army. When the Roman army became Christian, the implications of the maxim for the unconverted were very different. Augustine, having failed to persuade a sect of perfectionist Christians to rejoin the North African church, finally despairs of rhetoric and advocates the use of the sword: "Kill them or compel them to come into the Church." Some of the more vicious of the actions ascribed to the early adherents of Islam in the *Sunan Abu-Dawud* suggest the same mind-set toward persuasion:

> The Apostle of Allah said: If you gain a victory over the men of Jews, kill them. So Muhayyisah jumped over Shubaybah, a man of the Jewish merchants. He had close relations with them. He then killed him. At that time Huwayyisah (brother of Muhayyisah) had not embraced Islam. He was older than Muhayyisah. When he killed him, Huwayyisah beat him and said: O enemy of Allah, I swear by Allah, you have a good deal of fat in your belly from his property.[5]

The tradition reported here is not very different from this scene recounted from Hebron, a source of raw religious sentiment particularly because it is the only place in the world where both Jews and Muslims share the same place of worship: the Tomb of the Patriarchs, where Abraham, Jacob, and Rebecca are reportedly buried. In February 1994, an American Israeli named Baruch Goldstein walked into the mosque while Muslims were praying during the sacred month of Ramadan and opened fire with his submachine gun. At least forty worshipers were killed before Goldstein himself was killed by a crowd of over four hundred Muslims. In all such incidents, the historical causes of violence seem to have been subsumed by a more general, visceral license to violence based on traditional antipathies, social inequities, and land distribution questions, all conveniently given the label "issues." Yet land and rightful ownership of it, social distinctions, suspicion of enemies, and the right to revenge and defense are essential, not incidental, to the religious prose and poetry that support the Abrahamic faiths. No teacher among the Taliban, no professor of Judaic studies, and no liberal Anglican bishop wishes to sacrifice the sacred text in the crossfire between literalism and interpretation.

*   *   *

The question of religious violence is—as the literary critics like to say—multivalenced. It cannot be first of all a question of images, since images grow out of experience before experience utilizes images as rationales for action. In recent years, it has become a theological project of various churches to select, invent, or reform images thought to be violent, dehumanizing, or toxic. What we encounter in such programs is the familiar interpretative conviction with which we began: that religion is good, but some expressions of it better than others, and some expressions not acceptable at all. I am skeptical of these projects not because they are unwittingly rooted in the Absolute of Hegelian idealism—the notion that a religious essence perdures and sloughs off all of its imperfections over time. (The commercial equivalent is the ad for an arthritis medication a few years ago that told us "You're not getting older, you're getting better.") According to one school of thought, ritual precedes myth: the violent act is the precursor of the myths and doctrines that explain it—circumcision, sacrifice, the eating of the Lord's body in communion, the thirst for martyrdom, the latter-day commemorations of martyrs' deaths at Asherah, the Good Friday liturgy, jihadis-turned-suicides for the ideal of a perfected Islam. The clumping together of the "merely ritualistic" and the actually grotesque may seem unwarranted, even sloppy, because it seems to confuse rationalized acts of violence in ritual form, such as the eucharist, with actual forms of violence such as martyrdom and suicide. The distinction is not so clear. It is the question that psychologists and anthropologists ranging from Freud to Mary Douglas to Roy Rappaport and René Girard in the twentieth century have posed, but about which the theological establishment has been largely silent. The acknowledgment of exclusivism alerts us to the fact that religion has never been nonviolent, in essence or manifestation. The work of cultural anthropologists and philosophers, ranging from Braudel to René Girard, Konrad Lorenz, and theologians like Robert Hammerton Kelley have effectively leaked into the work of church historians, biblical scholars, and exegetes to the extent that it is no longer possible to deny the radical significance of violence as a constituent part of monotheistic tradition: simply put, violence is part of the human experience. Violence is fundamental, perhaps the defining element of social, religious, and cultural development. Hammerton-Kelly puts it succinctly: "The one thing that cannot be denied is that violence is ubiquitous and tenacious and must be accounted for if we are to understand humanity."[6] The sacrificial systems of ancient Israel, the apodictic doctrine of blood for blood, the apocalyptic vision of a John the Baptist, the martyrdom cults of ancient Christianity, the jihadist posture of the Muslim armies, the readiness to identify Holy Land and Holy People with one's homeland and closest kin, the doctrines of the eschaton (judgment, paradise, or everlasting torture), the bifurcation of the cosmos into a faithful brotherhood and reprobate majority, and the entirety of the images these evoke in the sacred writings of the Abrahamic traditions are violent, either directly in what they denote, or in the connative sense for modes of conduct they describe. To say this is not the same as asking the questions "How do religions become violent?" or "Why are some religions more violent than others?" but to confront in religious texts and traditions the story of human experience.

Attempts to hierarchize religious violence seem, of course, as naive as the pacific attempts to persuade a world now witnessing new holy wars that violence is aberrational or exceptional. Similarly, attempts to chronologize the question—Judaism and Christianity *used* to be violent, Islam *still* is—is a statement about the purchase of belief on ordinary lives in the modern era, not a statement about the nature of Christianity and Judaism.

Should we grant that the theories of social anthropology concerning the nature and origin of religion are offset by the "good they do" by virtue of being mature versions of what they once were? Perhaps. It was Augustine who argued, in his usual forceful way, that the child is the damned prototype of a being whose conduct would be universally condemned if it became the behavior of the mature human person: selfish, willful, disobedient—more like Cain than Adam. Are religions *naturally* violent in the way a baby is naturally but *incompetently* violent: is it the nature of religion to outgrow its violent infancy? Or is it, as Freud argued, the nature of religion to sustain us in a delusional state of selfish infancy where violence is always possible? Must we see the Augustinian and Freudian as opposites, since the adult state is not a steady state of maturity but always threatens to devolve into a state of whining self-love and aggressive self-protection? As J. D. Weaver suggested in a 2001 essay in the journal *Crosscurrents*, even a thoroughly rationalized article of faith—the Christian doctrine of the atonement—depends on the startling idea that God not only permitted but also somehow "required" the death of his own Son, and in making this its core belief, Christianity inadvertently presented to the world an image of God as an abusive parent. If a central doctrine can be assessed in this way, how much more obvious the implications of Jeremiah 20:7, the prophet talking about his experiences of revelation beginning at the age of nine: "O Lord thou hast seduced me and I am seduced; Thou hast raped me and I am filled up." In looking at doctrines, texts, myths, and images, we are looking at what religion says about itself, and it seems, again, deceptive or foolish, to suggest that the true character of a religion can be found only in the correction of its self-expression.

Catherine Madsen, in her interpretation of John Hollander's poem "The Mad Potter," offers this appraisal:

The violent God is not an image of our aspirations; he is an image of what happens when we fail. The Bible is not a blueprint for the ideal relationship between God and humanity, but a profound psychological portrait of a relationship that has been wretched from the start. A woman can walk away from a violent husband (sometimes, but not always, with the hope of escaping him), but we cannot leave the universe; there is no divorce from God. And here—in the least feminist, indeed the least ethical of situations, the one in which there is no choice—the terms of the problem become clear. A metaphor for God is not a preventative or a remedy. It may be a record of the irremediable: a marker for a disaster that has already happened, a pain for which there was no preventative, a wound for which there was no medicine. God is not the cure but the disease.[7]

Yet powerful as her image is, Madsen misses the point that religious texts do not try to disguise the "wretchedness" of the relationship: they alert us to it. The Christian doctrine of the atoning sacrifice of Jesus Christ is startling because it is startling that a violent act can be an expression of love, or perhaps more to the point, that sacrifice has merit. Theologically easy as this may be for the Christian to appropriate by custom, does he feel that the Martyrs of Palestine in the time of Eusebius have anything in common with the martyrs of Palestine today? When is violent death an expression of divine love and favor, and when is it not?

It seems then that the question about religious violence is really a question about the inherentism of violence to any consistent idea about God, a view that penetrates the three faiths here being discussed: God is creator, God is judge, God is merciful, God rewards, God saves, God slays *our* enemies, God punishes. In the particular traditions, God also reveals, commands, inspires, leads (as a general), and orders. T. S. Eliot asked in "The Four Quartets" whether the worship of this God means we must "Die of the absolute paternal care / That will not leave us, but prevents us everywhere."

The inherentism of religious violence describes or positions (it does not answer) the question we are wanting to ask: it is not really whether religion promotes violence, nor whether particular traditions are more violent than others, nor even whether some images of God are good for us and some toxic—that seems to me a jejune way to put the question. The question, rather, is what one is to do with the recognition that to the extent religion is not violent, it means a curbing of religion's natural symbolic appetite for images of the violent, for violent action—for war, capital punishment, and revenge against one's enemies—by suppression, erasure, or simply disbelief.

NOTES

1. *Al-Quds al-'Arabi* (London), February 23, 1998, p. 3.

2. Paper presented at "Genocide and Terrorism: Probing the Mind of the Perpetrator," Yale Center for Genocide Studies, New Haven, CT, April 9, 2003.

3. O. Thatcher, *Sourcebook for Medieval History* (New York: Scribners, 1905), pp. 513–15.

4. Cited in Joseph Telushkin, *Jewish Literacy* (New York: Morrow and Co., 1991), p. 111.

5. *Sunan abu-Dawud*, bk. 19, no. 2998.

6. Robert Hammerton-Kelly, *Violent Origins* (Stanford, CA: Stanford University Press, 1987), p. vi.

7. *Crosscurrents* 51 (Summer 2001): 5.

4

UNDERSTANDING VIOLENCE

THE NEW COPERNICAN REVOLUTION

Charles K. Bellinger

I n the Middle Ages, people did not have as clear a perspective on the shape of the earth and its place in the universe as we do today. They were in the dark regarding certain basic ideas about the movement of the sun, the earth, the moon, comets, and so forth that we now take for granted as common knowledge. Is there an analogous sense in which we today are in the dark and do not understand a vitally important aspect of the world? I submit that there is. We do not understand violence. We are in the dark about why we human beings are violent, to such an extent that the possibility of understanding the roots of violence doesn't commonly enter our consciousness as a live option for us. We don't even know enough to know that we do not know.

We are certainly aware of violence as a phenomenon of human culture. It saturates our news every day. But we don't typically think of violence as something that we could possibly come to understand, as scientists might strive to understand the origin of tornadoes, or the chemistry of DNA, or the complex ecology of a South American rainforest. Instead, our typical pattern of thinking about violence is moralistic. When violence is done to us, we think:

The people who did this are evildoers. When we consider the violence that we may be engaged in somewhere in the world, we think: our violence is justified because we are defending ourselves against the evildoers. Notice that the primary categories at work in this kind of thinking are good and evil. Human beings, generally speaking, see themselves as good and their enemies as evil. While Americans may be particularly adept at this way of thinking, it is not our exclusive possession. People from every corner of the globe representing a wide variety of religions and philosophies think that they are good and their opponents are evil.

Are the categories of good and evil the only ones that we can use as we think about violence? Certainly not. The plea that I present concerns the crucial need for another interpretive approach. My fervent hope is that we will gain the ability to expand the scope of our reflection to include a well-articulated psychological understanding of violence. The revolution in thought made possible by Copernicus, Kepler, and Galileo resulted in humanity making a transition from having faulty and incomplete *beliefs* about the heavens to *understanding clearly* the movement of the heavenly bodies in relation to one another. Today, we need a parallel shift from *moralizing unreflectively about the evil of others* to *understanding the psychological malformations and potentialities of all people.*

An important first step in this direction is provided for us by Aristotle, who began his *Ethics* with the observation that all action intends a good. In other words, whenever human beings act, their action is seeking to bring about some good, some benefit, for themselves. This observation may seem rather pedantic and obvious, yet its implications are truly revolutionary, and I would argue that even after more than twenty-three hundred years we still have not allowed this key philosophical insight to enter into general human consciousness. Consider the implications of this insight for the task at hand, understanding the phenomenon of violence. The moralistic way of thinking simply labels some people as "evildoers"; this shuts down any further reflection and leaves the "evildoers" as opaque objects which are simply responded to with fear and loathing. Aristotle's insight suggests that this way of labeling people is a substitute for clear thinking, not a contributor to it.

If we take the idea that all actions intend a good seriously, then we will have to ask what good is being intended by those who are violent. Notice that there are two principal ways this good can be specified and brought to articulation. The first is that we can ask those who are violent what their motives are. Their answer to this question will reveal what the good is that they think they are aiming at. They may say things like: "Our religion, our way of life, and our people are being attacked by the infidels who are spreading their spiritual cancer over the whole earth. We must defend ourselves and restore the glory of the true God." Or: "The Jews are an inferior race that must be eradicated in order to cleanse the world and allow the true superiority of the Aryan race to emerge." Or: "The bourgeois capitalists are a dying class that must be speedily liquidated so that a new society may be created in which there is no exploitation but only harmonious relations between free workers." So the first way to come to understand the good being aimed at is to ask the violent people what their motives are and then take their answers seriously.

The problem with this approach, however, is that it allows those whose actions raise serious questions about their mental health to establish the framework within which the diagnosis of their condition will be made. What would the alternative be? The alternative is to greet the pronouncements of the violent regarding their motives with a hermeneutic of suspicion. We know what the ostensible good is that their actions are aiming at in their own minds, but it may be the case that their actions are actually aiming at *another good* that they themselves are unaware of. To unearth this deeper motive will require a "depth" psychology that arises out of the understanding of a person who is not suffering from the same mental disease as the violent person. In other words, we need a form of consciousness that is higher, more mature, than the immature thinking of the violent actors if we are to have an effective diagnosis of the sickness of the human race.

Copernicus, Kepler, and Galileo had advanced insights into the movement of the earth in relation to other heavenly bodies before they became part of the general consciousness. Are there analogues to these three with regard to the possibility of understanding the roots of violent behavior? Are there thinkers who have articulated key insights into the human condition that can assist us in understanding violence? I believe that there are. The three analogues I will consider here are Søren Kierkegaard, Eric Voegelin, and René Girard.

*   *   *

In my opinion, Kierkegaard's book *The Sickness unto Death* is the most brilliant analysis of Nazism that has been published thus far. This is the case even though it was written in the middle of the nineteenth century. I need to explain what I mean by this somewhat odd claim.

In his earlier book *The Concept of Anxiety*, Kierkegaard had put his finger on the key difference between the psychology of human beings and that of the lower animals. Human beings have possibilities open to them that are not available to the lower animals; we have an open future that we can have a hand in shaping through our own choices. In other words, we are free. This may seem to be a great thing, but Kierkegaard is very realistic about the ramifications: we experience the emotions of angst, anxiety, and dread in a way that the other animals do not.[1] This anxiety that is the foundation of our psychology is deeply disturbing, painful, and burdensome. To a great extent, our lives are simply the strategies that we invent to manage our anxiety and keep it in check.

The Sickness unto Death builds on this understanding of human psychology by focusing on the various malformations of the human spirit that result from the many choices we make in managing our anxiety. Often, these choices are made at a mental level that is below full consciousness. Kierkegaard is wrestling with the paradox that we are free and are making choices, while at the same time remaining unaware of some of the most fundamental choices we are making. He analyzes with great subtlety the many variations of human psychological disorder that result from our tendency to veer toward the eternal and away from the temporal (or vice versa), or our tendency to soar into flights of imaginative fantasy, while ignoring the necessities of life (or vice versa). Underlying all of these malformations of the human spirit is the basic drumbeat of human disorder: the refusal to become the self that God wants us to become.[2] In other words, when we seek to manage our anxiety using our own methods, we are living in defiance of the Creator who calls us into the strenuous pathway of self-transcendent growth into maturity as human beings.

When we combine the message of this book with Kierkegaard's ethical treatise *Works of Love*, we can see how he comprehends Nazism at a greater depth than any of our historians have been able to do. The central message of *Works of Love* is that the matrix of our being, the creative pull of God, is directing us to love our neighbor just as we love ourselves.[3] But as long as human beings are living lives rooted in rebellion against the possibility of their own development as human beings, it will be impossible for us to love our neighbor. Instead, we will hate, attack, and kill our neighbors because the deepest motive of our being is to kill off the possibility of our own selfhood. Our animosity toward the human cultural Other arises out of our ill will toward the possibility that we could become an other to our self, the possibility of genuine growth into maturity.[4] In other words, human beings are violent not simply because they are immature, but because they insist upon remaining immature when an alternative is presented to them. Kierkegaard is bringing into philosophical articulation the idea that violence is a disease of selfhood. In my opinion, his understanding of this point was not simply ahead of his time; it is still ahead of our time.

The second author that I will put forward as an analogue to the Copernican astronomers is Eric Voegelin. His thought arises out of a reading of Kierkegaard and other modern and ancient thinkers who were able to express through their writings a vision of the health of the human soul, in contrast to that sickness of the soul that seems to be the default setting for human life. Kierkegaard had spoken of the tendency of human beings to make flights into fantasy worlds in their imaginations. Voegelin develops a similar line of thought in his critique of Gnosticism as a perpetual temptation for human beings. Gnosticism is the practice of refusing to live within the givenness of reality, with its ambiguities and anxieties. The Gnostic seeks release from doubt and pain by inhabiting an imaginary world of humanly invented salvific "truths." In the modern world, this tendency can be seen in both extreme left-wing and extreme right-wing movements. Marxism manifests the fantasy world of the classless society that will be created through a festival of supposedly temporary violence. In Voegelin's words: "Man cannot transform himself into a superman; the attempt to create a superman is the attempt to murder man. Historically, the murder of God is not followed by the superman, but by the murder of man: the deicide of the gnostic theoreticians is followed by the homicide of the revolutionary practitioners."[5] Marxism can be seen as the disease of the human spirit when it tries to live exclusively in the future, while rejecting the past and living unethically in the present. Nazism manifests the fantasy world of the master race that must continually convince itself of its superiority by murdering as many innocent victims as possible. Nazism was a kind of fundamentalist nationalism that tried to revive an image of the past through sacrificial action in the present. Al Qaeda is similar in relying on the sacrificial killing of innocent people to magically usher in an apocalyptic transformation of reality that will restore the glory of Islam.[6] Looked at from this perspective, we can see that at the root of violence is the refusal of human beings to live in the fullness of time: past, present, and future. The constructive side of Voegelin's thought sketches out what it means to do precisely this: to live as a creature, in time, in response to the pull of the divine toward ethical relations with other human beings.

The third author I will point to is René Girard, the self-styled anthropologist whose theories regarding the relationship between religion and violence have stimulated considerable scholarly conversation. Girard argues that human beings have a basic feeling of lack, of deprivation, in relation to others. We are continually comparing ourselves to others and writhing in pain because those others have things that we don't have. If we are to draw even with them or surpass them, then we must acquire the same things they possess. In other words, we must mimic their desires. But if I am imitating the desires of someone else, then by definition I am making myself into a rival of that other for the possession of those things. Rivalry leads to conflict and potentially to violence. If everyone in society has the same basic psychology, as Girard suggests they do, then we have just written the recipe for a war of all against all. How will society prevent itself from experiencing a meltdown into social chaos? By choosing a scapegoat to attack. By sacrificing a particular individual or members of a minority group within society, a culture finds a way for violent impulses to be channeled and controlled. According to Girard, this universal scapegoating mechanism is the origin not only of political structures, but also of religious structures. Of course, in the ancient world, this distinction was either unknown or highly ambiguous.

Girard argues that violence is a *skandalon*, in other words, an event that causes immense fascination in human beings. The initial acquisitive rivalry that arose out of mimetic desire can be transmuted into the conflictual rivalry of enemy brothers who seek to outdo one another in demonstrations of power and violence. This is how Girard interprets the never-ending cycle of violence and revenge in the Middle East, and the September 11 attacks and the response that they brought forward from the United States government. Implicit in his commentary is the faint hope that there is another way for human beings to relate to one another. We can break the satanic fascination of violence only if we begin to imitate a different kind of model—a nonviolent model such as Jesus.[7]

At first glance, it may look as though Girard's theory is worlds apart from Kierkegaard's. Girard is arguing that the key to understanding violence is social psychology, while Kierkegaard is resolutely focused on understanding individual psychology. In my view, these views are not incompatible; they are in fact two sides of the same coin. Kierkegaard's thought begins at a deeper level psychologically, with a description of how the human spirit becomes derailed if it does not respond to its native anxiety in a healthy way. This correlates with what Girard says about the feeling of lack that underlies mimetic desire. We feel lack because we are immature, we are unformed, and we are thrown out into the social world before we can fully comprehend our situation. Kierkegaard's thought, which has been unfairly labeled "individualistic," actually contains a very perceptive development of the social and political ramifications of the malformation of the human spirit. His essay on the theme "the crowd is untruth," for example, gives us a perfect epigraph for, and anticipation of, Girard's theory of society.[8]

*   *   *

I have been arguing that we cannot understand the motivations of violent persons if we simply listen to them talk about their motivations. That is like asking a mental patient to diagnose himself. But Kierkegaard, Voegelin, and Girard do give us the key philosophical tools we need to understand human motivations. For Kierkegaard, the good that is being intended through violent action is protection of the immature ego from the possibility of growth in selfhood. The pain that is involved in the process of growth is narcissistically rejected in favor of the comfort that results from believing that one is in control of one's own future. Voegelin's thought works within this basic framework, which has its roots in the Bible and Greek philosophy. He provides a highly elaborate philosophy of consciousness that outlines the "second realities," the comforting Gnostic dreamworlds that are created by those who refuse to rise up into the stature of what it means to be a human being living in time and with others. Girard's thought unveils the "good" of social peace and order that is generated through the scapegoating mechanism. Those who are supporting the act of scapegoating will always say that the victim deserved what he got and the world is better off without him. That is the official ideology. But what is really going on underneath the event of scapegoating is the unconscious logic of societal formation and preservation. The benefits of this process are enjoyed by all of those still in the land of the living who are now able to take their place within the new societal order of "justice."

In my view, the important insights into the deep springs of human behavior that are articulated by Kierkegaard, Voegelin, Girard, and many other authors constitute a crucial watershed in human intellectual history. In other words, we do not need to remain in the state of not comprehending violence forever, paralyzed by ignorance and fear. We can understand violence. The philosophical tools we need in order to understand it have already been forged. The time is ripe for us to pick up those tools and multiply their use throughout wider and wider circles of humanity. When we do so, we will be accomplishing the New Copernican Revolution.

*   *   *

Currently, people like Osama bin Laden are able to recruit at least some followers from within the Muslim world by preaching a message of love for Islam and hatred toward the United States and Jews. What would have to happen for a message such as that to be met with rejection by *everyone* within the Muslim world? What would have to happen—what would have to change—to bring that about?

What if all Muslim clerics and teachers and professors were to denounce violence at every opportunity? That's on the right track, but more is needed than simply denouncing violence. What we need is a real unveiling of the falseness of the way of thinking that justifies violence for a warped cause. What if every Christian and Jewish and Muslim and Hindu and Buddhist religious leader all over the world didn't merely denounce violence, but could actually speak articulately about the psychology of violent people? What if every history and social science teacher on the planet could do the same thing, and every politician, and every journalist, and every accountant, and every engineer, and every medical worker, and every soccer mom, and so forth. If people in general could not only *denounce*, but actually *explain* the nature of the mental distortions that lead people to commit acts of violence, and if they actually did do so on every appropriate occasion, imagine how the atmosphere of human culture would be changed dramatically. The advocates of violence would have to defend their positions against ideas they had never encountered before.

Violence thrives in the darkness. If the light of understanding were to shine brightly in more and more people, then the kind of moral retardation that we are familiar with will start to retreat into the shadows more and more until it is all gone. I realize that this is optimistic, but I'm not saying that this is going to happen in five years. It may take one hundred or two hundred years, but eventually *violence will be defeated by being understood.* Violence can't stand up to understanding in the long run, because the engine driving it is fear of self-knowledge.

We can summarize the modern natural sciences as trying to tackle the problem of natural evil. They are trying to be able to predict volcanic eruptions and tornadoes and asteroids, to cure cancer, and so forth. But moral evil, what we human beings do to ourselves through violence, is a much greater threat to our well-being than any natural events are. What we need are scientists of the spirit. We have them; it's only that most of the time we ignore them because we prefer to live in a medieval moral universe at the same time that we are living in a modern physical universe.

As I have been arguing, a considerable amount of thought has already gone into the problem of understanding the psychology of violent people. I have referred to Kierkegaard, Voegelin, and Girard as cutting-edge philosophical thinkers on this topic. There is also a large amount of literature on this topic written by social scientists, historians, and religionists. While this literature may not be as sophisticated and as deep as that written by the cutting-edge authors, it is still important and well worth reading. The question I ask now is this: how can the knowledge that is contained in this genre of literature make a real impact on human history? Here, we need to look at the sphere of education. Let's start with high school education. What subjects do people study in high school? Math, biology, literature, history, woodworking. But do they study violence? Violence will be referred to occasionally in history courses, but it isn't really studied in any intentional and careful way. I suggest that it should be. What if all high school students had a one-semester required course in which they were exposed to various theories about violent behavior? It would be a major step forward if high school students could start thinking along these lines, if they could start asking the right questions. The problem with education is that it often assumes that you need to give people the right answers, when it is really giving them the right questions that is crucial. We live in a world in which the adults have not been raised to ask questions about why people are violent. That is why events such as 9/11 leave people stunned and speechless. What would it take to have a society that would comprehend events like those? It would take a long, patient, generational process of education.

Let's consider higher education. A long time ago it was a tradition for college seniors to take a course in moral philosophy that was the capstone of their education. That idea has fallen into disuse, but it could be revived with a focus on violence. Even if it were an elective, rather than required, a course on violence could get ideas circulating among the students and faculty in a positive way. Colleges are supposed to give people the tools they need to be productive citizens in their society and ethical participants in the human race. But does that actually happen? How will it happen if something as important as violence isn't a part of the curriculum? After everything that has happened in the past century—the world wars, the Holocaust, Hiroshima, Stalin's purges, Rwanda, Bosnia, and so forth—is it really the case that the college experience is merely a glorified trade school? Is the academic world helpless and unable to come up with a plan for what needs to be taught to make things better in the future? I don't think so. I think we can educate people to become citizens of the planet who are capable of understanding what is involved in living in peace with one's neighbors.

What I'm suggesting is not that there must be an ethical doctrine that everyone is taught. I simply want important questions to be asked. If all people of goodwill were thinking about violence in new and creative ways, I think the ferment would be very beneficial. But for that to happen, the higher education culture needs to say clearly that reflecting on violence is a crucial part of the curriculum.

There should also be an intentional focus on the topic of violence within the sphere of theological education. Those who are training to become the religious teachers in their communities need to be equipped to be leaders in the spread of understanding regarding the roots of violence in human culture. The long history of entanglement between violence and religion needs to be well understood by the next generation of religious leaders, so that their efforts in interreligious dialogue and peacemaking will be grounded in a perceptive interpretation of the past and a realistic vision of the future.

*   *   *

The impulse to violence is to a great extent driven by emotions that are not under the control of the person's reason and understanding. So the new Copernican revolution we are talking about is not only a matter of intellectual understanding. It is much deeper than that, on the level of emotions. People usually think that emotions are things that happen to them, not things they have control over. If human beings are simply puppets manipulated by the strings of emotions they have no control over, then they are not truly free. I refuse to believe that. We are free, meaning that we can rise above our circumstances. We can think thoughts we haven't thought before; we can use our will and reason to shape our emotions in constructive directions rather than destructive ones. We can choose to relate to people in ways that are morally superior to the ways they are relating to us, instead of letting ourselves be dragged down to their level. Those possibilities are where our essential humanity shines through most clearly.

Violence is ultimately a war against the idea that human beings are free. Violence is the self's war against the possibility of the self's development, which is to say its freedom from the past. Violence says: "I'm going to kill this person I hate because I don't want to go through the pain of self-development that would be required for me to become a person whose emotions are free from the past and from my tribe or nation. I prefer to remain trapped in unfreedom and to impose this entrapment on others."

By explaining what is going on as clearly as possible, we can at least give spiritual and intellectual freedom a fighting chance to become attractive to people. Becoming a mature person can never be forced; it is always a free response to a call, an invitation. What I'm suggesting is that the call of freedom doesn't even have an opportunity to be heard where the intellectual horizons are so narrow that the true dimensions of the problems of violence can't even be seen. Making those dimensions clearer is something that thinking and education can do. But it isn't going to happen automatically or inevitably. It takes spiritual effort from individuals and groups to push these sorts of ideas forward in various venues: education, religion, the media, and so forth.

Spiritual effort, striving toward the good and overcoming the evil within oneself, is the basic meaning of the word "jihad." What we need is for people from all religions and philosophies to take up a jihad against violence itself. This is how we can put our finger on the most basic difference between false and true jihads. False jihads think that their struggle is against flesh and blood, against particular people or nations that have been moralistically labeled as evil. But the true jihad is one that sees *violence itself*, and the psychological ignorance that undergirds it, as the enemy that must be overcome. The path of the true jihad leads both oneself and others into a new way of living that has grown beyond violence. This is what Saint Paul was pointing toward when he wrote: "Do not be overcome by evil, but overcome evil with good" (Rom. 12:21).

NOTES

1. Søren Kierkegaard, *The Concept of Anxiety: A Simple Psychologically Orienting Deliberation on the Dogmatic Issue of Hereditary Sin* (Princeton, NJ: Princeton University Press, 1980), p. 42.

2. Søren Kierkegaard, *The Sickness Unto Death: A Christian Psychological Exposition for Upbuilding and Awakening* (Princeton, NJ: Princeton University Press, 1983), p. 74.

3. Søren Kierkegaard, *Works of Love* (Princeton, NJ: Princeton University Press, 1995), p. 24.

4. Charles K. Bellinger, *The Genealogy of Violence: Reflections on Creation, Freedom, and Evil* (Oxford and New York: Oxford University Press, 2001), p. 67.

5. Eric Voegelin, *Modernity without Restraint* (Columbia: University of Missouri Press, 2000), p. 284.

6. Political scientist Barry Cooper has perceptively applied Voegelin's thought to al Qaeda in Barry Cooper, *New Political Religions, Or, an Analysis of Modern Terrorism* (Columbia: University of Missouri Press, 2004).

7. For an overview of Girard's thought, see: René Girard, *The Girard Reader*, ed. James G. Williams (New York: Crossroad, 1996); and René Girard, *I See Satan Fall Like Lightning* (Maryknoll, NY: Orbis Books, 2001).

8. Søren Kierkegaard, *The Point of View* (Princeton, NJ: Princeton University Press, 1998), pp. 105–12.

5

WHO BROKE
THEIR VOW FIRST?

THE "THREE VOWS" AND
CONTEMPORARY THINKING ABOUT
JEWISH HOLY WAR

Reuven Firestone

According to the Hebrew Bible, God commands Israel[1] repeatedly to conquer the land that God promised to them. Early on in scriptural reference, this land is the "Land of Canaan."[2] Later, it is referred to as the "Land of Israel."[3] All these wars of conquest are authorized by God. In the West today, we would define them as "holy wars," despite the fact that biblical terminology does not include a term that would identify divinely authorized wars as "holy." On the contrary, the term "holy" (*qadosh, qodesh*), in traditional Jewish parlance, is reserved almost uniquely for the biblical sacrificial system. In fact, there is no consistent term to describe or differentiate divinely authorized wars from any others in the Hebrew Bible. The uniqueness of "holy wars" of conquest lies in the fact that they are commanded by God.[4] Nevertheless, although the Bible does not use the term "holy" to define its wars, the very fact that most of Israel's biblical wars were authorized or associated with the God of Israel makes them comparable to "holy war"—or divinely authorized warring in other religious systems and contexts.

According to biblical historiography, Israel's wars, whether initiated by Israel or for defense against attacking enemies, were successful when the people obeyed their God. But despite divine authority for engaging in war, Israel failed when it did not obey God. Thus, the People of Israel failed in their first collective attempt to fight their enemies because of their failure to listen to God.[5] All subsequent failures and defeats, as well as victories, were understood in biblical depictions as divinely prescribed, including the destruction of the Jerusalem Temple in 586 BCE and the associated massacres and population transfers by the Babylonian armies.[6]

According to biblical and postbiblical traditional Jewish historiography, history moves exclusively by way of God's will. When Israel's wars were successful it was seen as a sign that God looked at his people with satisfaction, but when they failed in their wars it was understood to signify God's anger against his people.

Because of this view of history, the destruction of the first Temple in 586 BCE was a huge shock to the self-concept of Israel. But God was understood to have repented in his anger by commanding the Persian king Cyrus to rebuild the Jerusalem Temple and bring the Judeans back from Babylonian captivity only two or three generations later.[7] The Maccabean military success against the Seleucids further reinforced the view that God helped Israel to defeat its enemies and conquer or reconquer the land promised to God's people.

When Rome entered the Middle East, however, the situation changed radically. All wars against Rome for control over the Land of Israel failed. The Temple was destroyed for the second time— this time by Rome—but no new Cyrus would serve as God's tool for the demolition of the hated empire. No one, whether Jewish or foreign, would bring Jews back to their land. On the contrary, the last Jewish rebellion against the Roman Empire, co-led by a rabbi named Akiva ben Yosef and a general named Bar Kosiba (also known as "Bar Kokhba"), failed miserably and with devastating effect upon the Jewish communities of Judea. According to the writer of Roman history, Dio Cassius (d. 235), hundreds of thousands of Jews were killed in the fighting, and many more were killed and sold into slavery.[8] Jewish sources confirm an appalling level of human depravation and destruction.[9] Jews were forbidden by Roman authorities from even entering the city of Jerusalem, and any Jews found there were killed on the spot. Most survivors were exiled from or simply fled Judea and found refuge in the north or in Babylonia (today's Iraq).

The surviving rabbis, it seems clear, felt the need to put an end to the expectation that pious warring would turn the tide against the enemies of Israel. They discouraged groups organized to return to the Land, and even discouraged individuals from returning, the former probably from the fear that an organized return such as occurred under the leadership of Ezra would have been considered threatening by the Roman authorities. The rabbis succeeded through a series of paradigmatic interpretations of scriptural verses. One such interpretation, or more correctly, family of interpretations, is known as the "Three Vows."[10]

Through the Three Vows paradigm, the rabbis forbade mass movements that might instigate a backlash by the various Gentile hegemonies under which the Jews lived even after the Christianization of the empire in the fourth century and in lands beyond its borders. The Three Vows refer to a phrase occurring three times in the Song of Songs: *I make you swear, o daughters of Jerusalem, by the gazelles and by the hinds of the field, do not wake or rouse love until it is wished.*[11]

The general rabbinic understanding of the repeated phrase is that God is making the daughters of Jerusalem, a metaphor for Israel, swear not to wake or rouse love—understood as attempting to bring the Messiah—until it is wished, meaning, until God decides the time is right. Attempting to bring the Messiah through human initiative rather than waiting patiently for God to do so is sometimes called "forcing God's hand," which would only bring God's wrath upon the Jewish people and further disasters. The discussion articulated in this Talmudic pericope became symbolic for Jews for well over a millennium.

Rabbi Yose in the name of Rabbi Hanina said: Why are there these three vows [in the Song of Songs]? One [teaches] that Israel should not ascend [to the Land of Israel] in a wall (*bechomah*), in one the Holy One made Israel swear that they would not rebel against the nations of the world, and in one the Holy One made the nations of the world swear that they would not subjugate Israel too harshly.

This paragraph explains the repeated phrase as articulating three divinely authorized requirements. Two relate to Israel and one to the rest of the world. The second and third requirements are quite clear, but "ascension in a wall" is not immediately comprehensible. Rashi (d. 1104), the great medieval Talmud commentator, explains the phrase simply as meaning ascension by force (*beyad chazaqah*). Later on in the Talmudic pericope, Rabbi Elazar is cited as explaining the phrase *by the gazelles and by the hinds of the field* as if in God's words: "If you carry out the vow, good. But if not, I will permit your flesh [to be consumed] like [that of] gazelles or hinds of the field."

This exegesis emerged as a paradigm of classical rabbinic thought: God requires through a series of vows made by Israel and by the Gentile peoples of the world that (1) Israel neither move or "ascend" to the Land of Israel en masse[12] (2) nor rebel against their inferior position under the rule of Gentiles. In response, (3) God will not allow the Gentiles to persecute the Jews "overly much" (*yoter midday*). If the Jews would not agree to these terms or break either of their vows in the future, then they would be subject to divinely authorized violence at the hands of the Gentiles, permitting their "flesh [to be consumed] like [that of] gazelles or hinds of the field." It should be observed that the rabbinic exegesis cited here did not consider the possibility that the Gentile nations might break *their* vow and persecute the Jews "overly much."

Moreover, these words should not be read out of context, for the Three Vows paradigm occurs within a Talmudic pericope that also conveys a number of statements strongly supporting living in the

Land of Israel. But after these pro-Land of Israel statements are articulated, the Three Vows contextualizes them by suggesting that, while living within the Land of Israel is good, rebelling against the exilic condition by doing so is dangerous and must not be allowed to occur.

The prohibitions against "going up in a wall" and "rebelling against the Gentiles" were not considered by the sages as having been articulated as direct divine commandments per se, though they were often considered authoritative.[13] Nevertheless, when Maimonides (d. 1204) wrote his *Book of the Commandments*[14] in which he gave his accounting of the 613 commandments assumed by rabbinic tradition to have been given by God in the first five books of the Hebrew Bible,[15] he did not include the Three Vows.[16] Nor did Nahmanides (d. 1270) mention the vows in his commentary on Maimonides when he argued, against Maimonides, that simply moving to the Land of Israel and settling there was a form of commanded war, a war of *mitzvah*, and still in force.[17]

Aviezer Ravitzky has shown how medieval Jews were divided over moving to the Land of Israel and settling it. Those who opposed it made the Land of Israel a symbolic, messianic category that remained off limits to Jews in real time. The final phrase of the verse from the biblical Song of Songs, *do not wake or rouse love until it is wished*, suggested to them that only when God wished in some unknown and unknowable time, would he rouse the divine love by bringing the Messiah. The full meaning of the repeated phrase, therefore, was that God has made Israel swear not to rebel against the Gentile nations or move en masse to the Land of Israel until the coming of the Messiah: *I make you swear, o daughters of Jerusalem, by the gazelles and by the hinds of the field, do not wake or rouse love until it is wished.*

On the other hand, proponents of relocation to the Land of Israel attempted to dissociate the Land of Israel from any sense of messianism and constructed barriers between their immigration and any expectations of a final divine redemption. Their move was not "in order to conquer," nor was it a mass immigration "ascending in a wall."[18]

Leaders of premodern Jewish communities observed occasional catastrophes that resulted from Jewish messianic mass movements, such as the devastating Sabbatean movement (1665–66). As mass movements that attempted to escape extremely difficult conditions under Gentile political control, they appeared to carry an element of rebellion against Gentile "nations of the world." Moreover, collective immigration to the traditional Land of Israel appeared to be a kind of "ascension in a wall." Because of such unpleasant premodern experiences, therefore, many in the Orthodox Jewish world condemned the early Zionists. Their proposed mass emigrations to Palestine under Turkish and then British mandate rule were considered dangerous and threatening to the well-being of the Jewish community.[19]

In fact, however, most of the earliest Zionists would be identified today as "Orthodox" Jews based on their traditional behaviors and obvious Eastern European Jewish culture. But within a short period, the leadership and then the rank and file of the Zionist movement were avowedly secular. To these nonobservant Jews, the Three Vows were meaningless. To the religiously Orthodox minority of Zionists, however, the vows remained a significant hindrance to their participation in the Zionism movement. Because of the profound implications associated with the vows, Orthodox religious Zionists were often accused by their Orthodox non-Zionist or anti-Zionist compatriots of trying to "force the hand of God" to bring the Messiah, an act that could only bring disaster upon the Jewish people.

In response, "Religious Zionists" (the term that has come to describe Zionists who are religiously Orthodox) claimed that their only goal in building up the Land of Israel was to provide a place of refuge for Jews in distress. The truly messianic nature of "Religious Zionism" only became publicly acknowledged by Religious Zionists (or perhaps only became recognized by most) after what was considered the divine miracle of victory in the June War of

1967. Until 1967, the intellectual organs of religious Zionism rarely suggested that the establishment of the State of Israel was part of the divine plan that would culminate in the messianic coming. Immediately after the victory it seemed as if a dam had burst and everyone in the Religious Zionist camp was writing about the beginning of messianic redemption.[20]

The discussion turned to national messianism, or the role of the State of Israel in God's design for a final redemption. Discussion regarding national messianism and war are not infrequently articulated in written discourse among religiously Orthodox Zionists in terms of the Three Vows, especially after the 1967 war. For this discourse, nagging questions continued to be asked. Was what became clearly recognized as the mass immigration of Jews to Israel through the Zionist movement "ascension in a wall"? Was the act of the State of Israel in setting its own independent political course, often directly against the United Nations, "rebellion against the nations"? Or are these justified in a cosmic sense by the Gentiles' breaking of *their* vow not to subjugate (or persecute— *yishta'abdu*) the Jews overly much in the modern period, and particularly during the Holocaust.

This is not an idle question from the perspective of traditional Judaism. For many, the stakes are extremely high. What is in the balance is the possible redemption of the Jewish people—or possibly another catastrophe along the lines of the destructions of the two Jerusalem Temples and the disaster of the Bar Kokhba Rebellion. Perhaps the best way to imagine the possible negative outcome of the wrong interpretation is another Holocaust, however one might imagine such a forbidden thought.

Rabbi Yisachar Shlomo Teichtel referred to the Three Vows in his book, *Em HaBanim Semeychah*, written during the Holocaust, which he witnessed from Budapest.[21] After writing his book, Teichtel died in a boxcar on his way to a death camp. Teichtel is notable because he changed course radically from anti-Zionism as a result of his personal observation of the systematic destruction of the Jewish communities of Europe, and he called for a concerted effort to move to the Land of Israel and settle there. According to Teichtel, Israel had become so accustomed to exile that it could not understand that it was being punished for rejecting the Land and having no faith in God's promise. "[W]e do not feel that sin is causing our suffering for so long, but it is because we do not push ourselves to return to the Land of our ancestors."[22]

In his brief treatment of the Three Vows, he understood the prohibition against "ascending in a wall" in a positive sense, meaning that "we are to use the natural means available to us, such as requesting that the rulers have mercy on us to end our exile and to conquer the Land through [legal] monetary acquisition . . . but not to rely on miracles."[23] This is a surprising repositioning of the interpretive responses to the paradigm. Traditionally, the Three Vows was understood as a requirement *not* to engage in natural means to ascend to the Land, for that would have been considered an act of human volition to attempt to "force" the coming of the Messiah. On the contrary, we have observed that the traditional position was to await the divine will. In most scenarios, that would be expressed in the miracle of the ingathering of Jewish exiles from throughout the world to the Land of Israel.

Teichtel begins with a qualified call to move to the Land of Israel: "It is commanded upon individuals to ascend, but not to the entire community, because we have been made to vow that we not ascend in a wall against the will of the political powers (*malkhuyot*)." But he moves from this to express assurance that it will soon become a mass movement. "[A]fter the political powers give us authorization to take possession of the Land of Israel and to ascend to it, then the commandment returns to becoming a communal commandment. In addition to the single individual being obligated to work diligently for this, it becomes again a communal obligation."[24]

Four years later in 1947, when war between Jews and Arabs seemed inevitable, Rabbi Isaac HaLevi Herzog (d. 1959), the chief rabbi of Palestine under the British mandate, took a similar position. In a responsum to the question as to whether the Three Vows remain in force, he replied: "There is no ruling (*halakhah*) that forbids us from establishing a Jewish state with the permission of the nations (*bireshut ha'umot*) before the coming of the Redeemer. . . . The Three Vows have validity, in my opinion, only in relation to the nations that rule over the Land of Israel. This is quite clear, that [the prohibition] not to rebel against the nations of the world has no validity in relation to the nations that do not rule,[25] for this is not their business."[26] He added that Jews who fight for the British holders of mandate Palestine against the enemies of Britain (and the Jews) in World War II do not transgress the Torah command against rebelling against the Gentiles. On the contrary, joining in the war on the side of the nations in power over the Land of Israel against ". . . the nations that do not have power over Israel . . . is not rebellion but rather, war, and it is not said that God made Israel swear not to war against the nations of the world."

Herzog thus opens the way for Orthodox Jews to volunteer to train and fight in the British army. In a discussion over Maimonides' decision to exclude the Three Vows from his compendium of official commandments, Herzog arrives at the following observation:

> In my view, [Maimonides] held that because it is said [in the paradigm of the Three Vows] that [God] made the nations swear they would not oppress Israel too much, and He made Israel swear that they would not rebel, the meaning is that the vows are dependent on one another. And since the nations transgressed their vow already and oppressed Israel too much, we are released from the two vows. . . . Maimonides, therefore, did not mention the Three Vows, because in his opinion we were already released from them after the nations transgressed the vow that was placed upon them. . . .[27]

One of the most venerable early thinkers in the postindependence activist Religious Zionist camp was Rabbi Sha'ul Yisraeli (d. 1995), who in 1957 was one of the first to write seriously and openly about both the halakhic and transcendent meaning of the

Jewish state. Like most Religious Zionists, he saw the international political process as a series of divinely established stepping stones along the path to Redemption. Decisions of the League of Nations, the United Nations and even individual governments were read as divine signs of impending salvation. "The essence of the return of [the people] Israel to the Land of Israel is not through an overt divine visitation (*peqidah geluyah*), for then the Vow would have been removed, but rather, through ascension with the permission and authority of the political powers."[28] Mass ascension to Palestine and, later, the State of Israel was therefore all part of the divine plan. As noted previously, the prohibition against ascending in a wall was defined by the authoritative medieval Ashkenazi commentator Rashi as "going up together by force" (*yachad beyad chazaqah*), which, according to Yisraeli, was neither the intent nor the modus operandi of the Zionist movement. In any case, the decision of the United Nations authorizing Jews to establish a Jewish state and declare national independence that would open the gates of the state to mass emigration nullified the vow not "to ascend in a wall." With the nullification of the vow, all of Israel became required to engage in settling the Land of Israel. The warning not to rebel against the nations of the world thus applied only in the lands of the exile, but not in the Land of Israel.[29]

> The establishment of the State in our days, which occurred according to the declaration of the nations to give the right to Israel, is the stage of which it is stated, "until [God] pleases," and it is the first stage in the way of Redemption, through which a strong public and independent rule in the Land of Israel is the establishment of the kingdom of the King Messiah.[30]

With the messianic suggestion associated with the conquest of most of the biblical lands in the 1967 war, Orthodox religious scholars, and particularly Religious Zionist activist thinkers, became far more invested in legitimating the right for the State of Israel to control those territories, and they naturally became more invested in the legitimacy of Jewish militancy in general. After 1967, Orthodox thinkers began to discover and cite a range of pre-modern thinkers and arguments that would support the messianic nature of the State of Israel. These include the view that not all Jews are required to return to traditional Jewish practice in order for the messianic Redemption to occur, and that the great agricultural successes of the modern Jewish state are signs of the immanent Salvation.[31] Despite the increased messianic feeling, establishment rabbis remained careful with their interpretation of the Three Vows. The chief rabbi of the Israel Defense Forces and later chief Ashkenazi rabbi of Israel, Shelomo Goren (d. 1995), provides three reasons for the cancellation of the force of the Three Vows, two of which rely on earlier authorities.[32]

For the first, Rabbi Goren cites Rabbi Chayim Vital (d. 1620), the student of Rabbi Moses Alshekh and the chief disciple and amanuensis of the great mystic Rabbi Isaac Luria, who placed a time limit of one thousand years on the vow, after which it was no longer operational. Goren cites Rabbi Meir Simchah HaCohen of Dvinsk (d. 1926) for the second reason that the Three Vows is no longer in force. According to Rabbi Meir Simchah, the Allied Powers' 1920 confirmation in San Remo of the Balfour Declaration concerning the establishment of a Jewish national home in Palestine was a public affirmation that mass immigration to Palestine could no longer be considered rebellion against the nations. The third reason is based on the requirement for the Jewish people to defend themselves from attack. The 1967 war was "an act of defense of the rights of the State of Israel to sail freely in the Red Sea Straits [which are] within the borders of the holy Land of Israel. . . . The Vow does not apply in any way to a war of survival such as this."[33]

Rabbi Goren cites Chayim Vital further in order to provide support for the Zionist project. Most traditional commentators understand the end of the applicability of the repeated Song of Songs verse *I make you swear, o daughters of Jerusalem . . . do not wake or rouse love until it is wished* to be an inscrutable decision of God into which humanity has absolutely no input. On the contrary, any human attempt to discern the divine will as to the time of the messianic Redemption is doomed to failure and catastrophe. Vital, on the other hand, suggests that God will be willing to bring Redemption only after the Jewish people communicates its intense desire for it: *"do not wake or rouse love until it is wished*, for the sparks of the Redemption need to be awakened by the spiritual will of the people, as it is written there, 'it is for this reason that *I make you swear o daughters of Jerusalem.'"* Goren understood Vital's comments to mean that Israel not attempt to awaken the Redemption until Jews are able to achieve the necessary spiritual will and desire. This is the meaning of *love* in the sentence. The conclusion therefore is that when Israel is truly ready, when its desire is great enough, then Israel will awaken the desire of God to bring the Redemption.[34] What does not need to be said by Rabbi Goren is that the Zionist project and the very existence of a vibrant Jewish state are demonstrations of Israel's readiness and desire, and that it has reached a point where it is indeed bringing on the process of Redemption.

Even after 1967, however, the Three Vows continued to have some force, and yeshiva students raised the question of whether they applied to the contemporary situation. The question continued to be asked very simply because non- or anti-Zionist rabbis continued to write and republish pamphlets and tracts condemning Zionism, and the ammunition of the Three Vows remained a powerful part of the anti-Zionist arsenal.[35]

By the 1970s, Rabbi Tzvi Yehudah Kook became the most symbolic leader of the activist camp of Religious Zionists. Rabbi Tzvi Yehudah, as he was often called, was the only child of Rabbi Abraham Isaac Kook, the first chief rabbi of Palestine under the British Mandate Authority and a great and beloved religious leader of the Jewish population of Palestine. Tzvi Yehudah became the head of Mosad HaRav, which developed into the intellectual center of activist Religious Zionism not long before the 1967 war.[36] When asked about the Three Vows shortly before the October war of 1973, he gave the following answer.[37]

> With regard to the rebellion against the nations of the world, when we were forced to expel English rule from here it was not rebellion against them, for they were not the legal rulers over our land. Rather [they were] temporary mandatory authorities [who were here] in order to prepare the rule of the People of Israel in its land as per the decision of the League of Nations, according to the word of God in the Bible. So when they abused that role, their time had arrived to depart from here. Lastly, ascension in a wall, about which we have been warned: this wall is nothing but the rule of the nations over our land and the place of our Temple. As long as that wall stands, [it does so] through the divine decree of exile. But in the course of the results of the revealed End [of history (*haqetz hameguleh*)], it was annulled and this wall fell, for "the mouth that forbids is the mouth that permits."[38] The Master of the Universe who set up this wall like "an iron partition that divides Israel from its Father in Heaven,"[39] is the one who annulled and took down that wall. And since there is no wall, there is no delay. The issue of ascension in a wall is like the one who vows not to enter a house. When the house falls down, he does not need an [official] annulment of his vow.[40]

Kook equates the proverbial wall of the Three Vows with foreign rule over the Land of Israel. God ordained this foreign rule in the past, but following Rabbi Sha'ul Yisraeli, Kook claims that God has since annulled the authority of foreign rule. This, according to both Yisraeli and Kook, can be proven from the very establishment of a Jewish polity in the State of Israel.

Tzvi Yehudah Kook was not an original thinker, but he is considered by many to have been the person most intimately familiar with the words and writings of his famous and extremely influential father. He thus became influential himself and came to symbolize a messianic activist approach to Zionism. His yeshiva students strove to live deeply traditional Jewish lives while carrying out the activist settlement.

In the early period of the vitalization of Religious Zionism in Kook's yeshiva and the yeshivas that grew out of its influence prior to the 1967 war, this invigorated sense of the need to ascend and settle the Land was activist, but it was nonviolent. It was associated with the agricultural settlements of the religious kibbutz and moshav movements and with a revitalization of Jewish learning.

After the 1967 war it became increasingly energized and aggressive. An organized political-religious movement emerged from the ideological mixture of religious orthodoxy and the well-known secular militant activism that had typified the pioneering ethos of the declining Socialist Zionist movement. The emerging movement was given a powerful push in the aftermath of the 1973 war, when there was increased discussion in Israeli government, military, and public circles about returning the territories conquered in the 1967 war. This new activist Religious Zionist movement became known as *Gush Emunim*, the "Faithful Block." That name has been discarded, but it still typifies what today is called the settler movement.[41] It is important to note that both parts of this combination—secular Socialist Zionism and religiously Orthodox Zionism—were neo-messianic movements. Combined, traditional religion and modern nationalism created a powerful, activist, and thoroughly postmodern messianism.

One result of the emergence of *Gush Emunim* and the settler movement that perpetuated the Gush's ideals was that the Three Vows have for all intents and purposes been annulled. Those in the Orthodox Jewish world who would disagree have long been overwhelmed by the fervor that grew out of the 1967 war, and especially the feverish activism that emerged after the 1973 war.

Even the huge failure of the 1973 war did not become a major setback. Ironically, it energized the movement. It marked a watershed in the fall of Socialist Zionism from ideological dominance in the Jewish state and the beginning of the rise of "Jewish" Zionisms.

Of course all expressions of Zionism are Jewish. Zionism is, by definition, a Jewish nationalist movement. But the dominant ideological force of Socialist Zionism was, theoretically, economic in nature, while the fluid coalition of ideological forces driving the "Jewish Zionisms" of the settler movement emerged out of a Jewish religious or neo-religious base, even among many Jews who would not define themselves as religiously observant.

As the humanistic ideologies emerging out of a socialist vision declined, the inward-looking beliefs of a particularist religious vision became increasingly instrumental in forming a new range of Israeli nationalist ideologies. Some of the thinking imbedded in these includes a reexamination of the meaning of divinely authorized war. According to the more militant activists in the settler movement, the advances marked by the establishment of the state, the success in conquering the biblical lands in the 1967 war and the establishment of Jewish settlements in these areas are all considered expressions of divinely ordained military conquest. During the period from 1967 into the 1980s, conquest became one sign of the coming divine Redemption.

This discourse of militant and military conquest of the Land of Israel is prominent in the more radical writings coming out of the settler movement. Many of these were collected into the short-lived motivational magazines, *Artzi* and *Tzefiyah*.[42] But religiously inspired military conquest in general has increasingly infiltrated the language of Zionist thinkers and teachers of the new pioneers that make up the settler movement and its supporters, and subsequently, increasingly in Zionist discourse in general.

Military conquest is, of course, not new to the State of Israel and its military, politicians, and citizens. The 1948 Israeli War of Independence included military victory over the lands allotted to the Jews by the United Nations Partition Plan and lands beyond those borders. The result of the 1967 war was a conquest of lands that extended the borders of Israeli control far beyond even those borders. But these conquests were hardly religiously inspired. They were considered to be necessary for military and political purposes —not for religious purposes.

It may seem impossible to raise the stakes of war higher than those of the life and death of a nation's noncombatant citizen population. But within the religious thinking of the activists among the Religious Zionist settler movement, the meaning of war is closely associated with the meaning of redemption—and annihilation. To some, the failure of the Jewish people to obey the divine message of the imminent arrival of the Messiah is not simply another missed opportunity for redemption in the long history of Israel. A failure of this magnitude would bring down God's wrath and perhaps unprecedented destruction. In other words, the miracle of the Six-Day War is considered by some to be a sign that God designed for Israel to conquer and settle all of the Bible Land of Israel, including those lands extending far beyond the borders established by the United Nations Partition Plan of 1947, the armistice agreements following the 1948 war, and to some, even beyond the borders established by the 1967 war. Failure to carry out the divine will would therefore be disastrous.

This discourse of conquest is a discourse of "holy war." In reference to the 1973 war, Yehudah Amital writes:

> Every war of Israel is a war for the unity of God.[43] . . . Israel represents by its very existence the divine concept of the unity of God and the divine way of righteousness and justice. The meaning of the victory of Israel is the victory of the divine concept, and also, heaven forbid, the opposite.[44]

In conclusion, we have observed how the Talmudic sages of Rabbinic Judaism were successful for a time in removing an important but dangerous and self-destructive aspect of religion from application in the "real time" of history. But their program was possible only within a particular historical context. The history of Jewish existential and political exile ended with the rise of modernity in the West and the concomitant emergence of nationalisms. These brought a new historical age that required new ways for Jews to cope. As in all periods of Jewish history, the interpretive strategies employed by contemporary religious thinkers responded to the exigencies of their own age. These historical changes enabled them to reexamine the notion of commanded war in the light of the needs of the times.

But not all interpretation, even by respected religious leaders, results in benefits for the community at large. In the case of interpretation of the Three Vows examined above, some Talmudic sages succeeded in radically reducing Jewish anger and violence directed against the Roman authorities, the acts of which had provoked an overwhelming Roman military response and catastrophes suffered by the Jews of Roman Judea. In retrospect and with historical hindsight, the consensus position would certainly consider this good for the survival and continuity of the Jewish people. But the exegesis of these Talmudic sages was largely a reaction to the dangerous and destructive position taken by the greatest Talmudic sage of his generation, Rabbi Akiba (and others), which led to the failed and calamitous rebellion against Rome known as the Bar Kokhba Rebellion. The current revival of Jewish religious fervor, militancy, and violence among Religious Zionists active in the settler movement may finally bring the desired result of divine intervention and messianic redemption. Or it may not.

NOTES

1. The term "Israel" always refers to the People of Israel or Children of Israel ('am yisra'el or beney yisra'el) in Jewish discourse before the establishment of the State of Israel. The actual name of the modern Jewish state is Medinat Yisrael, "the State of [the People of] Israel." In this essay, I use the traditional vocabulary of "Israel" to refer to the Jewish people from the biblical to the modern periods.

2. Gen. 17:8, 45:25; Exod. 6:4, 16:35; Lev. 14:34, 18:3, 25:38; Num. 13:2, 13:17; Deut. 32:29, etc.

3. 1 Sam. 13:19; Ezek. 40:2, 47:18; 2 Chron. 34:7.

4. Num. 33:50–53; Deut. 7:1–2, 20:1–17; Josh. 6:2–5, 8:1, etc.

5. Num. 14:44–45/Deut. 1:42–44.

6. 2 Kings 24:1–4; Jer. 37:27–31, 38:2–3, 39:15–17; 2 Chron. 36:11–21.

7. Isa. 24:26–25:5; Ezra 1:1–8; 2 Chron. 36:22–23.

8. Doron Mendels, *The Rise and Fall of Jewish Nationalism* (Grand Rapids, MI: Eerdmans, 1992), p. 388.

9. Gedalia Alon, *The Jews in Their Land in the Talmudic Age* (Cambridge, MA: Harvard University Press, 1980), pp. 627–37.

10. *Ketubot* 110b–111a, paralleled in the Midrash, *Song of Songs Rabbah* 2:7. For an examination of the impact of the Three Oaths in history, see Aviezer Ravitzky, *Messianism, Zionism, and Jewish Religious Radicalism*, trans. Michael Swirsky and Jonathan Chipman (Chicago: University of Chicago Press, 1996), pp. 211–34.

11. Song of Songs 2:7, 3:5, 8:4. The last rendering of the sentence, in 8:4, does not include "by the gazelles and by the hinds of the field," but the rabbis include it in 8:4 by analogy.

12. "Ascension" or "going up" refers to moving from outside the Land of Israel to within the biblical borders (from whence the modern Hebrew term for emigration to the State of Israel, *'aliyah*). Some considered this a collective prohibition but not a prohibition against individuals who wished to move their families to the Land of Israel.

13. Mordechai Breuer, "The Discussion Concerning the Three Oaths in Recent Generations" (Hebrew), *Ge'ulah uMedinah* (Jerusalem, 1979), pp. 49–57.

14. Jersusalem: Mosad HaRav Kook, 1981, and printed elsewhere in many formats in Hebrew. English translation in two volumes by Charles Chavel (London: Soncino Press, 1967).

15. BT Shabbat 87a.

16. Maimonides did invoke the Three Vows in his Letter to the Yemen, however. He was trying to dissuade the agitated Jewish community of Yemen from following a messianic pretender (*Crisis and Leadership: Epistles of Maimonides* [Philadelphia: JPS, 1985], pp. 130–31.

17. Nahmanides, *Hasagot* or "Comments" on Maimonides' *Book of Commandments*, positive #4 (found in the traditional Hebrew folio editions). The difference between Maimonides and Nahmanides forms part of virtually all contemporary discussions of divinely authorized war in

Judaism. The tension between the Three Vows paradigm and that of "Commanded War" (*milchemet mitzvah*, Babylonian Talmud Sota 45b) will be developed further in an upcoming article.

18. Ravitzky, *Messianism, Zionism, and Jewish Religious Radicalism*, p. 221.

19. *Light for the Righteous* [in Hebrew] (Warsaw, 1900); *Position of the Rabbis* [in Hebrew] (Warsaw, 1902). In the West, anti-Zionism included Orthodox as well as Reform and secular Jewish seekers of emancipation. Rabbi Samson Raphael Hirsch, the leader of German neo-Orthodoxy, understood the Three Vows to mean that the Jews should not seek to create their own nation-state (Ravitzky, *Messianism, Zionism, and Jewish Religious Radicalism*, p. 231).

20. This is clear from newsletters and journals of Orthodox Zionism, such as *Amudim*, the newsletter of *Hakkibutz Haddati*, *Zera'im*, the newsletter of the *Beney Akiva* youth movement, *Machanayim*, the publication of the Chief Military Rabbinate of the Israel Defense Forces, and many other less influential publications.

21. Yisachar Shlomo Teichtel, *Em HaBanim Semeychah* (Jerusalem: Kol Mevaser, 1998). Translated by Pesach Schindler as *Restoration of Zion as a Response During the Holocaust* (Hoboken, NJ: Ktav, 1999). Citations are from the Hebrew edition.

22. Ibid., p. 8.

23. Ibid., pp. 194–95.

24. Ibid., pp. 307–308.

25. This is a reference to the local Palestinian Arabs and neighboring Arab states.

26. *The Collected Writings of Rabbi Yitzhaq Isaac HaLevi Herzog* [in Hebrew], vol. 1 (Jerusalem: Mosad HaRav Kook/Yad HaRav Herzog, n.d.), p. 121. This responsum appears in a slightly different version in *Techumin* 4 (1983), and *Sefer HaTzionut HaDatit*, 2 vols. (Jerusalem: Mosad HaRav Kook, 1977), 1:60f.

27. *Sefer HaTziyonut Hadatit* 1:62–63.

28. *Sefer Eretz Chemdah* (1957; Jerusalem: Mossad Harav Kook, 1999), p. 31.

29. Isaac Axelrad, "The Halakhic Problem of Giving Back Territories from the Land of Israel: Law and Ideology" [in Hebrew], *HaPeraklit* 41 (1993): 21.

30. *Eretz Chemdah*, p. 35.

31. Shelomo Aviner, *Am Kelavi'* (Jerusalem, 1983), 2:114–15, 119–20. See also Rabbi Meir Blumenfeld, "On the Vow Not to Go Up as a Wall," *Shanah BeShanah* (1974): 151–55; Rabbi Menachem M. Kasher, "Torah Position on the Vow that Israel Not Go Up as a Wall to the Land of Israel," *Shanah BeShanah* (1977): 213–28; Rabbi Moshe Tzvi Neria, "Our Right to the Land of Israel," *Torah sheBe`al-Peh* (1974): 149–80, etc. Abraham Isaac Kook was an exception who wrote about the messianic implications of the new Jewish settlements' agricultural attainments even before the Balfour Declaration (Zvi Yaron, *The Philosophy of Rabbi Kook* [Jerusalem: World Zionist Organization, 1991], pp. 234–35.

32. *Torat HaMedinah* (Jerusalem: Chemed, 1996), pp. 36–42.

33. *Torat HaMedinah*, p. 42.

34. Shelomo Goren, *Mishnat HaMedinah* [in Hebrew] (Jerusalem: Chemed, 1999), p. 23.

35. See, for example, Rabbi Yoel Teitelbaum, *On the Redemption and Recompense* (Jerusalem, 1982, 5th printing). First printing in Brooklyn: Jerusalem Publishing, 1967. Teitelbaum is the head of the Satmer Hasidim, a community that is adamantly opposed to Zionism and the establishment of a Jewish polity for reasons cited above.

36. G. Aran, "From Religious Zionism to Zionist Religion," in *Social Foundations of Judaism*, ed. Calvin Goldscheider and Jacob Neusner (Englewood Cliffs, NJ: Prentice Hall, 1990), pp. 259–81; Menahem Friedman, "Jewish Zealots: Conservative versus Innovative," in *Jewish Fundamentalism in Comparative Perspective*, ed. Laurence Silberstein, (New York: New York University Press, 1983), pp. 148–63; Myron J. Aaronoff, "The Institutionalisation and Cooptation of a Charismatic, Messianic, Religious-Political Revitalisation Movement," in *The Impact of Gush Emunim: Politics and Settlement in the West Bank*, ed. David Newman (New York: St. Martin's Press, 1985), pp. 46–69.

37. Rabbi Tzvi Yehudah Kook, "Clarification About the Claim of the Three Vows" [in Hebrew], in *Lenetivot Yisrael*, 3 vols., 3:217–18. This brief statement was originally published in *HaTzofeh*, the daily Hebrew newspaper of the Israeli National Religious Party, September 15, 1973, one month before the October war.

38. A reference to God (this is a citation from the Jerusalem Talmud, *Terumot* chap. 9).

39. A slight variation from the Babylonian Talmud, *Pesachim* 85b and Sota 38a.

40. Cf. *Shulchan Arukh, Yoreh De'ah*, 216:6.

41. Aran, "From Religious Zionism to Zionist Religion."

42. *Artzi* 1 and 2 (1982), 3 (1983), 4 (1986), 5 (1991), and *Tzefiyah*, which published two issues in 1985 and occasionally thereafter (no. 3 was released in 1988, no. 5 in 1996). Both supported the radical end of the settler movement, and *Tzefiyah* served as a magazine of a radical group that supported the "Jewish Underground" (*mahteret*) and related issues and groups from the mid-1980s into the 1990s.

43. This is based on Maimonides, *Mishneh Torah, Kings* 7:15.

44. Yehuda Amital, *Rising Up from the Depths* [in Hebrew] (Jerusalem, 1986), pp. 18–19, see also pp. 55–61. Parentheses in original.

6

RETHINKING RELIGIOUS VIOLENCE

FIGHTING OVER NOTHING

Hector Avalos

Religious violence has preoccupied me ever since I began to ask myself, as a teenager, how I could hold sacred the Bible, a book filled with so much violence. Eventually, I began to ask how anyone today could still deem sacred those books that endorse any level of violence. By early 2001, I had already published an article comparing violence in the Bible and the Bhagavad Gita.[1] By the time I had completed the manuscript of *Fighting Words: The Origins of Religious Violence*, I had concluded that academic biblical scholars bore some responsibility for maintaining the value of scriptures despite the endorsement of violence in those texts.

Some of my thinking was influenced by a book by Regina Schwartz, *The Curse of Cain: The Violent Legacy of Monotheism* (1997).[2] She argued that monotheism was inherently violent. Since monotheism advocates only one legitimate deity, then the worship of anything else is a violation of boundaries. The creation of a group of outsiders then becomes the prime ingredient for violence. The life of outsiders may be devalued, and so killing them can be justified. But more intriguing was her allusion to the scarce resources created by monotheism.

I wondered if similar mechanisms were at work not only in monotheism, but also in religion as a whole. I asked myself whether religion is inherently violent. If not, what are the mechanisms by which religion results in violence? Are those factors the same as the ones that cause other types of violence? Is there something special about religion that makes it prone to violence? Or are we misperceiving religion by focusing too much on its violent side?

The questions seemed particularly important because there is a definite stream of popular opinion and scholarship which denies that religion is the cause of some specific conflict or of violence in general. Shortly after the attack of September 11, 2001, Andrew Sullivan noted in a *New York Times Magazine* article that "there has been a general reluctance to call it a religious war."[3] Similarly, there have been efforts to deny that the Nazi holocaust had any religious roots, some preferring to place responsibility on evolutionary theory or atheism. Alan Jacobs has even argued that "the whole notion of religion as a cause of violence is . . . a function of the desire to believe that religion is eliminable."[4]

Along the way, I concluded that religion, while not always causing violence, is inherently prone to violence.[5] But more importantly, I came to wonder *how* and *why* religions could be prone to violence. After much thought and comparison of many religions, I formulated what will be the main elements of my thesis, which I can summarize succinctly as follows:

1. Most violence is due to scarce resources, real or perceived.

Whenever people perceive that there is not enough of something they value, then conflict may ensue to maintain or acquire that resource. This can range from love in a family to oil on a global scale.

2. When religion causes violence, it often does so because it has *created new scarce resources*.

DEFINITIONS

Any claim that religion is inherently prone to violence must begin with definitions. The first pertains to religion, which I define as a mode of life and thought which presupposes the existence of, and relationship with, unverifiable forces and/or beings. As such, our definition is squarely and unapologetically within the empirico-rationalist tradition.

All definitions of violence are value-laden insofar as we choose the type of suffering and violence we value.[6] Our definition is somatocentric insofar as it values the physical human body and regards any sort of "soul" or "spirit" as nonexistent. As we will see, religions often espouse a pneumatocentric justification for violence in which the values of the entities called the "soul" or "spirit" are paramount to those of the body. Accordingly, *we define violence as the act of modifying and/or inflicting pain upon the human body in order to express or impose power differentials.*[7]

By this definition, pain or bodily modification can be inflicted upon a person by others or it can be self-inflicted, as in the case of self-flagellation and martyrdom. There are degrees of violence so that a haircut or a tattoo, both bodily modifications, are not always regarded as very violent. At the same time, our definition allows for the fact that depilation and tattooing can be painful forms of torture.[8] Likewise, circumcision could be subsumed under violence in that it modifies a body for the purpose of expressing power differentials. Circumcision also imposes a power differential upon a child, as it is not the result of a mutual decision between parent and child. Killing, of course, is regarded as the ultimate imposition of a power differential on the body.

Under our concept of violence, we can also distinguish between justified and unjustified violence. Violence in self-defense or the defense of the physical well-being of others is acceptable. The surgical modification of the body for the purposes of saving a life or empowering an individual, especially if the individual so chose to be modified, is justified violence. Below, we develop the argument that any violence not based on verifiable causes and phenomena is senseless and immoral.

CAUSALITY AND HISTORICAL EXPLANATION

Since at least the time of David Hume (1711–1776), the notion of causality has undergone severe scrutiny. In the realm of historical explanation, the notion of cause has produced a crisis that is still underway. So what does it mean to say that religion "causes" violence or can cause violence? We may say that *religion causes violence if and when the perpetration of violence is a logical consequence of beliefs in unverifiable forces and/or beings.* The expression "logical consequence" can be represented in a more formal manner: *Religious Belief X, therefore Act of Violence Y.*[9] Accordingly, attribution of religious causation requires demonstration that an act of violence had a necessary precedent in a religious belief. Without that causational belief, the specific act of violence would not have taken place.

For example, suppose Person A really believes that God has commanded him to kill homosexuals, and this person then kills a homosexual. In this case, we can say that Belief X (God has commanded Person A to kill a homosexual) caused the killing of the homosexual. In such a case, we may say that the religious belief was necessary, if not sufficient, to perpetrate this act of violence. In the clearest cases, the perpetrators may themselves cite such beliefs.

Accordingly, the reader must realize that *our thesis does not claim that religion is the cause of all violence.* We certainly recognize that poverty, politics, nationalism, and even neuropsychological factors may generate violence. Rather, our thesis proposes that when religion causes violence, it usually does so because it has created a scarce resource. *The creation of a scarce resource by religion occurs when belief in supernatural forces and/or beings are held responsible for identifying a resource as scarce in some manner.* Accordingly, we must also extend our argument to include scarcity in the chain of causation.

A resource is any entity that persons utilize in the enterprise of living. Not all resources are of equal value, of course. One can live without a Rolex watch. We focus on those resources that are of high value, or at least of a value high enough to fight for. A resource may be described as scarce when it meets one or more of the following requirements: (1) it is not immediately available; (2) accessing it, maintaining it, or acquiring it requires the expense of a significant amount of social or physical capital and labor. A Scarce Resource X created by religion may cause violence when at least one of two or more persons or groups *(1) desires to acquire or maintain X; and (2) believes violence is an allowable and proper method to acquire and/or maintain X.*

Demonstration of our thesis consists of at least two main types of evidence. The first centers on the words of perpetrators of violence themselves. Too often, in debates about religion and conflict, the attribution of motives is based on secondary sources or faulty deductions. One example of a clear attribution of violence to religious reasons can be seen in the following Hadith reported by al-Bukhari, perhaps the most authoritative collector of traditions about Muhammad. Al-Bukhari tells us:

> The prophet said, "Allah . . . assigns for a person who participates in (holy battles) in Allah's Cause and nothing causes him to do so except belief in Allah and in His Messengers, that he will be recompensed by Allah with a reward, or booty (if he survives) or will be admitted to Paradise (if he is killed in the battle as a martyr).[10]

Here is a clear attribution of the reason for violence from a Muslim himself. This sort of self-attribution by practitioners of a religion certainly would count as strong evidence that violence was due to religious beliefs.

We need not study every religion in the world to establish our thesis. While most religions may be prone to violence, not all religions have an equal impact on the quality or quantity of violence that we see in the world. Here we focus on the so-called Abrahamic religions: Judaism, Christianity, and Islam, which are related insofar as they see Abraham, the biblical patriarch, as an exemplar of righteousness and as a progenitor of monotheists. We discuss how religion creates scarce resources, and then focus on the following: (1) access to the divine will, particularly through enscripturation, (2) sacred space, (3) group privileging, and (4) salvation.

Enscripturation

Enscripturation refers to the reduction to writing of what is believed to be authoritative information about or from supernatural forces and/or beings. William Schniedewind has recently written on the process of textualization, which may generally refer to the process of transitioning from oral to written media.[11] However, our thesis holds that it is important to distinguish textualization from enscripturation, as the latter has more specific features beyond those borne by simply the production of a text. A sacred scripture is created when someone puts into writing what writers/readers believe to be the thoughts and actions of a deity or supernatural forces.

All Abrahamic religions purport to have a record of supernatural revelations in some form of writing. For Jews, it is the Tanakh. In Exodus 34:1, God himself is said to have written at least part of the Bible: "The LORD said to Moses, 'Cut two tablets of stone like the former ones, and I will write on the tablets the words that were on the former tablets, which you broke.'" Muslims have the Qur'an as a basic document of revelation. Christians use both the Jewish Tanakh, reconceptualized as the "Old Testament" as well as what they call a New Testament.

In terms of scarce resource theory, writing becomes a scarce resource when not everyone has access to the writings or lacks the ability to read those writings. In the ancient Near East most people never mastered some of the more complicated writing systems of Mesopotamia.[12] Most people would not be able to read anything regarded as sacred scripture. If these books are the basis of authority, then they are a scarce resource to those who cannot read them. But by far the most conflictive aspect of enscripturation comes when it is claimed that only one particular book or set of books contains authoritative divine revelation.

The fact that violence can result from disagreements about who has the proper access to divine communication is clear in Deuteronomy 18:20: "But any prophet who speaks in the name of other gods, or who presumes to speak in my name a word that I have not commanded the prophet to speak—that prophet shall die." Divine communication is a scarce resource, and violence must be used to maintain access to what is perceived to be the right conduit.

An example of violence between Christianity and Judaism on the issue of holy scripture can be found in the Hebrew chronicles of anti-Jewish violence in 1096, during the movements associated with the Crusades.[13] Emicho of Leinigen was the leader of the anti-Jewish mobs, which rampaged through a number of Jewish communities, including those in Cologne, Mainz, and Worms. The Chronicle of Solomon bar Simson tells what happens when a Christian destroys the Torah of a Jewish household:

> There was also a Torah Scroll in the room; the errant ones [= Christians] came into the room, found it, and tore it to shreds. When the holy and pure women, daughters of kings, saw that the Torah had been torn, they called in a loud voice to their husbands: "Look, see, the Holy Torah—it is being torn by the enemy!" . . . "Alas, the Holy Torah, the perfection of beauty, the delight of our eyes, to which we used to bow in the synagogue, honoring it; our little children would kiss it. How has it now fallen into the hands of these impure uncircumcised ones?"
>
> When the men heard the words of these pious women, they were moved with zeal for the Lord, our God, and for His holy and

precious Torah. . . . They found one of the errant ones in the room, and all of them, men and women, threw stones at him till he fell dead.[14]

It is very seldom that we have such a detailed rationale for violence perpetrated because of the perceived holiness of a text. The example certainly can be reduced to the form: "Belief X, therefore Act of Violence Y." In this case, the belief that the Torah is holy and cannot be desecrated is explicitly stated to be the reason for the killing of the Christian who desecrated that text. At the same time, the Christian desecrated the Torah because he did not regard it as holy.

The attacks upon sacred scriptures continue today. According to a report posted on the CNN Web site on April 1, 2002, a synagogue in Marseilles, France, was attacked: "'All the religious objects, books, the Torah, all of it burned,' Sydney Maimoun, the synagogue's president, told the Associated Press, adding there's 'really nothing left.'"[15] While most of the perpetrators in this case are thought to be Muslims, the truth is that violence against scriptures can involve all sorts of permutations within the Abrahamic traditions.

Sacred Space

All of the major world religions share the idea of sacred space. We may define sacred space as a bounded space whose value is placed above surrounding space for religious reasons. Since not everyone has access to, or can live in, a sacred space, then it becomes a scarce resource. And since sacred space is a scarce resource, then it becomes a potential center of conflict.

Some spaces may be sacralized because they possess economic and political value first. In the Abrahamic religions, the value of one sacred space, Jerusalem, is almost entirely the creation of religion. Jerusalem has no great economic or strategic value other than what is derived from the sacrality bestowed upon it by the sacred scriptures of these religions. Ultimately, the sacrality of Jerusalem originates in the Hebrew Bible (see Zech. 2:12, Ps. 76:1–2).[16] Judaism, Christianity, and Islam all have had members willing to die for the supposed holiness of Jerusalem (and the broader space called the "Holy Land").

In Christian history, some of the clearest examples of the relationship between violence and sacred space may be found in the First Crusade and the propaganda meant to incite Christians to join it. The speech delivered by Urban II at Clermont has not been directly preserved, but we do have various versions of it from supposed witnesses or recorders. These testimonies are all gathered in the monumental *Recueil des Historiens des Croisades* (henceforth, RHC), which still forms a basic source for all studies of the early Crusades.[17]

We must be cautious in representing these testimonies as a stenographic record of the speech and thought of Urban II. Rather they are to be seen, in part, as retrospective narratives colored by regionalism and the success of the First Crusade.[18] Otherwise, these testimonies constitute evidence of what the authors understood to be the motives for the First Crusade. Urban's motivation for this Crusade is clear in the version of Robert the Monk:

> Let the holy sepulchre of the Lord our Saviour, which is possessed by unclean nations, especially incite you, and the holy places which are now treated with ignominy and irreverently polluted with their filthiness.[19]

Another version of Urban II's speech begins by arguing that not all space is of equal value:

> If among the churches scattered about over the whole world some, because of persons or location, deserve reverence above others (for persons, I say, since greater privileges are accorded to apostolic sees; for places, indeed, since the same dignity which is accorded to persons is also shown to regal cities, such as Constantinople), we owe most to that church from which we received the grace of redemption and the source of all Christianity.[20]

The speech subsequently outlines the various reasons why Jerusalem is holy. Not one of the reasons is economic or even outwardly political. Instead, the speech harkens to scriptural warrants for declaring Jerusalem holy. Note the following argument:

> If this land is spoken of in the sacred writings of the prophets as the inheritance and the holy temple of God before ever the Lord walked about in it, or was revealed, what sanctity, what reverence has it not acquired since God in His majesty was there clothed in the flesh, nourished, grew up, and in bodily form there walked about, or was carried about; and, to compress in fitting brevity all that might be told in a long series of words, since there the blood of the Son of God, more holy than heaven and earth, was poured forth, and His body, its quivering members dead, rested in the tomb. What veneration do we think it deserves?[21]

In short, if the city was holy before Jesus walked its streets, it should be even holier after that. Yet, Jesus need not have lived or died in Jerusalem to render it holy. As the speech argues:

> Let us suppose, for the moment, that Christ was not dead and buried, and had never lived any length of time in Jerusalem. Surely, if all this were lacking, this fact alone ought still to arouse you to go to the aid of the land and city—the fact that "Out of Zion shall go forth the law and the word of the Lord from Jerusalem!"[22]

Similar rationales are given on the Muslim side by 'Imad ad-Din, who says:

> Islam wooed Jerusalem, ready to lay down lives for her as a bride-price. . . . Saladin marched forth . . . to remove the heavy hand of unbelief with the right hands of Faith, to purify Jerusalem of the pollution of those races, of the filth of the dregs of humanity.[23]

Today, the sacrality of Jerusalem and other spaces in the Middle East still fuels much violence in the world. Osama bin Laden says as much in his infamous 1998 fatwa, which outlines some of his reasons for his jihad against the United States:

> First, for over seven years the United States has been occupying the lands of Islam *in the holiest of places*, the Arabian Peninsula, plundering its riches, dictating to its rulers, humiliating its people, terrorizing its neighbors, and turning its bases in the Peninsula into a spearhead through which to fight the neighboring Muslim peoples.[24]

In short, sacred space continues to be a generator of violence in Abrahamic religions. As long as people deem certain spaces sacred, the potential for violence will be there.

Group Privileging

Closely linked to enscripturation and sacred space is group privileging, which refers to the idea that certain groups have privileges and rights not granted to those outside of the group. As such, those privileges become a scarce resource to outsiders.[25] In some cases, the privileges need not cause conflict if the outsider does not value them. For example, not all outsiders care that only priests can enter the Holy of Holies of the Temple of Solomon. If outsiders live far away, it may not matter to them.

However, if belonging to one religious group means that one receives certain economic benefits that others in proximity don't, then conflict may ensue. Those economic benefits are now unequally distributed, and so constitute scarce resources. Violence may follow attempts to acquire those benefits or attempts to prevent the loss of those benefits.

At the most extreme level of violence, group privileging resulted in the extermination of at least some groups of people that were seen to threaten the privileged group in power. This is most clear in a number of passages, such as the following:

(Deut. 7:1) When the LORD your God brings you into the land that you are about to enter and occupy, and he clears away many nations before you—the Hittites, the Girgashites, the Amorites, the Canaanites, the Perizzites, the Hivites, and the Jebusites, seven nations mightier and more numerous than you

(Deut. 7:2) and when the LORD your God gives them over to you and you defeat them, then you must utterly destroy them. Make no covenant with them and show them no mercy.

(Deut. 7:3) Do not intermarry with them, giving your daughters to their sons or taking their daughters for your sons,

(Deut. 7:4) for that would turn away your children from following me, to serve other gods. Then the anger of the LORD would be kindled against you, and he would destroy you quickly.

(Deut. 7:5) But this is how you must deal with them: break down their altars, smash their pillars, hew down their sacred poles, and burn their idols with fire.

(Deut. 7:6) For you are a people holy to the LORD your God; the LORD your God has chosen you out of all the peoples on earth to be his people, his treasured possession.

Note that this passage links the "choseness" of Israel with the destruction of the particular outsiders. Note that destruction of others is attributed to Israel's "holiness."

Likewise, Hadith, the traditions about Muhammad, are permeated by the feeling of superiority among Muslims. Thus, Al-Bukhari records one tradition in which the religious status of a boy is at issue. The boy has a non-Muslim mother and a Muslim father. A group of Muslims state that custody must be given to the Muslim parent. The episode concludes with the statement "Islam is always superior and never inferior" (al-Islâm ya'alû wa-lâ yu-lâ).[26] Such a view, in turn, has led to the subjugation and killing of non-Muslims throughout Islamic history.[27]

Salvation

The ultimate supernatural prize in the Abrahamic religions is "salvation," a term that is highly complex and often ambiguous. Salvation, for our purposes, refers to the idea that one receives a supernaturally favorable status or permanent benefit by belonging to a particular religion. It is closely allied with group privileging, except that the reward called "salvation" is ultimately not tangible or verifiable. "Salvation" only exists insofar as people believe in it.

In any event, salvation is a scarce resource insofar as it is not equally distributed. Within the Catholic tradition there developed the concept of *Extra Ecclesiam nulla salus* (Outside of the Church there is no salvation). As Hans Küng notes, the Council of Florence (1442) was unequivocal:

> The Holy Roman Church . . . firmly believes, confesses and proclaims that outside the Catholic Church no one, neither heathen nor Jew nor unbeliever nor schismatic will have a share in eternal life, but will, rather, be the subject to everlasting fire. . . .[28]

René Girard has argued that the salvific sacrifice of Christ, the god-man, could effect the complete overthrow of scapegoating violence.[29] In reality, the notion that salvation of humankind had been achieved through such a trauma to the deity spawned a number of rationales for violence, whose consequences echoed in many forms. For example, a most persistent rationale for violence used the violent death of Christ to justify forcing the conversion of others. Since God had made such a great sacrifice, it behooved human beings to be grateful. To not convert after knowing of the suffering of the Christ meant that one was ungrateful. That lack of gratefulness needs to be punished, as indicated in Hebrews 10:29: "How much worse punishment do you think will be deserved by those who have spurned the Son of God, profaned the blood of the covenant by which they were sanctified, and outraged the Spirit of grace?"

Thomas Aquinas, the most influential theologian of the Middle Ages, used rationales for violence that were linked to the maintenance and expansion of the scarce resource we call salvation. One main reason that Aquinas gives for waging war and imprisoning unbelievers is not so that those unbelievers will convert, but rather so that those unbelievers do not hinder the salvation of others.[30] Here we can clearly see how salvation is a scarce resource, not available except through sanctioned means. Violence may be used in order to allow or maintain access to this scarce resource.

Aquinas likewise favored bodily compulsion for heretics who strayed from Christianity.[31] One of the main biblical texts used by Aquinas, among others, to sanction such compulsion was Luke 14:23: "Then the master said to the slave, 'Go out into the roads and lanes, and compel people to come in, so that my house may be filled.'" This instruction is part of a parable given by Jesus, who is speaking of a rich man who gave a feast, but the invitees did not come. The master of the house told his servants to force people off the street into the banquet. By analogy, if Christians are the servants, and Jesus is the Master of the House, then Christians must compel nonbelievers to enter the kingdom of God. Violence in order to preserve the salvation of the favored group can also be found in ancient Judaism and Islam.

Other violent rationales generated by the idea of Christ's sacrifice are less well appreciated. In a magisterial study, Timothy Gorringe argued that Anselm's theory of the atonement had wide influence on justice systems in Europe. He notes that the need to hang or torture criminals was never self-evident. Often there were debates about the necessity of such practices. However, when they were upheld it was often because of allusions to Anselm's theory or New Testament ideas of the atonement. As Gorringe phrases it, "the theology of satisfaction, I contend, provided one of the subtlest and most profound of such justifications, not only for hanging but for retributive punishment in general."[32]

AN ETHICAL CRITIQUE OF RELIGIOUS VIOLENCE

Although we focus on how scarce resources cause religious violence, an overarching theme of our thesis is that the lack of verifiability in religious belief differentiates ethically the violence attributed to religion from the violence attributed to nonreligious factors. The quality of any scarcity created by religion is fundamentally different from scarcities created by natural means.

Within a moral relativistic frame that accepts empirico-rationalism as providing reliable data, our argument that religious violence is always immoral begins by positing the seemingly obvious proposition that what exists has more value than what does not exist. Only what exists can be said to have any value, if it has any value for us. If that is the case, then life, as an existent phenomenon, must have more value than what does not exist. We can schematize our rationale as follows:

1. What exists is worth more than what does not exist.
2. Life exists;
3. Therefore, life is worth more than what does not exist.

Accordingly, we may deem immoral any action that places the value of life as equal to, or below, the value of nothing. Therefore, it would always be immoral to kill for something that does not exist.

We can also extend this argument to what cannot be proven, on empirico-rationalist grounds, to exist. For example, if I were to say that I am killing because undetectable Martians have declared it obligatory to kill, the argument would be regarded rightly as absurd. But, the *possibility* of undetectable Martians existing is not what would declare such a statement absurd. It is perfectly possible that undetectable Martians exist and order people to kill other people. The main reason that we do not accept this rationale as moral is that we, as observers, cannot verify that undetectable Martians exist, and so we would regard the perpetrator's claims as absurd. Lack of evidence for the existence of invisible Martians, and not merely the possibility of their existence, provides the basis for our ethical judgment here.

This is not to deny that secular violence certainly may be immoral *sometimes.* Let's say even most of the time. Killing for something that is not necessary to human existence, for example, may be deemed immoral. Yet, killing in self-defense is usually not considered immoral. Killing when there is no other way to survive is not considered immoral. As long as a person needs a basic resource (food, water) to survive, then it may be morally permissible to fight and kill for it. In contrast, any violence for religious reasons is *always immoral because bodily well-being is being traded for the acquisition or loss of an entity that does not exist or cannot be verified to exist.* The fact that religious violence *is always immoral,* and the fact that nonreligious violence is *not always immoral,* is the fundamental ethical distinction between religious and nonreligious violence.

SOLUTIONS AND CONCLUSIONS

If religious violence is always immoral, then how do we solve the problem of religious violence? Two obvious logical choices present themselves: (1) retain religion, but modify it so that scarcities are not created; (2) remove religion from human life. Each of these choices has its own advantages and disadvantages.

First, note that we indicate "minimization" is the key, as violence cannot be eliminated for the simple reason that scarce resources will probably always exist. Competing interests will always exist. In some cases, violence should not be eliminated, as self-defense is a legitimate use of violence. Minimization means that we concentrate on ridding ourselves of unnecessary violence.

Since religious violence is mainly caused by competition for resources that are actually not scarce at all, then part of the solution must involve making religious believers aware of how they have created belief in scarce resources. Nonbelievers must challenge believers to explain why they believe in such resources in the first place. We should challenge believers to explain why they believe a certain space is sacred. Nonbelievers should challenge believers to explain how their notion of salvation is any more verifiable than the notion offered by another religion. Of course, it is naive to expect believers to automatically examine their beliefs and abandon them. However, making believers aware of how religion can create scarce resources must be a starting point if there is a solution at all.

One can object that eliminating the notions of salvation, sacred space, divine revelation, and group privileging would eliminate religion itself. This is only the case if one judges religion to "essentially" consist of these elements. Of all of these elements, however, I can only think of "divine revelation" as the only essential feature of all religions. That is to say, a person who believes that there is some sort of god or even transcendent force must have some notion that he or she is able to perceive those entities. Sacred space, salvation, and group privileging are not so clearly "essential," though they certainly may seem so. The notion of the "holy land" had been redefined or abandoned by many Jews and Christians who could still call themselves "religious" at some level. Such redefinitions, in effect, made competition for a physical space irrelevant sometimes.

The second logical solution, removing religion from life, is of course much more complicated. But, we should note that academic biblical scholars and scholars of religion, more often than not, actually maintain the value of religious texts that promote or endorse violence. This maintenance is accomplished by hermeneutic strategies that sanitize the violence, claim to espouse multivocality in readings, or claim aesthetic value to texts, even if historical aspects of the texts are minimized. In this regard, we are influenced by theories that see the academic study of literature itself as a locus and instrument of power.[33]

One obstacle in the way that biblical scholars approach religious violence resides in the perceived mission of religious studies, particularly in secular institutions of higher learning. Noam Chomsky argued cogently, during the Vietnam War, that "it is the responsibility of intellectuals to speak truth and to expose lies."[34] However, since public universities are funded by taxpayers, the mission of religious studies is perceived to mean that scholars must be sympathetic or neutral toward religion. Religions must be understood but not criticized. Any research indicating that religion is injurious or that particular religions are injurious can bring a response that universities, as publicly funded institutions, cannot seek to undermine the faith of constituents.

Otherwise, the notion of academic responsibility has not been consistent from field to field. Professors in the sciences, for example, routinely are expected to help solve problems in society, ranging from finding a new medication for cancer to learning how to suppress odor produced by swine containment facilities. This is particularly the case in so-called land-grant universities, which are expected to be involved directly in the betterment of the society around them. In the case of science, academics are encouraged to identify a "problem," and then help to solve it.

Within religious/biblical studies, John J. Collins, president of the Society of Biblical Literature in 2002, urged an activist stance when he concluded: "Perhaps the most constructive thing a biblical critic can do toward lessening the contribution of the Bible to violence in the world, is to show that certitude is an illusion."[35] I would go much further. As an academic scholar of religion, it is my responsibility to analyze, on the basis of verifiable facts and reason, how religion may contribute to the detriment or well-being of humanity.[36]

If empirico-rationalism and naturalism are held to be the proper approaches to truth, then it becomes feasible to argue that the best way to deal with religious violence is to undermine religion itself. Just as we undermined the religious belief that Genesis 1 is scientifically true, academic biblical scholars should continue to undermine any religious belief that can result in violence. Indeed, even if it can never be achieved, the most ethical mission of academic religious studies may be to end religion as we know it.

NOTES

*Unless noted otherwise, all of the author's biblical quotations are those of the *New Revised Standard Version* (National Council of Churches of Christ in the United States of America; Nashville, TN: Thomas Nelson, 1989).

1. Hector Avalos, "Violence in the Bible and the *Bhagavad Gita*," *Journal of Vaishnava Studies* 9, no. 2 (2001): 67–83.
2. Regina Schwartz, *The Curse of Cain: The Violent Legacy of Monotheism* (Chicago: University of Chicago Press, 1997).
3. Andrew Sullivan, "This *Is* a Religious War," *New York Times Magazine* (October 7, 2001): 47.
4. Kenneth R. Chase and Alan Jacobs, eds., *Must Christianity Be Violent? Reflections on History, Practice and Theology* (Grand Rapids, MI: Brazos Press, 2003), p. 231.
5. For recent similar observations, see James K. Wellman Jr. and Kyoto Tokuno, "Is Religious Violence Inevitable?" *Journal for the Scientific Study of Religion* 43, no. 3 (2004): 291–96.
6. For the political implications of defining violence, see also Stephen J. Casey, "Defining Violence," *Thought: A Review of Culture and Idea* 56, no. 220 (1981): 5–16.
7. There is now a vast literature on the social role of the body and embodiment. Among some of these studies are: Chris Shilling, *The Body and Social Theory*, 2nd ed. (London: Sage, 2003); Barbara Maria Stafford, *Body Criticism: Imaging the Unseen in Enlightenment Art and Medicine* (Cambridge, MA: MIT Press, 1997); Simon J. Williams and Gillian Bendelow, *The Lived Body: Sociological Themes, Embodied Issues* (New York: Routledge, 1998); Jon L. Berquist, *Controlling Corporeality: The Body and the Household in Ancient Israel* (New Brunswick, NJ: Rutgers University Press, 2002); Dale B. Martin, *The Corinthian Body* (New Haven, CT: Yale University Press, 1995); Howard

Eilberg-Schwartz, *People of the Body: Jews and Judaism from an Embodied Perspective* (Albany: State University of New York Press, 1992); Benedict Ashley, *Theologies of the Body: Humanist and Christian* (Braintree, MA: Pope John XXIII Medical-Moral Research and Education Center, 1985).

8. For some examples, see Frances E. Mascia-Lees and Patricia Sharpe, eds., *Tattoo, Torture, Mutilation, and Adornment: The Denaturalization of the Body in Culture and Text* (Albany: State University of New York Press, 1992); Alfred Gell, *Wrapping in Images: Tattooing in Polynesia* (Oxford: Clarendon, 1993).

9. For further comments on establishing religious causality, see J. Milton Yinger, *The Scientific Study of Religion* (New York: Macmillan Company, 1971), pp. 93–98.

10. Al-Bukhari, 36/Book of Belief, 26. Citations of al-Bukhari are from the Arabic-English edition of *Shahih Al-Bukhari*, trans. Muhammad Muhsin Khan, 9 vols. (Riyadh, Saudi Arabia: Darussalam Publishers and Distributors), 1:73.

11. William Schniedewind, *How the Bible Became a Book* (Cambridge: Cambridge University Press, 2004).

12. See further Giuseppe Visicato, *The Power and the Writing: The Early Scribes of Mesopotamia* (Bethesda, MD: CDL Press, 2000).

13. For an edition of these chronicles, I depend on Shlomo Eidelberg, *The Jews and the Crusaders: The Hebrew Chronicles of the First and Second Crusades* (Madison: University of Wisconsin Press, 1977).

14. Eidelberg, *The Jews and the Crusaders*, p. 37.

15. http://edition.cnn.com/2002/WORLD/europe/04/01/synagogue .attacks/?related (accessed July 14, 2004).

16. See further, J. M. Roberts, "Zion in the Theology of the Davidic-Solomonic Empire," in *Studies in the Period of David and Solomon and other Essays*, ed. Tomoo Ishida (Winona Lake, IN: Eisenbrauns, 1982), pp. 93–108.

17. *Recueil des Historiens des Croisades* (Paris: L'Académie impériale des inscriptions et Belles-Lettres, 1841–1906), from which all our Latin citations are drawn. The report of Fulcher of Chartres is available in English as Fulcher of Chartres, *A History of the Expeditions to Jerusalem, 1095–1127*, trans. Frances Rita Ryan and ed. Harold S. Fink (New York: W. W. Norton, 1969).

18. See further, Hans Eberhard Mayer, *The Crusades*, trans. John Gillingham (New York: Oxford, 1972), pp. 10–11; Christopher Tyerman, *The Invention of the Crusades* (Toronto: University of Toronto Press, 1998), pp. 8–29.

19. RHC 3.728: "Prasertim moveat vos sanctum Domini Salvatoris nostri Sepulcrum, quod ab immundis gentibus possidetur, et loca sancta, quae nunc inhoneste tractantur et irreverenter eorum immundiciis sordidantur."

20. RHC 4.137: "Si inter ecclesias toto orbe diffusas alieae prae aliis reverentiam pro personis locisque merentur; pro personis, inquam, dum apostolicis sedibus privilegia majora traduntur uti est civitas Constantinopolitana, praebetur: illi potissimum ecclessiae deberemus ex qua gratiam redemptionis et totius originem Christianitatis accepimus."

21. RHC 4.137–138: "Si enim haec terra Dei haereditas et templum sanctum, antequam ibi obambularet ac pateretur Dominus, in sacris et propheticis paginis legitur, quid sanctitatis, quid reverentiae obtinuisse tunc creditur, quum Deus majestatis ibidem incorporatur, nutritur, adolescit, corporali, vegetatione hac illacque perambulat aut gestatur; et, ut cuncta quae longo verborum gyro narrari possunt, digna brevitate constringam, ubi Filii Dei sanguis, coelo terraque sanctior, effusus est, ubi corpus, paventibus elementis mortuum, in sepulchro quievit? quid putamus venerationis emeruit?"

22. RHC 4.138: "Ponamus modo in Iherusalem Christum neque mortuum, nec sepultum, nec ibidem aliquando vixisse. Certe, si haec deessent omnia, solum illud ad subveniendum terrae et civitati vos excitare debuerat, quia de Syon exierit lex et verbum Domini de Iherusalem." The biblical quotation is from Isaiah 2:3 (paralleled in Micah 4:2).

23. Francesco Gabrieli, *Arab Historians of the Crusades*, trans. E. J. Costello (New York: Barnes & Noble, 1969), p. 147.

24. For this translation and the Arabic text, see http://www.library.cornell.edu/colldev/mideast/wif.htm. Emphasis mine.

25. For a classic treatment of group privilege, see Gerhard E. Lenski, *Power and Privilege: A Theory of Social Stratification* (Chapel Hill: University of North Carolina Press, 1984). Lenski, however, still sees Judaism and Christianity as providing a "basis for an ethical criticism of the existing order" (p. 39). Lenski, therefore, still has assimilated uncrit-

ically benign views of how Judaism and Christianity create and maintain privilege.

26. Al-Bhukari, 1353/Book of Funerals 79/Darussalam edition 2.250. Yohanan Friedmann (*Tolerance and Coercion in Islam: Interfaith Relations in the Muslim Tradition* [Cambridge: Cambridge University Press, 2003], p. 35), translates this as "Islam is exalted and nothing is exalted above it."

27. For detailed cases, see Friedmann, *Tolerance and Coercion.*

28. Hans Küng, *Christianity and the World Religions: Paths to Dialogue with Islam, Hinduism, and Buddhism* (New York: Doubleday, 1986), p. 23.

29. See René Girard, *Violence and the Sacred*, trans. Patrick Gregory (Baltimore: Johns Hopkins University Press, 1977).

30. *Summa Theologica*, Part II-II, Question 10, Article 8, Obj. 4. Our citation of the *Summa Theologica* is from the first complete American edition in three volumes translated by Fathers of the English Dominican Province (New York: Benziger Brothers, 1947), 2:1219: "They should be compelled by the faithful, if it be possible to do so, so that they do not hinder the faith by their blasphemies, or by their evil persuasions, or even by their open persecutions."

31. See *Summa Theologica*, Part II-II, Question 10, Article 8, Reply Obj. 3; Benziger edition 2:1219.

32. Timothy Gorringe, *God's Just Vengeance: Crime, Violence, and the Rhetoric of Salvation* (Cambridge: Cambridge University Press, 1996), p. 12.

33. A principal theoretician here is John Guillory, *Cultural Capital: The Problem of Literary Canon Formation* (Chicago: University of Chicago Press, 1993).

34. Noam Chomsky, "The Responsibility of Intellectuals," in *The Chomsky Reader*, ed. James Peck (New York: Pantheon Books, 1987), p. 60.

35. John J. Collins, "The Zeal of Phinehas: The Bible and the Legitimation of Violence," *Journal of Biblical Literature* 122, no. 1 (2003): 21.

36. For a discussion of the responsibility of scholars of religion, see Russell T. McCutcheon, *Critics not Caretakers: Redescribing the Public Study of Religion* (Albany: State University of New York Press, 2001), esp. pp. 155–77.

7

VIOLENCE IN THE TEXT

VIOLENCE THROUGH THE TEXT
Bahar Davary

When I set out, he[1] is my goal.
When I look in my heart, he is its ravisher.
When I seek justice, he is the judge.
When I go to war, he is my weapon.
When I join the celebration,
He is the wine and sweetmeats.
. . . .
When I fight a battle,
He is the commander in chief.
When I enter the banquet hall,
He is the *saaqi*, the minstrel, and the cup.

Rumi (d. 1273)

The face of your religion
Covers the face of his love
. . . .
If a mirror shows you your own ugliness
what is the use
of breaking the mirror with your fist?

Rumi (d. 1273)

Monotheistic religions in general and Islam in particular have been charged with the tendency toward legitimating and ensuing of violence. The Judeo-Christian commandment "Thou shalt have no other gods before me" and its Islamic parallel "There is no god but God" have been regarded as an uncompromising statement of faith that has led to a legacy of intolerance toward those who do not adhere to strict monotheism. Under the guise of the will of God, frontiers are made clear.[2] Those who believe in the one true God are saved and those who do not are out of this realm and are therefore damned. Is it true that the belief in God the deliverer inevitably entails the trust in God the conqueror? Does religion promote intolerance and violence? And more specifically, does it violate the rights of women and the ideal of gender equality? Although these questions are broad in their scope and in the extent that each draws upon the religious discourse, the framework in which I situate them is common to both themes. My focus, however, will be on the second question, that of religion as a justification for violating gender equality or of encouraging belligerence toward women. While the framework that I will be using can be applied to Judeo-Christian tradition, my formulation will be specifically based on Islamic textual and oral tradition, with few references to Christianity.

This essay consists of two parts. The first and shorter segment can be labeled "monotheism the misunderstood faith" and establishes the foundation for the second part. How is monotheism misunderstood? What does misunderstanding mean in this context? Who is partaking in this misunderstanding and who is liable for it? The misunderstanding of monotheism is not always and not only enacted and sanctioned by those outside the realm of belief, but at times it takes place in the minds of its adherents. This dichotomy between those who believe and those who do not is at some level an artificial one. According to the twelfth-century Spanish Muslim philosopher Ibn 'Arabi, to be human is to have a belief or to have a view of reality that shapes one's understanding of the world. Any view of reality or belief is literally "a knot tied in the heart"—one that refers to "the whole range of cognitions, ideas, theories, doctrines, dogmas, prejudices, feelings, and inclinations that allow people to make sense of the world."[3] In other words, "to be human is to have a perspective on self and other, even if one is unaware of one's underlying mind-set" and that "belief is unavoidable."[4] In his interpretation of Ibn 'Arabi's *Futuhat al-Makkiyya*, William Chittick explains that one can not conclude that this exposition has "no relevance for those who have no beliefs about God, or who reject the idea of God altogether" for "God after all is *wujud*; [being] and *wujud* embraces all of reality on whatever level it is envisaged."[5] In other words, anyone who adheres to being adheres to Infinite being, because "each existent thing represents a particular self-disclosure of non-delimited *wujud*."[6] Everyone realizes certain aspects and attributes of the nondelimited *wujud* and in a sense everyone is a believer; some only realize the form and others the meaning beyond the form.

A good place to start the clarification of the meaning of monotheism is the distinction between different realms of reality: that of the form and of the meaning, the outer appearances and the inward nuances. Mawlana Jalal al-din Rumi speaks of this differentiation as distinguishing the pearl from the shell.

Having seen the form, you are unaware of the meaning,
If you are wise pick out the pearl from the shell!

Rumi's dichotomy of form and meaning is similar to Wilfred Cantwell Smith's distinction between "cumulative tradition" and "faith."[7] Monotheisms each encompass a cumulative tradition, at times even multiple versions of it. At the heart of the cumulative tradition lies the faith or the truth of that message. The question of whether religion justifies or calls to violent action can have different responses depending on whether one perceives religion as faith/meaning or as cumulative tradition/form. Religion as form/ cumulative tradition would give quite a different response than religion as meaning/faith. To conceive of religion as faith or meaning is to be aware of the limitations of the form/accumulative tradition. It is being able to pick out the pearl from the shell, an act that requires an involvement with reality rather than a passive acceptance of the form. Monotheism that mistakes the form for the meaning is no monotheism; that is the misunderstood monotheism.

It is this attention to the inner meaning oneness of the Divine that has been emphasized in Islamic terminology where involvement with reality is either founded on *shirk* (multitheism) or on *tawhid* (monotheism). Both *shirk* and *tawhid* are religions, they both direct their followers to an object or objects of worship. This dichotomy is most commonly professed as a divide between religions that worship many gods, such as Hinduism, and those that emphasize the worship of one God, such as Judaism, Christianity, and Islam. Such dichotomy, however, only regards the form and not the inner meaning of the two terms. *Shirk* correctly understood is not simply the worship of other gods, but the worship of anything other than God. Therefore, in rejecting *shirk* it is not enough to reject the explicit forms of multitheism (and sometimes not required either, for it is possible that explicitly multitheistic traditions practice *tawhid*; monotheism inwardly), but rather, all idols must be denounced.

One of the most common idols to be overturned is the idol of the self, the one that all monotheistic religions emphasize. To kill the idol of the self is the most legitimate violence prescribed by religion. Oscar Romero writes:

> . . . the only legitimate violence,
> the violence that he [Christ] does to himself
> and that he invites us to do to ourselves:
> "let those who would follow me deny themselves"
> be violent to themselves,
> repress in themselves the outbursts of pride,

kill in their hearts the outbursts of greed,
of avarice, of conceit, of arrogance.
Let them kill it in their hearts.
This is what must be killed, this is the violence that must be done,
So that out of it a new person may rise,
The only one who can build,
A new civilization:
A civilization of love.[8]

The prominent Iranian sociologist of religion Ali Shari'ati characterized the religion of *shirk* as the worship of self, in its complex forms appearing in the worship of "a system, an emotion, a thought, a possession" as well as in the form of "cultural colonialism, religious deception, class exploitation, mass media."[9] The religion of *shirk* can take the form of "bureaucracy, technocracy, chauvinism, nationalism, racism, or sexism; the egotism of Nazism . . . or militarism's love of coercion. Sometimes it is the worship of pleasure . . . of a subjective idealism or objective materialism."[10] These are the idols of the new multitheism and not the worship of Shiva, Ganesha, and Vishnu and a host of other gods. *Shirk* is adherence to a belief that elevates a person, a system, a group of people, or a nation above others at the price of the integrity of the rest. Monotheism in its exclusivist form can become a form of *shirk*, and goes hand in hand with the gods of mechanized industry, militarism, and scientism. While all these forces threaten peace and harmony, it is the latter tendencies that are often overlooked in discussions on violence and peace.

Jalal Ale-Ahmad in his notable work *Gharbzadegi = West-struckness*, written over forty years ago, spelled out the impetus behind most conflicts throughout the world.

These days any school child not only sees the expansionists aims of mechanized industry . . . but also sees things that were happening in Cuba, the Congo, the Suez Canal and Algeria were disputes over sugar, diamonds, and oil. The bloodshed in Cypress,

Zanzibar . . . Vietnam was for achieving a bridgehead to protect trade routes.[11]

The outward battle for God is often driven by a host of other gods disguised in a variety of forms.[12] Monotheism (*tawhid*) correctly understood goes far beyond an adherence to one God in matters of worship; rather, it manifests itself in "belief in the unity of humanity, the unity of all races, all classes, all families and all individuals, the unity of rights and the unity of honor."[13] In Islam the declaration of faith is not about emphasis on limiting the number of deities to one but about saying no to all other powers. This saying no is a way "to resist the structures of injustice that are built into the very societies in which we live."[14] Not adhering to the religion of *tawhid* (its meaning rather than its form) is submission to the religion of *shirk*, which is "surrender and slavery to hundreds of other powers . . . other polarizations and forces, where each pole, each power . . . is a god."[15] One meaning of *jihad* is the constant struggle to distinguish *tawhid* from *shirk*. This struggle does not pertain to Islam alone; it is a universal struggle so well characterized in Arthur Miller's classic *The Crucible*.[16] The idols of *The Crucible* were those of wealth, fear, public image, and power, which remain to be the most ominous along with the gods of technology and the gods of the stock market with their violence against nature, women, and the poor.

Consumerism, the dominant and fastest-growing world faith, is another manifestation of the religion of *shirk*. Consumer culture is one of "the planet's most sophisticated religious preachers" to whom we submit.[17] In the religion of consumerism "we exist to work, to earn money to get stuff. . . . The ultimate meaning of human existence is getting all this stuff. That's paradise."[18] What is the harm in that? We do not realize that this paradise comes at the cost of much violence. "We are so blinded by the all-encompassing propaganda we never think to confront the advertisers and demand they cease. On the contrary, as if the believers of the religion of consumerism ourselves we pay them lucrative salaries and hand over our children in the bargain."[19] The religion that supports this religion of *shirk* is the religion of legitimation, of immobility, and limitations, and is a religion, which is indifferent to the lives of the people.[20]

The misunderstanding of monotheism and the great hypocrisy of history has been the transmutation of religion through religion; disguising *shirk* as *tawhid*.[21] The religion that has ruled over history and has been a force for stagnation and oppression is that of *shirk*. It looks at the world with an "arrogant eye which objectifies the other for its own benefit."[22] This "arrogant eye is the colonial, imperialistic, patriarchal eye that simplifies and controls the other."[23] To believe in the religion of *tawhid* is to stand against oppression. The focal point of *tawhid* is to resist submission to all forms of *shirk* rather than to satisfy a jealous self-promoting God. One of the underlying implications of *tawhid* is to be mindful and "critical of the arrogance of modernity," which suggests the end of history and claims that "free trade and free markets have proven their ability to lift whole societies out of poverty."[24] It is a simplification of the Qur'anic statement: "Do you worship things which you (yourselves) carve?" (Qur'an, 37:95) to view it as limited to physical idols rather than to the idols of the mind. In the words of Oscar Romero, "many indeed would like . . . a pocket God, a God to get along with their idols, a God satisfied with the way they pay their workers, a God who approves of their atrocities."[25] These are the gods that the prophets have come to denounce and destroy. If their message contains violence, it is the violence of love, Romero writes:

> The violence we preach is not
> The violence of the sword,
> The violence of hatred
> It is the violence of love,
> Of brotherhood,
> The violence that wills to beat weapons
> into sickles for work.[26]

Religion as Shari'ati and Romero depict it lays out not just a beatific vision of social justice and peace, but also aims to transform hearts and societies, a transformation that all religions require of their adherents and one that is much needed. It is not a conversion from one religion to another, and not from religion to secularism or to the absence of religion, but a change from looking at the world with arrogance to looking at it with courtesy. Violence begins with looking with an eye to objectifying for its own benefit. Women, nature, and the poverty-stricken masses of the world suffer from the same culprit: "the male gaze, the anthropocentric gaze and the colonial gaze are similar."[27]

Discrimination and violence against women[28] are not limited to geographical or cultural boundaries; they are universal and rooted in a global culture of violence based on discrimination on various grounds, including race, ethnicity, sexual orientation, social status, class, and age.[29] What role does religion play in atrocities against women? A German scholar once said about the peculiar relationship between women and religion: "Women have always been the best friends of religion, but religion has generally not been a friend of women."[30] Does this imply that religion perpetrates violence toward women and imposes limitation on their rights? Has religion betrayed its best friends? To answer these questions in the framework of Islam, we must turn to the textual and oral traditions. Foremost among these is the Qur'an itself. Wilfred Cantwell Smith pertinently refers to the Qur'an as an inlibration—that is, God becoming book—which he deems comparable to the Christian concept of incarnation, God becoming flesh. Indeed, from a Muslim viewpoint the Qur'an is the word of God, and therefore is absolute and coeternal with God. Qur'anic interpretation (*tafsir*) has been understood as "the humanization of the divine word and the divinization of human spirit,"[31] at times indistinguishable from the Qur'an. This is part of the dilemma.

It is absolutely true that the Qur'an is a book and does not speak; therefore, it needs interpreters, and people alone can be interpreters.[32] It is of the utmost importance to distinguish the Qur'an from its multiple representations (the commentarial tradition).[33] There is a double quandary involved here. On the one hand, the interpretations have been viewed as the word of God. On the other hand, the absoluteness of God has been transferred to the absoluteness of the word of God, the Qur'an. *Tawhid*, with its emphasis on the absoluteness of God, signifies that nothing else is absolute, not even the Qur'an. Inlibration itself can be viewed as a form of *shirk*. How does our understanding of the Qur'an, an understanding that is human and not divine, which evolves in time and space and is filtered through one's cognitive universe, reveal absolute truth? Is not the human understanding of the sacred text time-bound?

Past interpreters have made an invaluable contribution to the ongoing understanding of the Qur'an. Yet their views should not be perceived as the absolute authoritative interpretation of the text. Doing so will deprive the Qur'an of its semantic autonomy.[34]

In short, "traditions do not arrive from heaven fully formed, but are subject to the vicissitudes of human history. Every tradition is always a tradition in becoming, and Islam is no exception."[35] One of the predicaments in understanding the place of women in Islam is the high emphasis placed (by Western intellectual reasoning) on textual Islam. In her autobiography, *A Border Passage: From Cairo to America—A Woman's Journey*, Leila Ahmed rejects the dissemination and promotion of textual Islam as the *true* and *authentic* Islam simply because it represents that which has been considered to be true by Muslim male powers for centuries. She makes a distinction between textual Islam, which is associated with men, and oral/aural Islam, which is associated with women: "The Islam of the text . . . is the Islam of the arcane mostly medieval written heritage . . . erected by the minority of men."[36] It is this classical Islamic textual heritage that continues to determine the Muslim law in our time. In contrast with the textual Islam is the oral/aural Islam or women's Islam, that of the common folk. These adherents, she argues, bring their deepest thoughts, feelings, and moral imagination into the shaping of the consciousness of others and thereby create texts out of their own lives, texts that are oral and evanescent yet "every bit as rich and sustaining as the most celebrated written texts."[37] In short, textual Islam is static and inert and unchanging while oral/aural Islam is a way of living and being. In the former the most recurring themes of the Qur'an, that is, peace, compassion, mercy, justice, kindness, fairness, and truthfulness, "are smothered and buried under a welter of obscure and abstruse learning . . . filtered through . . . only now and then in a body of law otherwise overwhelmingly skewed in favor of men."[38]

One of the essential implications of the emphasis on textual Islam, which has been influenced by Western intellectual reasoning, is that "the textual authority is treated as superior knowledge."[39] It further assumes that "female religious activity and knowledge is nonexistent" or that Muslim women are "protectors of religion in the home."[40] At times Muslim women's self-perception, as well as men's perception of their image and role, has been and continues to be affected by textual Islam. It is the study of this self-perception that renders significance to the analysis of the textual heritage. It goes without saying that such studies do not negate the fact that the varieties of Islam and especially the untold stories of Muslim women need to be discovered and revealed. In fact, women's awareness of false self-perception is the first step toward such revelations. One way of achieving it is to engage in a dialogue with tradition. It is in this dialogue that understanding occurs and not in its rejection in toto.[41] There is today an increasing number of women in Iran, Egypt, Turkey, and other parts of the Muslim world embracing Islamic orthodoxy and intellectualism, leading to the creation of a new identity model and "new spaces for debate about religious and political issues through the negotiation of relevant texts and scriptural traditions . . . and men's control of the relevant information can no longer remain exclusive to them."[42]

Every interpretation brings the past text into life, and is therefore the living conversation between past and present. One example of the encounter of past and present is the way in which the reformist approach within Western feminist theology engages in dialogue with tradition in order to unravel its liberating elements and to eradicate those that are conducive to oppression and violence. While Christology often makes naive use of the maleness of Jesus as a universal principle viewed as the maleness of God, leading to the paradigm that maleness is closer to God than femaleness, R. R. Ruether argues that Jesus' ability to be a liberator does not reside in his maleness but in the fact that he has renounced this system of domination and seeks to embody in his person the new humanity of service and mutual empowerment. Elizabeth Johnson charges the androcentric images of God as idolatrous in that they maintain that maleness is constitutive for the incarnation and redemption.[43]

In like vein, the inlibration of the word of God has at some levels violated women's rights. The elevation of the *Shari'a* as the absolute word despite the element of *ijtihad,* which guarantees the dynamism of the tradition and the law, is indeed generating an idol to God. Religious text, be it the *Shari'a* or the text of the Qur'an is uplifted in a way that a single statement is taken out of context to make a universal claim. Muslim scholars today express no doubt that slavery is inherently opposed by principles of justice presented in Islam; yet the Qur'an set rules and regulations regarding the just treatment of slaves. No Muslim jurist today suggests a return to slavery simply because the Qur'an states certain rules regarding the treatment of slaves. How is the decree on women different? In chapter 4, in a section titled an-*nissa* (Women), on inheritance and distribution of wealth, the Qur'an states: "Men are *qawwamun*[44] over women because God has made some of them superior to others" (4:34). Is this an absolute statement that applies to all women, at all times, and in all contexts? The verse continues: "and because they spend their wealth to maintain them" (4:34). In a section on divorce, it states: "Women have rights similar to those of

men over them in kindness, and men are a degree above them"
(2:228). Is this degree given to men in accordance with their duty
to maintain financial support? Does that mean that if one part of the
statement (financial maintenance) does not apply, it invalidates the
other part (having a degree above)? It is indeed difficult to render
fewer rights to women than to men if one reads the Qur'an holisti-
cally. The Muslim public discourse at times generalizes what is
implied by parts as what is implied by the whole using those parts
to lend a measure of authority to their opinions, suggesting that
what they are saying is simply common sense. They gain the power
that proverbs have as marvelous means of rationalizing. In other
words, what one wants to maintain as truth can be justified with
communal approval and maybe as age-old wisdom. Here are a few
examples: we say that absence makes the heart grow fonder, but we
also say out of sight, out of mind. When we want help we say many
hands make light work; when we don't, we say that too many cooks
spoil the broth. I realize that proverbs are not universal truth, but
neither are the sections and verses of the sacred text in separation
from the whole. The selections from the sacred text, just like
proverbial wisdom, can be contradictory. Therefore, adaptation of
certain parts of the text out of the whole without regard for the
whole is violence to the text itself. While with proverbs we can pick
and choose whatever fits the occasion, one cannot do the same with
the sacred text. Any interpretation of the text that is not holistic is
violence to the text itself.

According to all traditional sources, the message of the Qur'an
is universal and timeless. If it is to be meaningful in multiple historical horizons and in innumerable cultural settings, it must not be
imprisoned in a single historical or cultural perspective.[45]

In its original form the language of the Qur'an is dialogical, that
is to say that it discloses itself in the immediate historical relation
between God and the believer. It speaks *to* and addresses us; it is
not merely a text that speaks *about* something. It reveals itself in
the form of I-thou relationship; in other words, it constructs a com-

municative space within which God and human beings share common subject matter. One of the essential features of dialogical language is its ability to provide an opportunity for imaginative thinking, allowing the partners in dialogue to be active participants in the subject matter. The language of the classical textual interpretations becomes something for the interpreters to speak about. It becomes something narrated to someone.

Thus, the interpretations as metanarrative reduce the multiple levels (or pluralistic nature) of dialogical language of the Qur'an to a single level such as rational, metaphysical, or political, each according to its own historical context. This reduction can be specifically observed when the interpretations deduce a universal claim from the Qur'anic text by means of syllogism or deductive reasoning. The radical reduction of multiple levels of meaning of the Qur'anic language into a single level of discourse of interpretation has enormous religious, social, and political consequences. In other words, by elaborating and magnifying one or the other aspect of the text and by drawing sharp lines and images, this reduction eliminates the communicative space provided by the Qur'anic language and limits the possibilities of understanding. The most common positive aspect of the interpretations is that they provide a realm in which one can raise new questions in regard to the role of women and gender relations relevant to the present situation. The language that they practice creates new perspectives and possibilities for us, enabling us to understand the role of women more historically than we could possibly understand by the word "history" today. In establishing a basis for raising new questions, they not only enable us to question what they claim to be true, but also help us develop our insight into the subject matter more efficiently, ushering a way to a more authentic understanding of the present.

If language is tradition or the locus of history, then putting the past interpretations which shaped Islamic tradition into mutual conversation is to further the living history; and furthering the living history in terms of dialogical language is the most efficient way of becoming a more authentic human being. Thus, reconsidering and questioning the past interpretations as language-events needs to be an ongoing thing. It is by active participation in interpretation that women become subjects in conversation with the text and not merely passive objects. These mutual conversations can be enlightening for those interested in women's emancipation, for emancipation does not ensue from changing the audience as much as it is changing one's self.

NOTES

1. In the original Persian there is no gender marker, there is one pronoun "ou" for the English he and she, yet the translators often use the masculine pronoun perhaps for two reasons. First, because the references, although they bear double meaning, point to God, the Beloved and traditionally the Arabic Islamic texts use the masculine pronoun to refer to God. Second, and more important, because of the intentional double meaning in the verses of Rumi between reference to God, the Beloved on the one hand, and his master of 'irfan, Shams, the beloved on the other. It is for this second reason that the masculine pronoun is used.

2. Regina M. Schwartz, *The Curse of Cain: The Violent Legacy of Monotheism* (Chicago: University of Chicago Press, 1997).

3. William C. Chittick, *Imaginal World: Ibn al-'Arabi and the Problem of Religious Diversity* (Albany: State University of New York Press, 1994), pp. 138–40.

4. Ibid., p. 138.

5. Ibid., p. 139.

6. Ibid., p. 140.

7. William C. Chittick, *Sufism: A Short Introduction* (Oxford: One World Publications, 2000), pp. 21–22.

8. Oscar Romero, *Violence of Love* (Farmington, PA: Plough Publishing House, 1998), p. 38.

9. Ali Shari'ati, *Religion vs. Religion* (Albuquerque, NM: Abjad Publishers, 1988), p. 17.

10. Ibid.

11. Jalal Ale-Ahmad, *Weststruckness*, trans. J. Green and Ahmad Alizadeh (Costa Mesa, CA: Mazda Publishers, 1997), p. 14.

12. Ale-Ahmad writes: "Something else is obvious to us as well, and that is that since the time the West called us from the eastern shores of the Mediterranean to India–the east as it arose from its hibernation of the dark ages seeking the sunlight, spices, silk and other goods, they have been coming to the east, first as pilgrims to the holy shrines, then in the armor of the crusades, then in the guise of tradesmen, then under the protection of their . . . warships, then as Christian missionaries, and finally in the name of promoting civilizations" (*Weststruckness*, p. 17).

13. Shari'ati, *Religion vs. Religion*, p. 27.

14. Omid Safi, ed., *Progressive Muslims* (Oxford: One World Publishers, 2003), p. 4.

15. Shari'ati, *Religion vs. Religion*, p. 30.

16. Reverend Parris and John Proctor are respectively examples of the practice of the religion of *shirk* and that of the struggle for moving from *shirk* to *tawhid*. Should Elizabeth and John Proctor have submitted to the words of the minister, the Reverend Hale, who said: "cleave to no faith when faith brings blood"? Is it the mistaken law that leads one to sacrifice? Should Proctor had confessed and given the lie that was demanded of him simply to abide by the priest's principle that "life is God's most precious gift" and that "no principle, however glorious, may justify the taking of it"? Arthur Miller, *The Crucible* (New York: Penguin, 1976), p. 132.

17. Brian Swimme, *The Hidden Heart of the Cosmos: Humanity and the New Story* (New York: Orbis Books, 2001), p. 19.

18. Ibid., p. 18.

19. Ibid., p. 19.

20. Shari'ati, *Religion vs. Religion*, p. 37.

21. Ibid., p. 15.

22. Sallie McFague, "The Loving Eye vs. the Arrogant Eye: Christian Critique of the Western Gaze on Nature and the Third World," *Ecumenical Review* 49, no. 2 (April 1997): 185.

23. Ibid., p. 187.

24. Safi, *Progressive Muslims*, pp. 4–5.

25. Oscar Romero, *The Violence of Love* (Farmington, PA: Plough Publishing House, 1998), p. 90.

26. Ibid.

27. McFague, "The Loving Eye vs. the Arrogant Eye," p. 185.

28. The majority of women throughout the world are deprived of their basic human rights; they constitute more than half of the world's population and perform two-thirds of the world's work, yet they receive 10 percent of the world's income and own less than 1 percent of the world's property. Jeanne Vickers, *Women and War* (London: Zed Books, 1993), p. 88.

29. The majority of the victims of the global structural violence of poverty are women and children. Perpetrators of violence against women are rarely held accountable for their actions. In the United States, a woman is raped every six minutes; a woman is battered every fifteen seconds. In North Africa, six thousand women are genitally mutilated each day. This year, more than fifteen thousand women will be sold into sexual slavery in China. Two hundred women in Bangladesh will be horribly disfigured when their spurned husbands or suitors burn them with acid. More than seven thousand women in India will be murdered by their families and in-laws in disputes over dowries. (*Broken Bodies, Shattered Minds: Torture and Ill Treatment of Women* [Amnesty International, 2001].)

30. Sachiko Murata, *The Tao of Islam: A Sourcebook for Gender Relationship in Islamic Thought* (Albany: State University of New York Press, 1992).

31. Andrew Rippin, ed., *Approaches to the History of the Interpretation of the Qur'an* (Oxford: Clarendon Press, 1988), p. 177.

32. *Nahj-ulBalaqa: Peak of Eloquence* (New York: Tahrike Tarsile Qur'an, 1985), Sermon 124.

33. The distinction between the Qur'an and its interpretations is a significant one because the Qur'an reveals itself differently in different contexts and historical contexts cannot be transcended. In other words, the timeless nature of the Qur'an cannot be surpassed in one or a number of particular contexts. Understanding is historically bound and therefore there is no absolute end point in interpretation where absolute truth of the text discloses itself in its totality.

34. This view is not new in the history of interpretation of the Qur'an. Twelfth-century Sufi-theologian 'Ayn al-Qudat Hamadani, a disciple of Ahmad Ghazali, makes a similar point. In his tafsir *al-Haqayiq al-Qur'an* (*Truths of the Qur'an*) he confirms the basic Islamic precept

that the Qur'an is addressed to different people and different times. Concurrently, he maintains that we receive from the text of the Qur'an according to our personal development. Realizing the prejudices of the mind, he adds that our eyes are veiled by norms and conventions, which he interprets as the idols of our time. For him the text of the Qur'an is a means to get to the uncreated Qur'an. The greatest master of the Sufi tradition, Muhyi al-din al-Arabi, had declared an analogous view. According to Ibn Arabi, "to be human is to have a perspective on self and other, even if one is unaware of one's underlying mind-set or is unable to articulate it . . . the human being . . . is not able to go beyond knowledge of himself in his knowledge of the other. . . . You do not know other than yourself." See William C. Chittick, *Imaginal Worlds: Ibn al-'Arabi and the Problem of Religious Diversity* (Albany: State University of New York Press, 1994), pp. 138–63.

35. Safi, *Progressive Muslims*, p. 6.

36. Leila Ahmed, *A Border Passage: From Cairo to America—A Woman's Journey* (New York: Penguin Books, 2000), p. 129.

37. Ibid., pp.125–26.

38. Ibid., p. 75.

39. Ibid., pp. 126–27.

40. Zahra Kamalkhani, *Women's Islam: Religious Practice Among Women in Today's Iran* (London: Kegan Paul International, 1998), p. 8.

41. Most critics of Islamic tradition argue that the tradition can be objectified and criticized on the basis of reflective thinking. Yet the inseparable relation between past and present suggests that the past interpretations do not stand as mere objects to be analyzed in themselves; rather, they condition the present, while the present conditions the way we look at the past (interpretations). Therefore, to objectify the past meaning in its totality is not possible since the past is dissolved in the present. To claim to understand the past meaning in its total objectivity is tantamount to claiming the ability to transcend history. Hans-Georg Gadamer, *Truth and Method* (New York: Continuum, 1997), p. 276.

42. Ibid., p. 7. In her study representing Shirazi women in Iran Kamalkhani concludes that the religious participation of women is far from being marginal or muted, and that "they are even more involved in religious and socio-ritual activity than the average male family member." She further states that "the religious arenas have neither traditionally nor

in the context of the contemporary Islamic revivalism hampered women's active participation as religious followers and as experts, but rather encouraged it" (p. 179).

43. Elizabeth Johnson, *She Who Is: The Mystery of God in Feminist Theological Discourse* (New York: Crossroad Publishing Company, 1992).

44. The word has been translated invariably as "those who have authority," "those who provide maintenance," "protectors," "those in charge of"—each meaning implying a different outlook.

45. The Qur'an reveals itself differently in different contexts: historical contexts cannot be transcended. In other words, the timeless nature of the Qur'an cannot be surpassed in one or a number of particular contexts, for understanding it is historically bound.

8

CRITICS OF JUST WAR THEORIES

CHARLES E. RAVEN AND A. J. MUSTE

Robert B. Tapp

P eople are usually shocked when I say that my lifetime of studying religions has paralleled that of a medical researcher working with viruses. Most of them *are* toxic from a human standpoint but we ignore them at our peril. To understand their effects and to find ways to modify them—that is the paramount task.

One of the greats in my field of comparative religion was Wilfred Cantwell Smith. He reminded us that words such as "religion" and "Christianity" and "Islam" are meaningless abstractions that should be abandoned. There are only humans who, at particular times and places, choose to call themselves Christians or Muslims or Jews and scratch new meanings for those words on the slate of history.

Sixty years ago the *Christian Century* magazine featured an article by the president of the major Protestant seminary titled "The Invisible Religion." He referred to fundamentalism! After all, his version of Christianity had founded many of our great universities, adjusted to science and democracy, and moved forward with the times. This 2004 election reminds us again how wrong he was. Any form of religion really is whatever its current adherents do—and think. Even when their "thinking" prides itself on being irrational!

Fareed Zakaria, remembering the India of his youth, knew this when he defined democracy as the downshifting of power, and then went on to detail ways in which US evangelicals had dropped their theological nuances and simply united their flocks on the issues of abortion and homophobia (Zakaria 2003). Jerry Falwell once spoke of hell and original sin, now that it has been simplified. This made for an easy political alliance with the once-hated Catholics who had become polarized by what Rosemary Ruether called "the pelvic fixation" of the American bishops. Since one voter in five defined "morality" in this simplistic fashion, scholars need to be more empirical in making their map.

When we analyze what some Christians have meant by a "just" war, we also need to attend both to the theologians and to "the Christian street." Of course political leaders prefer to have ecclesiastical blessing when they send forth their troops. But if they know Western history they know full well that the powerful domestic priests will always sanction the war—and the citizenry that will tolerate nothing less.

I am not arguing here that Jews, Christians, and Muslims should not continue analyzing and criticizing our human propensities to use violence. But once the armies march, that potential educative function of religious organizations is essentially suspended. Cynics often criticize military generals for fighting today's war with yesterday's strategies. In modem wars, technology has consistently outpaced moral reflections—think high-level bombers, smart missiles, nuclear weaponry, space weaponry, and biological weaponry.

Until the end of World War I, Christian doubts about calls to war were confined to a fairly narrow spectrum. If one focuses on ordinary Christians and not theologians, the spectrum is even narrower. Duty to country trumped all other considerations, for almost all those in the pews. After the institution of a draft, the small minority of US males who belonged to the historic peace churches and whose convictions resisted the war drums sought forms of alternative service such as the ambulance corps or medical corps.

AMERICAN BEGINNINGS

The Revolutionary War, after all, had been a war of liberation fought against an enemy that was too similar for full demonization. The Civil War had, for each side, been cast as a war for territory—preserving either a new Confederacy or an older and larger Union. In this case, the subsequent Spanish war required a slightly different rationale. That Catholic country had been treating its colonial subjects "badly," and they needed liberation. Participation in the subsequent First World War required considerable demonization of the coreligious "Hun." Church leaders fell in line, however, as documented in *Preachers Present Arms*.[1]

Just war theories were a minor part of this process both in the United States and in the rest of Christendom. Since Augustine's formulations, they had remained a kind of ecclesiastical exercise—interesting between wars but inapplicable in wartime. At least the church leaders of no nation had ever found that they had to denounce the activities of their own government as unjust.

THE APOCALYPTIC BACKGROUND[2]

This becomes more understandable when we think of the several end-time scenarios that underlay theological reflections. Augustine's two cities—one here and quite human; the other, there and quite divine—would persist in their separate ways until the end of time. Moreover, his earthly city was metaphorical of those several actual civilizations that would have their days and then wane. In other words, the very imminent kingdom of God once expected by sectarian Judaism and primitive Christianity was reduced to a far-off event. And all problems of the here and now could be explained by a pervasive sinfulness inherited from Adam. (Even though Eve was seen as the apple passer, the patriarchal traditions could not allow her a central transmissive role!)

More "realized" eschatologies emerged as Christians assimilated Greco-Roman thinking. Their fictionalized Jesus no longer
expected a divine kingdom; he was it. Whoever became "in him"
was already in that kingdom. The creeds of the fourth century
embraced both versions, incongruously affirming immortality of
the soul (entering "life everlasting" at death, presumably) and a resurrection of the body (in the final day of judgment of "living and
dead," presumably). Maybe this illogicality was the reason the late
Bishop Pike said that he could still sing the Creed but no longer say
it! Augustine's view persisted through the centuries. Reformation
thinkers spoke of a double predestination. The god knew the destiny of all humans before they were born, and no earthly virtue or
vice could alter this. To think otherwise would be to deny divine
omniscience. Luther, after all, had been an Augustinian monk.
Ignatius Loyola prudently advised his Jesuits to preach this predes-
tinarian truth very cautiously. Luther and Calvin, however, almost
rejoiced in it as showing the "grace" of god. Since Augustine's cal-
culation had been that only 144,000 seats remained in heaven
(abandoned by the fallen angels), this meant that the chances of
having been chosen reduced with every moment of time. Calvin's
suggestion was that, since none could know whether they had been
designated as saint or damned, all should try to behave as saints.
Some of the reformers on the left found this too pessimistic and
suggested that humans had some measure of free will, and that virtuous living would certainly deserve divine reward. Eventually,
groups such as the Methodists began claiming that all humans were
capable of earthly perfection and would be rewarded for it.

These three significantly differing positions—salvation before
birth, salvation after a final judgment, and salvation at death for
some—have persisted in Christian thought. Based on them, human
virtue was irrelevant, secondary, or primary. To understand today's
fundamentalisms, we must attend to this apocalyptic backdrop.

THE EMERGENCE OF A SOCIAL GOSPEL AND ITS COMPETITORS

It was this newer group of liberal Christians, with their focus on free will, that began a series of moral crusades to improve human society. If humans were capable of achieving a moral perfectionism, it followed that improving society was one way of supporting this. Some of the sixteenth-century reform groups had withdrawn from society in order to pursue a perfectionism—but the next century saw this impulse directed toward society itself.

The good society would not simply be one where sinfulness was restrained but instead would be one where changes reflecting a higher morality were achieved in the public arena. This new theology surfaced in the wake of an industrial revolution in Protestant areas such as Germany, Scandinavia, the Netherlands, Switzerland, England, and the United States. The religious pluralism of the latter three countries facilitated matters in the sense that competition among sects supported innovations. One of the earliest causes was the abolition of slavery. Conservatives clung to biblical supports, the weight of historical custom, and the obduracy of sin. The new reformers reached back to the biblical "kingdom of God" image but transformed it into a blueprint to be achieved by human virtue, in earthly space, by humans who had heard the call.

Take the case of Walter Raushenbusch, a Baptist. The Civil War had made it clear to many that any talk of some single "Christian ethic" was futile, and a new beginning had to be made. Raushenbusch called it "Christianizing the social order." Early efforts to end slavery had begun among Quakers but had spread to Congregationalists, Unitarians, Universalists in the North, and thence to Methodists, Baptists, and Presbyterians. Most of these groups experienced splits on this issue, and in some cases have never reunited. The Civil War ended slavery, of course, but certainly not racism. New causes emerged in this broad social gospel movement—rights of women, workers, and children. The eschatological underlay here was a subtle shifting to immortality beginning at individual death.

In many ways this movement was new in that it aimed at transforming the whole social order. Well, almost. Until the First World War, little was done regarding any reevaluation of international violence. Charles Howard Hopkins, in *The Rise of the Social Gospel in American Protestantism, 1865–1915*, covered the movement well (Hopkins 1940).

In America, particularly, this period from 1870 to 1914 was a complex one. Various nativisms reacted against the immigrations encouraged by industrialism and European social conditions. Most of these were also anti-Catholic, and the Vatican added to the strains by suppressing an Americanist movement among progressive Catholics.

Religious proliferations were probably the greatest brake on progressivism, however. Methodists and Baptists created waves of evangelism that swept the land, stressing an imminent end-time and judgment. Sin was being refocused to drinking, sex, and gambling (rum, Romanism, and rebellion was a variant on these themes). Seventh-Day Adventism and Mormonism grew rapidly. Various types of "positive thinking" (Christian Science is a good example) flourished in other class and educational niches, and spiritualisms were rampant. And a Pentecostalism surfaced that emphasized bodily ecstasies. No historians of the time, to my knowledge, were betting on the bright futures that Mormons and Pentecostals have experienced! Nor of the even greater success of those very angry Protestants who called themselves fundamentalists.

THE WAR TO END ALL WARS

If 1910 was the summit of liberal and social gospel expectations, 1918 began the descent. The United States retreated into isolationism, dooming the League of Nations to impotence. Widespread economic depressions made conventional economics dubious. Revolutions, right and left, doomed any rational political development.

Perhaps the most disappointing fact was the continuance of military violence as a means of resolving disputes and extending ambitions. Bolsheviks unseated Mensheviks, and defeated White Russians and their European allies; a disassembled Ottoman empire was ruled by imperial militarisms; Italy attacked Ethiopia; Franco's troops overthrew the Spanish republic.

Within non-Catholic Christian circles, cooperative "ecumenical" movements emerged, stimulated in part by this chaotic historic backdrop. At first the focus was on building a united front against secularism. But the rise of Nazism complicated matters, and a 1938 organizing meeting in the Netherlands was torn by competing German factions. The non-Nazi Confessing (*Bekennende*) group was critical of the cooperative liberalism of the new organization, moving in a Barthian direction and labeling itself neoorthodox. The German invasion of Poland in 1939 triggered numerous military alliances that effectively shelved any international theological cooperation.

This interwar period saw many movements questioning whether any war could be "just" from any Christian standpoint. New armaments—tanks, aerial bombardments, poison gases—were forcing rethinking. The historic peace churches (Quaker, Brethren, Mennonite) had always argued this but now mainstream Christians were rethinking their reflex patriotisms. A Dutch historian had termed his book *The Fall of Christianity*, and he dated it with Constantine.[3] The problem, he argued, was any link to state power. I would add, however, that Heering felt a modernization of received theologies would be redemptive.

COMMUNAL PACIFISM

For my purposes here, it will be important to distinguish among personal pacifism; communal pacifism; Christian, Jewish, Hindu, and Buddhist pacifisms; and universal pacifism. All are reactions to human uses of violence against other humans, but their rootages vary, and all but the last may be situational.

Most individuals learn to avoid violence when possible, if only because they have learned that retaliations in kind may not be worth enduring. Most individuals have also learned to extend this avoidance to certain in-groups—family, neighborhood, or legal community.

Communal pacifisms within Christianity clearly reach back to the earliest periods. When the Roman ruler has all the weapons and all the power, violent resistance is dangerous. When a group of Jews in Jerusalem rebelled against Roman power in 66 CE, the small Jewish-Christian community clearly abstained and fled. Assuming these were the followers of Jesus' brother James, we never hear from them again. New converts from the activities of Paul and those like him were not known for violence against Rome. Their reasons, however, may have been more eschatological than ethical. If Jesus will be returning momentarily to establish the divine kingdom, there is no need to bother either attacking or defending doomed earthly kingdoms. As time transpired and this event disappointed, the ethical reasons not to support Rome no doubt became more prominent, and a kind of Christian pacifism appeared. By the end of the second century, some Christians were clearly serving in the Roman armies and Tertullian was assessing whether this could be accepted.

As the percentage and distribution of Christians within the empire grew, these original communal pacifisms became confined to bands of hermits who were retreating from the new worldliness of their fellow Christians. Monasteries emerged from this impulse. In subsequent centuries reform movements translated this intense ethic for new communities—Lollards, Cathars, Anabaptists, Third-order Franciscans, Mennonites, Quakers.

CHRISTIAN PACIFISM

My third kind of pacifism contends that all "true" Christians should renounce violence. Historically, it is a recent emergent. One might see Erasmus as an early proponent, but the century of religious wars doomed his message. And the ensuing truce slogan, *cujus regio, ejus religio* (the religion of the prince is the religion of the realm), retained the linkage of Christianity to power and thus to violence. Umphrey Lee's *The Historic Church and Modern Pacifism* is a good guide to this history (Lee 1943).

Why do we not see Christian pacifism until the period between the wars of the twentieth century? One reason is that Napoleon's innovation of citizen armies brought the problems of killing into every household. The senseless slaughter of the First World War made thoughtful theologians rethink their relationship to state power. And the impact of scientific advances upon doctrines had already pushed them away from easy traditionalism. The spread of graduate universities forced much theological transformation. Comparative religion, critical history of religions, anthropology, psychology, and sociology of religion all flourished apart from the colleges and seminaries. Secularization and laicization resulted. And, not least, the spread of democratic ideas opened new social and economic solutions.

The ensuing Christian liberalism moved on several fronts. For one thing, Christian origins were being scrutinized with new tools and new freedom. Albert Schweitzer's *Quest for the Historical Jesus* hit Germany in 1902, summarizing fifty years of scholarship. An issue of the *Hibbert Journal* in 1902 was titled "Jesus or Christ?" and assumed readers would know what was the problem. A few years before, an American poet had written: "Some call it Evolution, others call it God." A few Christian writers in the late nineteenth century were praising a Christian socialism.

Typically the liberal theologian would reach back through the centuries of theological constructions to a "historic Jesus" whose ethic would be seen as universally relevant. Adolph Harnack, the great Berlin historian, argued around 1900 that Christianity began to decline when it absorbed Hellenistic ideas. The liberal theologian would then weave elements of a scientific worldview and progressive politics around this ethic.

A good example is G. H. C. Macgregor's *New Testament Basis of Pacifism* (Macgregor 1936). It was hard for people to read this brief treatise by the Scottish theologian and continue singing "Onward Christian Soldiers." Similarly, George Bernard Shaw's *Heartbreak House* affected readers as well as playgoers at the end of the war. Shaw had prudently delayed staging until then.

Other occasions for rethinking were the weakness of the League of Nations, the realization that the Versailles Treaty included more revenge than was useful in rebuilding Europe, and the emergence of authoritarian governments across Europe in response to social and economic disappointments.

PEACE PLEDGERS

The many peace marches and movements in the interwar period of 1918–39 indicate that pacifist thinking was no longer confined to seminaries and pulpits. After all, that bloody war had been among Christians who all invoked the same deity! It wasn't even a Catholic versus Protestant encounter, much less a crusade against some other religion. While Napoleon had started a tradition of citizen armies, the slaughter here in trench warfare exceeded all past conflicts. The property destruction and economic disruptions were equally unacceptable to most people.

In the United Kingdom, and to a lesser degree in the United States, liberal Protestants, with their sympathy for a social gospel including this extension of social gospel concerns, supported pacifist interpretations of their faith. Just-war traditions seemed an arcane archaism best left to molder in Catholic circles.

NEO-ORTHODOXY'S "REALISM"

In Europe, a growing ecumenical movement, stemming from a cooperative movement among those who had been engaged in worldwide Protestant missionary movements, found itself embroiled in murkier theological waters. In 1928, meeting in Jerusalem, it had been clear that the enemy of the faith was to be found in secularism. While the Soviet Union was most aggressive in this, much of Europe was tired of religious strife and further disenchanted by the common religiosity of Germany and the Allies in the First World War.

This shared liberalism was being challenged by sophisticated returns to a chastened orthodoxy. Karl Barth was a key figure in this. Disillusioned by conventional religiosity in the trenches, he had turned to Kierkegaard and Augustine and was reviving a version of human sinfulness to explain what he felt was the inevitable ambiguity of history in the times before a divine finale.

Hitler's rise to power, and the subservience of many of Germany's Protestants, further solidified this viewpoint. Barth shifted to Basle and a postliberal career of questioning human rationality. In the United States, his best-known disciple was Reinhold Niebuhr. Moving from a social gospel and pacifist orientation, and a frustrating experience in a parish racked by industry-union tensions, Niebuhr began speaking of "moral man" surrounded by "immoral society." No ethical fulfillment could be expected in history, even though we could still speak of an "impossible ideal."

Therefore, totalitarianism (his focus was primarily on Germany) would have to be countered with force—and pacifism would prove too idealistic and important for this. Military response would need endorsement as a "lesser evil." The church could never stand with a political power but must, in some sense, remain critical. Believers, living in this imperfect world, might well have to take up arms against evils. Thus, when Hitler invaded Poland in 1939, and particularly when Japan attacked the United States in 1941, a significant body of theologians and all major church leaders were ready to endorse military responses on theological grounds. The more cynical observation that no national church had ever opposed the war activities of its nation remained intact.

TWO DISSENTERS

Along with this nationalistic unanimity, there were, of course, opponents and critics. We will examine two prominent ones—one in England and the other in the United States. With parallel life-spans, both rejected just-war theories and moved into forms of pacifism before 1939. Thus, there are certain parallels and certain differences that we must examine to understand their impact both during their lifetimes and beyond.

Charles E. Raven (1885–1964)

Charles Raven had a multiple career as academic and radical. He was a key figure in the Modern Churchman's Union, the theologically liberal Anglican association. He not only did science "on the side," he published bird studies, butterfly studies, and flower studies and made significant forays into the history of science. In 1910, at the age of twenty-four, he became dean of Emmanuel College where his theological radicalism was continually challenged. Pacifist, socialist, and feminist, he was nonetheless a chaplain to the king as of 1920. For most of his career he was Regius Professor of Divinity at Cambridge.

Eventually Raven became master of Christ's College, and then served as vice chancellor in 1947 until his 1950 retirement. I. T. Ramsey recalls one incident during this distinguished academic career:

> After his last dinner as Master, undergraduates carried him shoulder-high back to the lodge—a tribute to the deep affection

in which he was held. When Christ's College commemorated its Quincentenary in 1948—the middle of his time as Vice-Chancellor—he made, on successive evenings, two masterly after-dinner speeches on the college and its history, and on the purpose of a university education, and not a phrase was duplicated. On one of the evenings, turning to portraits behind High Table he pointed to Milton and Darwin as representing two cosmic perspectives which the metaphysics of William Paley, well intentioned, well informed, and clearly argued though it be, could never contain, but which, he believed, might well be harmonized by rehabilitating in our own day some of the distinctive ideas and themes of Ralph Cudworth, the Cambridge Platonist.[4]

These referents illustrate clearly the dominant foci of Raven's career—science and religion. His time as university administrator brought him wider contacts, and these further qualified his estimates of much theological discourse:

I have been working for the past three years in as close touch with biologists, botanists, and zoologists as, with my own theologians. Once again I was impressed by the quality of the scientific outlook; its freedom to grow, sloughing off ideas outworn or disproven; its primary concern for truth and its willingness to stand unreservedly by the verdict of the evidence; its enthusiasm in welcoming novelty and in tracking down elusory data; and in consequence, the kindliness and co-operation of its workers.[5]

Throughout his long and productive career he wrote detailed monographs on items of church history, the history of science, and modern social problems. His modernism disdained dualisms. In his Gifford Lectures, he would rephrase this emphasis:

The fact is, of course, as we shall consider later, that the whole story of our universe is a serial and that the volume dealing with the evolution and character of life on this planet begins (perhaps) with the amoeba and ends (at present) with the saint. . . . But if, as most scientists and all Christians would surely agree, the creative process in nature and history shows not only continuity but the emergence of real novelty, there is more in the saint than in the amoeba; and we shall form a truer concept of the process if we study it from its end, rather than from its beginning.[6]

These forays into science and its history clearly tempted him to avoid theological arguments, but he once commented upon his abiding obsession with the human scene:

Nature, perhaps because of its strangeness, fills us with an awe that we cannot feel for humanity: we turn to it with a sense of relief at escaping from the folly and meanness of our kindred: and for a moment we believe that God is nearer and more manifest in it than among them. This is of course only a mood of unreasoning paganism: but there is a pagan in most of us, especially if we live in cities. Yet to urge it seriously should be for a thinking person impossible: it is a reversion to animism and idolatry, to the personification of sacred symbols, to the "pathetic fallacy" which finds in Nature a sympathy undiscovered in mankind: or else it is to reckon the inanimate as more representative of reality than the animate.[7]

Part of Raven's intellectual freedom stemmed from the fact that for most of his career he was ordained but not under any bishop. Thus his forays into the sciences and Christian history, to say nothing of social issues, were relatively unfettered. He had not only mastered the biblical scholars of his time and the church fathers, but he moved freely through every stage of Christian history. His treatment of the great British biologist John Ray remains useful in our time.

Raven as pacifist

With many misgivings, Raven had seen military duty in the First World War, but he returned a convinced Christian pacifist. This appears regularly in his writings. A good place to look at his attitudes regarding church and war is with his *War and the Christian*.[8] Here he reviews the earlier history and focuses on the ecumenical movement and the 1937 Oxford Conference.

> Most of us would regard the tradition as entitled to respect, few would consider it sacrosanct, both because of the change in the character of war, and because today in every church there exists an influential body of opinion definitely opposed to it. This minority is no longer negligible in any British denominations, and in America is most certainly a majority; and it consists not of any one section of extremists or rebels, but of men and women differing widely in their doctrinal and ethical outlook on other matters.[9]

Raven reviews the various attempts to find biblical justifications for war and cites approvingly Macgregor's treatment of the New Testament.[10] Raven's own conclusion was: "It is, in fact, more than doubtful whether any single utterance or action of Jesus gives any sort of sanction to war in any form: it is absurd, to suppose that they justify the mass murders of modern conflict."[11]

Raven interprets the doctrine of incarnation to lay upon humans a quest for perfection, however long and gradual it may be:

> The quest for perfection will present itself as a series of stages to be travelled, of concrete and limited objectives to be attained. In the individual and in the race, attainment consists in maintaining loyalty to an absolute demand and striving to fulfil that obligation in the particular circumstances of each day.[12]

Events the next year challenged all of these assumptions. Raven's pacifism was prepared for this eventuality, however, and he kept arguing that Christians should oppose military ventures. Throughout the Second World War his pacifist writing and activities continued unabated. In 1950 he delivered in the Robert Treat Paine Lectures his fullest statement of the case, *Theological Basis of Christian Pacifism.*[13] Raven reminded his US audiences that the British obliteration bombing of Lubeck set the stage for American actions at Hiroshima and Nagasaki, and that the churches in both countries had not taken the new situation seriously but had instead moved through the old excuses of lesser evil, halting oppression, and inevitability of compromise. The essay is a long critique of Reinhold Niebuhr's position as failing to build the communal aspect of a full Christian faith.

> The theological situation was now new, however. Theologies of "crisis" now prevailed. Has all our theology of crisis and of denunciation merely brought us to the point at which because we are fallen sinners we can excuse ourselves for any sin, however monstrous and diabolical? If so, let us repent of it and return to the liberalism which for all its tolerance never pretended that evil was good or that men could reject moral standards without abjuring Christ.[14]

If war is the central issue, Christians must come to terms with what is already being discovered in the world—the archaism of the sexism and racism that have been so dominant. Incidentally, Raven calls the emancipation of women " the greatest achievement of our modern age.[15] This echoes what he was saying in 1940.

> A world rent by conflicts of race and class and sex; a Church which has accepted and sanctioned these conflicts and added to them its own sectarian rivalries; these do not provide material for communal sympathies or an integrative way of life.[16]

As far back as 1930, his list had included "racial prejudice, economic exploitation, political injustice, national pride, industrial unrest, social change, mental confusion, moral anarchy"—these and not the rival claims of other religions.[17]

In the second set of his Gifford Lectures, he reiterates the pacifist position in full strength:

. . . the advent of new weapons and particularly the use of chemical and bacteriological techniques, of obliteration bombing, of nuclear fission and the so-called hydrogen bomb for indiscriminate massacre, has produced a situation in which there can be no pretence of a just war in the traditional meaning of those words and small possibility of reconciling warfare with any religious or moral valuation of mankind.[18]

Critique

No British thinker better embodied scholarship and activism than Charles Raven. Because of both his theological modernism and his interest in the sciences, he was out of the mainstream after 1939. Yet none could match his steady output. Verbally, he avoided being labeled a humanist or naturalist in any philosophical sense. His goal was to bring the Church of England into the modern world. His academic posting gave him enormous freedom to work at this. While his formulations regularly used the terms "Incarnation" and "Holy Spirit," his reworking of those terms into a universe open to scientific study was consistent.

During much of this period, his scientific and philosophical friends operated within forms of logical positivism, viewing many of his ideas as nonsense. From Raven's point of view, they were simply viewing nature from the wrong point. One needs to start with the upper end of evolutionary development and not the lower. And even there, one should focus on the saints and not just ordinary folk. Raven's Jesus is found here, and his Cross is a path and not a onetime divine event.

The pacifism centers here, and Raven's ethic is consistently put in Christian terms rather than rational or universal ones. He may have criticized his friend William Temple for failing to move fully into pacifism but his familiarity with other religious systems fell short of Temple's, and this gives a sort of parochial quality to his ethical stances.

A. J. Muste (1885–1967)

My second critic of just wars operated in the United States where denominational and theological pluralism was the rule and not the exception. He and Raven knew each other, but their ethical journeys had many differences. One of the most obvious was the ways in which Muste could absorb and adapt lessons from Gandhi's trajectory.[19]

Immigrant Calvinist

Muste, as a young Dutch immigrant to Michigan, living among many in a similar situation, did the normal thing. He went to Hope College, where he distinguished himself academically. The ministry seemed a logical profession and he went to New Brunswick (New Jersey) Theological Seminary where he graduated with distinction.

Reformed Minister

Muste spent his second seminary summer at a Manhattan church and after ordination moved to a Fort Washington parish with parishioners on many social and intellectual levels. He enrolled at Union Theological Seminary and his intellectual flowering and leftward movement, religiously and politically, intensified. Two years later he resigned his position and sought fellowship with the Congregationalists.

Liberalized Social Gospeler and Labor Educator

In Muste's new parish in Newtonville, Massachusetts, his intellectual broadening continued. He had discovered Tolstoy while in Manhattan and now was finding kinship with Emerson and Thoreau, and reading Rufus Jones. He moved toward pacifism and joined the Fellowship of Reconciliation (FOR). After being disappointed that the United States had entered the war, he resigned that pulpit in 1917. His new orientation had narrowed his search to the Quakers, and Muste now moved to Providence, Rhode Island. He kept up a relationship with Norman Thomas, whom he had known at Union, and with Roger Baldwin, who had founded the National Civil Liberties Bureau. In 1919 mill workers at Lawrence went out on strike, led by the Industrial Workers of the World. The AFL denounced the strike, and the radicalization Muste underwent made it necessary for him to sever his relationship with the Quakers. An outcome of the mill strike was the creation of a second union, the Amalgamated Textile Workers, and Muste became its general secretary. In 1921 the Brookwood Labor College was founded in Katonah, New York, with Muste as director. The college combined intellectual studies, leadership training, and manual labor in an intense community. Inevitably the more conservative labor movement viewed it with suspicion. By 1928 the AFL called upon its unions to drop support. In 1929 those close to Muste organized the Conference for Progressive Labor Action (CLPA) with its own journal in order to protect the original ideas of Brookwood. As the CLPA became involved with strike support, Muste's own original pacifism became tempered, and he saw Brookwoood falling into reactionary hands. The college closed in 1937.

Labor Radical

As the Great Depression spread in the United States, the problems of unemployment loomed. The Communist Party set up its own organizational structure and the CLPA did the same. Even though some consultations between the two groups had taken place, Muste's distrust prevailed. In 1933, in Pittsburgh, Pennsylvania, the American Workers Party (AWP) was formed. Musteites claimed a million members in seven hundred locals.[20] The next year the AWP became involved in a successful strike of the Auto-Lite workers in Toledo, Ohio, and a Teamsters strike in Minneapolis, Minnesota. In both cases their efforts paralleled those of the Trotskyites.

Trotskyite

In that same year the AWP merged with James Cannon's Communist League of America, a Trotskyist organization, to become the Workers Party of the United States. At this time, the Trotskyists, it must be remembered, considered themselves to be the true inheritors of the Bolshevik Revolution. Muste now began to speak of the class struggle and revolution. Trotsky himself, then living in France, had approved the merger and admired Muste (despite Muste's still-clinging religiousness). The merger was short-lived since the order had come, from Trotsky, to infiltrate the local socialist parties, a move that Muste opposed. Muste was further disillusioned when his close colleague Louis Budenz defected to the Communist Party. Muste also worked with Max Schachtman during this period, and sympathized with him when he split with Cannon and formed the Workers Party.

Religion Again

In 1936 Muste took a European vacation and spent a week with Trotsky in Norway. They disagreed about the US effects of the Socialist infiltration but parted amicably. While in Paris Muste wandered into St. Sulpice and had a kind of religious experience that turned him back toward his earlier orientation. Several weeks later his American friends learned that he had turned away from Trotskyism and was once again a Christian Socialist. Seeing events in Europe at close hand, he had become convinced that war was the central problem.

Labor Intellectual

For the rest of his long and active life, Muste would keep these two foci—pacifism and social revolution. In this sense, his experiences made him unique. But they also made him somewhat marginal. His secular friends engaged in social change would always be wary of his religious side while his Christian friends would have problems with his expansive and revolutionary approach to their commitments.

> I do not essentially regret the course I took, not that regret would do any good. And I did put the theories of "lesser evil," of "realism," of the inescapability or necessity of violence, or revolutionary dictatorship, and so on, to the test of experience. I am, therefore, not beguiled by contemporary expressions of them. I am sure my earlier experience has been helpful to me in my attempts to develop nonviolent methods and a more revolutionary pacifist movement in later years.[21]

Pacifist Organizer

In 1936 Muste became industrial secretary of the Fellowship of Reconciliation, the US branch of the organization founded during the First World War, and in 1937 he became director of Manhattan's Presbyterian Labor Temple. These two jobs provided support for his family and a good platform for his dual interests. In 1940 the FOR named him national secretary.

Pacifist Critic of Neo-orthodoxy

As Europe became embroiled in the Second World War, many Protestant Christian pacifists shifted to support military constraints on Nazism. Theologically, many moved toward the "realistic" position with Reinhold Niebuhr. Muste was clearly the sharpest critic of this shift. In 1940 his *Non-Violence in an Aggressive World* appeared.[22] He addressed himself to three groups—religious persons, workers-movement activists, and those concerned in preserving democracy. His description of his Christianity here focuses on a historic Jesus who struggled against power and ultimately died on a cross for his efforts. He rejects the idea that this religion is utopian or an "impossible ideal," contending that it represents a new and correct way of changing history. To accept war, especially modern war, is to accept un-Christian activities. Thus the pacifist who refuses is the real realist. Muste cites as allies those Catholics who have rejected "just war" in the PAX movement and Emil Brunner, the Swiss theologian who differed with Barth.[23]

Turning to his political friends, Muste recognizes the linkage between militarism and capitalism and imperialism:

> [It is] the possession of a military machine, its maintenance, the possibility of resorting to war, which keep an exploiting capitalism and a predatory imperialism alive, which constantly interfere with the movement for social justice, and make it possible for ruling groups to evade facing and dealing with the economic evils which bring suffering upon the masses.[24]

His chapter 6 is unique in its shift from political argument to literary buttressing. Reading it today reminds us of many writers now no longer read but powerful and popular in their times—Ignacio Silone, Charles Rann Kennedy, and Franz Werfel. Muste then turns to democracy, arguing that something other than force holds it together: It is of the very essence of the democratic way of life that society is thought of as held together not by violence but by the justice which is embodied in the organization of any given society and the human community, the fellowship, which it makes possible.[25]

Muste would substitute for armies a police function, arguing

> Police function under a reign of law. It is, furthermore, a law which is on the whole accepted by society, by those who live under it, and this because it embodies an approximation to justice, because men find mutual advantage under the set-up, some degree of real "community" is achieved.[26]

Muste then discusses the various economic injustices that lead to wars and suggests ways to resolve these without resorting to violence. Turning to the church, he insists that it must develop sound theology if this is to take place, and be flexible in the symbols used within this philosophy. There follows a long discussion of "Party" in Leninism as having some parallels with the committed community of theologies. The book concludes with a call to revolution led by a party-church of those who are fully convinced that violence is self-defeating.

Nonviolent Revolutionary

In 1939 a visit from Krishnalal Shridharani helped many US radicals evaluate Gandhian strategies and tactics.[27] Given Muste's revolutionary stances and his intellectual commitment to broad social change, the Indian experience had for years been important in his work. Muste's revolutionary commitments were more than many pacifists were ready to make, and he was continually developing outreach programs. These were often spurred on by colleagues that he was able to bring into FOR staff positions. Glenn Smiley, Bayard Rustin, James Farmer, James Lawson, John Swomley, David McReynolds, and David Dellinger are among the most important names in this regard. Add to this his influence on those who were never on his staff—Roger Baldwin, Norman Thomas, Walter Muelder, Martin Luther King Jr., Homer Jack, Sidney Lens, Paul Goodman, A. Phillip Randolph, Paul Jacobs, and Nat Hentoff.

Not everyone shared his particular religious views but all were drawn to his broad vision of social changes. The Congress on Racial Equality was founded in 1942, in order to develop nonviolent solutions to US racism. In 1948, restless over the less-than-revolutionary stance of some FOR members, Muste helped create Peacemakers, whose organization was through cells rather than on an individual basis; they accepted nonviolence in all aspects of life "as the means for resisting totalitarianism and achieving basic social change."

In 1949 Muste and Victor Paschkis created the Society for Social Responsibility in Science. In 1950 Muste was a key figure in creating the Church Peace Mission that produced *The Christian Conscience and War*. A widely read booklet of the American Friends Service Committee, *Speak Truth to Power*, was produced in 1955 with major input from Muste. In 1957 the Committee for a Sane Nuclear Policy was formed. Muste was a central figure in the World Peace Brigade, bringing nonviolent strategies to nationalists in Africa. In 1960 he was instrumental in organizing the San Francisco to Moscow Peace Walk, proceeding from the United States to the Kremlin. In 1966 he led a group to Saigon in the midst of America's war in Vietnam, where they were quickly deported. He then made a trip to Hanoi.

Muste's commitments kept him involved until the very end. Whether it was organizing marches from America to the Kremlin or trespassing on US nuclear sites, he was there. Without doubt he was the key figure in creating a nonviolent civil rights movement in the United States. He was also the key figure in expanding American pacifism beyond the religious few to the secular many. After Muste, few would use pejorative terms such as "passivism" to describe peace efforts. His influence remains worldwide. Testimonials from two who were inspired by him but did not share his religious commitments illustrate this. First, Nat Hentoff:

> The contrast is between violent hatred and the nonviolence of determined resistance to that hatred. During the Vietnam War— influenced by A. J. Muste; Dorothy Day, the Catholic speaker of truth to power; and others—I committed civil disobedience in front of a draft registration center, along with hundreds of others that day.[28]

And then from David McReynolds:

> . . . one of the things which most deeply impressed me about the late A. J. Muste was his ability to listen with respect to those with whom he deeply disagreed, not as a tactic but because he hoped to catch in their remarks some truth he himself had missed. Most

of us, in arguing, can hardly wait for our "opponent" to finish so that we can "correct" him (or her).[29]

When Muste died, his death notice read: "in lieu of flowers, friends are requested to get out and work—for peace, human rights, for a better world."

Critique

Looking back on their long friendship, Harold Fey had to say that Muste was a "loser." Yet he was also one of the most influential figures of the twentieth century in labor, civil rights, and antiwar activities. His blend of religious pacifism attracted many and put off some. Yet he could work with the secular radicals just as easily. And his indebtedness to Gandhi took the edge off his earlier Christian narrowness.

Raven's pacifism certainly stayed within the boundaries of a liberal Christianity, even though he worked hard to restate a theology based on modern science. Muste's theology was more mainstream, even though he moved beyond the conservative Calvinism of his youth.

What would a "universal pacifism" be like? It would be an ethical position that could stand on its own, based on reasoning and consequences. That is, it would be viewed as a desired alternative to violence that was more likely to achieve the ends that were already desired. It might use the symbols and rituals and emotional elements of various particular religions but it would also be able to exist on various secular bases.

In this direction, Muste's activism and organizational brilliance becomes exemplary. The fact that he could work together with the Dellingers, the Hentoffs, the McReynoldses, the Jacks, and the Housers exemplifies this universality.

PERSISTENT LESSONS

The three Abrahamic faiths are still too closely tied to their own histories to reverse course effectively in regard to violence. In the case of Judaism this is more recent, but the messianism of the settlements will not disappear quickly. Nor is there much hope in the resources of the other world religions. Each has its own "strong" streak and its employment and justification of violence to deal with. What we need is an ethic so universal that it can be rephrased in specific religious terminologies and then resonate more effectively with groups of believers.

Along with such a universal ethic, we need to re-present two histories. Both are neglected in the interests of current political powers. On the one hand, the failures of violence in the modern world are usually obscured by claims of success. World War II becomes the "great war." But only if one overlooks the stupidities that allowed the rise of Mussolini, Tojo, and Hitler and the terrible aftermath ensured by the expansion of Stalinism. Careful analysis of US military campaigns alone in ensuing years makes clear that violence is a very blunt and ineffective weapon. Korea, Vietnam, Somalia, Latin America, Afghanistan, and Iraq—amass the total human and property costs—without any national tags—and these were disasters.

The other history, even more neglected, is the increasing use of nonviolence as a change technique. The underlying pacifism has often been only situational, but the results have been impressive. Poland, Chile, Yugoslavia, Czechoslovakia, South Africa, and the Philippines. The two figures best known to US readers will be Mohandas Gandhi and Martin Luther King Jr. Both showed how effective nonviolence could be as a tool of within-country change for dispossessed peoples.

NOTES

1. Ray Hamilton Abrams, *Preachers Present Arms; a Study of the War-Time Attitudes and Activities of the Churches and the Clergy in the United States, 1914–1918* (Philadelphia, 1933).

2. The term "eschatological" would be more accurate here as a reference to "end times," but popular usages have tended to employ "apocalyptic" for these connotations. While that term more properly designates hidden matters, its appearance in the title of the last book of Christianity's bible blurs this distinction. An example is Robert Jay Lifton's new book: *Superpower Syndrome: America's Apocalyptic Confrontation with the World* (New York: Thunder's Mouth Press/Nation Books, 2003).

3. Gerrit Jan Heering and J. W. Thompson, *The Fall of Christianity* (London: G. Allen & Unwin, 1930).

4. I. T. Ramsey, "Charles Earle Raven," *Proceedings of the British Academy* (1965).

5. Charles E. Raven, *Good News of God* (London: Hodder and Stoughton, 1943), p. 5.

6. Charles E. Raven, *Natural Religion and Christian Theology, Gifford Lectures, 1951–52* (Cambridge, England: University Press, 1953), p. 12.

7. Charles Raven, *Christianity and Science* (New York: Association Press, 1953), p. 425.

8. Charles E. Raven, *War and the Christian* (New York: Garland, 1972).

9. Ibid., p. 92

10. G. H. C. Macgregor, *The New Testament Basis of Pacifism* (London: J. Clarke & Co., 1936).

11. Ibid., p. 133.

12. Ibid., p. 139.

13. Charles E. Raven, *The Theological Basis of Christian Pacifism, The Robert Treat Paine Lectures, 1950* (New York: Fellowship Publications, 1950).

14. Ibid., p. 14.

15. Ibid., p. 85.

16. Charles E. Raven, *The Gospel and the Church; A Study of Dis-*

tortion and Its Remedy (New York: Charles Scribner's Sons, 1940), p. 247.

17. Percival Gardner-Smith, Francis Crawford Burkitt, and Charles E. Raven, *The Church of To-Day* (Cambridge, England: University Press, 1930), p. 355.

18. Raven, *Natural Religion and Christian Theology*, p. 183.

19. The most detailed biography of Muste is Jo Ann Robinson, *Abraham Went Out: A Biography of A. J. Muste* (Philadelphia: Temple University Press, 1981). A much briefer biographer is Nat Hentoff, *Peace Agitator* (New York: Macmillan, 1963). Hentoff has also edited a large section of Muste's writings: Abraham John Muste, *The Essays of A. J. Muste*, ed. Nat Hentoff (Indianapolis: Bobbs-Merrill, 1967).

20. Robinson, *Abraham Went Out*, p. 50.

21. Hentoff, *Peace Agitator*, p. 93.

22. Abraham John Muste, *Non-Violence in an Aggressive World* (New York and London: Harper & Brothers, 1940).

23. Ibid., pp. 49ff.

24. Ibid., p. 58

25. Ibid., p. 109.

26. Ibid., p. 111.

27. See Krishnalal Jethalal Shridharani, *War without Violence* (New York: Harcourt, Brace and Company, 1939).

28. Nat Hentoff, "The Power of Nonviolence," *Jewish World Review*, September 6, 2000.

29. http://www.nonviolence.org/issues/philosophy-nonviolence.php

BIBLIOGRAPHY

Abrams, Ray Hamilton. *Preachers Present Arms; A Study of the War-Time Attitudes and Activities of the Churches and the Clergy in the United States, 1914–1918.* Philadelphia, 1933.

Gardner-Smith, Percival, Francis Crawford Burkitt, and Charles E. Raven. *The Church of To-Day.* Cambridge, England: University Press, 1930.

Heering, Gerrit Jan, and J. W. Thompson. *The Fall of Christianity.* London: G. Allen & Unwin, 1930.

Hentoff, Nat. *Peace Agitator*. New York: Macmillan, 1963.

———. "The Power of Nonviolence." *Jewish World Review*, September 6, 2000.

Hopkins, Charles Howard. *The Rise of the Social Gospel in American Protestantism, 1865–1915*. New Haven, CT: Yale University Press, 1940.

Lee, Umphrey. *The Historic Church and Modern Pacifism*. New York: Abingdon-Cokesbury Press, 1943.

Lifton, Robert Jay. *Superpower Syndrome: America's Apocalyptic Confrontation with the World*. New York: Thunder's Mouth Press/Nation Books, 2003.

Macgregor, G. H. C. *The New Testament Basis of Pacifism*. London: J. Clarke, 1936.

Muste, Abraham John. *The Essays of A. J. Muste*, edited by Nat Hentoff. Indianapolis: Bobbs-Merrill Co., 1967.

———. *Non-Violence in an Aggressive World*. New York and London: Harper & Brothers, 1940.

Ramsey, I. T. "Charles Earle Raven." *Proceedings of the British Academy* (1965): 467–84.

Raven, Charles. *Christianity and Science*. New York: Association Press, 1953.

Raven, Charles E. *Good News of God*. London: Hodder and Stoughton, 1943.

———. *The Gospel and the Church; a Study of Distortion and Its Remedy*. New York: Charles Scribner's Sons, 1940.

———. *Natural Religion and Christian Theology, Gifford Lectures, 1951–52*. Cambridge, England: University Press, 1953.

———. *The Theological Basis of Christian Pacifism, The Robert Treat Paine Lectures, 1950*. New York: Fellowship Publications, 1950.

———. *War and the Christian*. New York: Garland, 1972.

Robinson, Jo Ann. *Abraham Went Out: A Biography of A. J. Muste*. Philadelphia: Temple University Press, 1981.

Shridharani, Krishnalal Jethalal. *War without Violence*. New York: Harcourt, Brace and Company, 1939.

9

RELIGIOUS WARFARE ON THE GLOBAL BATTLEFIELD

Pauletta Otis

"A man with an idea is more powerful than 100 men with interests," according to John Locke, but when ideas and interests combine, the chemistry may be lethal.

Religion is a powerful force and factor in twenty-first-century warfare. Although leaders from major religious traditions vigorously reiterate that the purpose of religion is love and peace, not killing, it is irrefutable that religious warfare is a global "fact of life."[1]

"Religion, politics, and warfare" are the reality of global discussion and discourse yet public understanding of the religious factor has been noticeably deficient in clarity and sophistication.[2] Journalists, academics, policymakers, and the American public are generally unfamiliar and uncomfortable with language that combines religion, politics, and warfare. Church, mosque, temple, synagogue, and shrine seem far from modern killing fields. Ever fearful of an inappropriate overlap of church and state, the secular and sacred, government officials tread ever so lightly in conversations with religious content. Scholars of international relations, security studies, and foreign and defense policy are similarly hesitant and have provided little enlightenment or guidance. Much public information has reflected subjective ad hoc, haphazard, and superficial explanation perhaps reflecting the historically marginalized, sensitive, volatile nature of the topic.[3]

The fact that religion is a part of contemporary war can no longer be avoided, however politely. One way or another, religious theology and religious factors have had a significant impact on twenty-first-century theories of social justice, changing governmental arrangements, and shifting international power—and violence. It is apparent that religion plays a critical role in human security, both in preventing and provoking various forms of conflict and war.

Religion in warfare is evident all over the globe, involves all religious traditions, is related to all forms of modern warfare, and is a factor for rich and poor, weak and powerful, democratic and autocratic regimes.

In the global arena, the combination of religious ideology and interests that use religious factors in violence are becoming an increasingly potent force in Africa, Asia, the Middle East, and even the Americas. As the world's hegemonic power, the United States has been involved in conflict most notably in the Balkans, Somalia, Afghanistan, and Iraq. In each of these cases, religious factors were a significant part of the enemy's motivation, intent, capabilities, and goals. In addition, global terrorism is increasingly characterized by violence perpetuated by individuals and small groups, with religious motivation, using nonconventional weapons, choosing symbolic targets, and judging success by obedience to God.[4]

At the beginning of the twenty-first century, it is evident that religious factors play a role in conflict and war on all continents and involve all major religious traditions.[5] Additionally, each "type" of conflict has a religious dimension: conventional warfare, fourth-generation warfare, ethnic conflict, insurgency, suicide bombing, genocide, and terrorism.

The scope and substance of violence and warfare associated with religion is global. Each continent, each military Area of Operations (AOR), has situations in which religion is a factor in conflict:[6] Examples include: Europe (EUCOM)—the Balkans, the Middle East; (CENTCOM)—Egypt, Iraq, and Iran; Asia and the Pacific (PACOM) —Indonesia, East Timor, and China; South America (SOUTHCOM) —Peru, Brazil, and Mexico. This list merely scratches the surface as wherever there is war, religious factors help define and contribute to violence; wherever there is war and instability, the hegemonic military power of the United States is involved.

Current media reporting suggests that every major religious tradition is involved in some sort of warfare. Warfare is both a historical and a contemporary experience of individuals and groups claiming adherence to Islam, Christianity, Judaism, Hinduism, Buddhism, and the "minor" religions.[7] Hindu and Muslim strains are apparent in Gujurat. Buddhists and Hindus continue a bloody conflict in Sri Lanka. The Shia-Sunni divisions continue to factor in the Iraq conflict. The Lord's Resistance Army in Uganda pits Christians against Christians. Christians fight Christians in Serbia and Croatia and both turn on Bosnian Muslims. In Sudan, the Muslims are said to repress and enslave Christians and animists but in Chad the situation seems to be reversed. In Nigeria, the many ethnic groups have gradually polarized and redefined the ethnic-tribal-governmental conflict in terms of religious identity. The Aum Shinrikyo, associated with Japanese Buddhism, was responsible for the use of chemical weapons in a 1995 terrorist attack in a Tokyo subway and continues to be of concern in Australia and New Zealand where it claims over sixteen thousand adherents. The conflict between Israel and Palestine is often held to be a religiously complicated war between Jews and Muslims; Lebanon pits groups identified as religious—Druze, Maronite, Catholic, and Shi'a. In eastern Europe, various Christian groups, including Greek Orthodox, Russian Orthodox, Armenian, Catholic, Protestant, have evidenced levels of hatred and hostility not seen since the seventeenth century.[8]

A frightening modern addition to "religious warfare" is the reality of modern weapons and the nature of contemporary warfare. There are two major factors in this: (1) the hegemonic state has formal control of nuclear weapons based on a premise of conventional warfare. This is premised on the assumption that states have ultimate control of "security," including rights and responsibilities of controlling the use of force within a defined territory. Nuclear weapons in the hands of either an irresponsible state or an independent terrorist group could wreak havoc on the entire world for purposes known only to them. This implies that there is a potential for devastation and destruction unknown in human history. (2) The second factor is more difficult to conceptualize. The weaponry of less powerful groups, whether state-based or organized around religious ideology, is that of unconventional warfare, or "fourth-generation" warfare. Weapons, strategies, and tactics are designed to resist the power of states and propel other agendas including those of a political, economic, and religious nature. The actors, groups, or organizations, are nonstate, global in nature, and tend to be amorphous, that is, networked rather than hierarchical. The weapons used to support the struggle against the more powerful are those designed to be attritional—suicide/human bombing, guerrilla and insurgency movements, and global terrorism.

A grim picture emerges of warfare of two types: state-based conventional warfare with weapons of mass destruction designed for warfare between sovereign states, and fourth-generation warfare based on social forces using weapons of convenience with low lethality but high consequence designed to destabilize the state system in support of global social agendas. The grim picture emerges of the largely conventional forces of the world hegemonic powers fighting various groups of global religious *mujahadeen* in asymmetrical wars where the stakes include economic, political, and cultural power and the weapons are mismatched. It is not possible to eradicate "religious warriors" using conventional weapons; it is not possible to "kill" ideas or beliefs. The National Security

Strategy (2004) is defined as "prevent, protect, and prevail." The concepts are far removed from conventional warfare where the idea is to conquer land and people or defend against being conquered.[9]

Current studies of how religious ideology frames conflict or how religious factors contribute to warfare are notoriously subjective. However, the literature seems to support the following statements:[10]

- Religion is present in all conflict—as religion provides reason for individual life and death, and provides rationale for killing or sacrificing for group good;
- Religious conflicts tend to have higher levels of intensity, severity, brutality, and lethality than other forms of war;
- Wars are longer in duration when religion is a major factor;
- Over half of all contemporary conflicts have a significant religious dimension;[11]
- Religious leaders emerge as primary authority figures under conditions of state failure;
- Religious factors are invariably related to ethnic group identity, language, territory, politics, and economics;
- Religious factors are an essential component of effective conflict prevention, management, and resolution.

No one would seriously suggest that religion is the only explanatory factor in explaining warfare. Religion relates and overlaps other explanatory variables, specifically economic and political factors. But, whether religion is treated as causal in ideological explanations, or as a contributing factor to other variables, it is an integral piece of the security puzzle and, as such, deserves focused attention.

UNDERSTANDING RELIGION AND WAR

Approaches to the Study of Religious Warfare

Religious scholars and military leaders must take the political risk of addressing religion and violence in a meaningful way. The first challenge is to provide minimal definitions of the terms "religion," "warfare," and "religious war." This will contribute to understanding the ways in which contemporary global conflicts are—and are not— religious. The second challenge is to find ways of studying religious warfare that make sense of the reality both in a theoretical and applied sense. Only when these challenges are addressed in meaningful ways can the world community either counter the negative effects of religion as it contributes to conflict or support the aspects of religion that contribute to peace and survival.

The following definitions are offered:[12]

- Religion is the codification of values in a society with reference to a transcendent being; religious beliefs and behaviors are learned, social, and generational. Religion provides reason for life and death, systematizes life experiences, and symbolizes the transition from birth to death in symbolic "rite of passage" such as those that a society celebrates at birth, puberty, marriage, and death.
- War is a social group behavior that results in death and violence for other groups.
- Religious war is a group behavior that uses the ideology, codes, and behaviors of a religious system in the perpetuation of violence resulting in killing of the members of other groups.

There are two fundamentally different but overlapping approaches to the subject of religion and warfare (1) an approach based on the premise that religious theology is the basis for a particularly powerful ideology or philosophy and the associated "mind-set" form a basis for conflict, and (2) an approach that identifies particular religious factors that contribute to warfare. When religion is defined as the enveloping idea and that which maintains the essential mind-set of a group, individual behaviors are essentially derivative. When religion is defined as a part of culture, individual and group behaviors are viewed as part of a range of alternative actions available in the complexity of an identifiable social group or culture.

Religion as philosophy and based in specific theologies provides large understandings of how the world works and a relationship to transcendental Supreme Being, or God. Scholars who address religious violence as based in theology assume that religion has always been a contributing factor in warfare and provides the parameters of *jus bello* and *jus in bello*, and look for reasons why it is emerging (or reemerging) as the single most important political-ideological default mechanism in global conflict.[13]

Many well-known authors use this framework: for example, Samuel Huntington's controversial *Clash of Civilizations* is premised on the idea that civilizations or societies somehow "think" in reasonably predictable patterns. Differences are explained through historical artifacts, contemporary adaptation, economic and political arrangements, and the "reflective identity" of the good "us" and the bad "them." Behaviors are inextricably linked to the mind-set and are derivative of basic cultural assumptions. Individual behaviors are reflective of the ideology of the group and/or the religious theology of the major cultural/social group with an identifiable religious mind-set. Bernard Lewis and Thomas Friedman also use this intellectual strategy to logically inform their audiences why certain religious groups premise their behaviors on a religious/cultural "mind-set" with the assumption that those mind-sets produce peace and conflict.

There is some dispute as to whether cultures/civilizations and the respective mind-sets are immutable and simply "givens," or are changeable by forms of social engineering. Much of the current US government policy seems to be directed toward "addressing Islam on its own terms," or supporting moderate elements, or even strategic influence campaigns designed to "change the minds and hearts" of Islamic populations. When this perspective is extant, the literature is a bit depressing: an individual mind is a hard thing to change, let alone that of the "masses" of civilizations. Changing ideologies or reinterpreting theology is a bit complicated. Most conclude that the task is daunting or perhaps impossible. Some even reach the conclusion that since a mind-set cannot be changed, or changed "in time," the only recourse is killing and war.

For individual "mind-sets" religious ideology/theology provides comprehensive ideals for life and principles that govern both life and death. This is a universal premise that includes all religions in all times and in all places. Religion gives individuals and individuals in social groups reason for "being born, dying, killing and offering to be killed" for the good of the group. This phenomenon is apparent in both the "suicide bombers" of the Tamil Tigers and for the US Marine who for no "good reason" throws himself on a grenade in order to save the life of a friend.[14]

Religion as ideology is derived from an external framework that links individuals to the greater whole and provides formal institutions that help define and organize that whole. It provides a meaningful worldview as well as the rules and standards of behavior that connect individual actions and goals to the worldview. It has the ability to legitimize actions and institutions.

A second way of addressing religious warfare is to define religion as a part of human behavior as found and adapted by specific sociocultural groups. In this framework, religious ideas provide a framework for group adaptation to the social environment, and religious behaviors are seen as related to all other aspects of culture: territory, language, economics, authority, endogamy, and identity. The ideals and actualities of the "religious beliefs and practices" can be studied and analyzed separately. Conflict or war is the manifestation result of a complex of identifiable factors—religiously identified beliefs and behaviors, codified by a society, studied as belief sets of a group, and observable in a range of individual behaviors—in relationship to in-group factors and to the way in which that group interacts with others in a sociocultural environment.[15]

Religious factors are "power resources" in the sense that religious institutions and leaders control resources, define interpersonal relationships, establish and maintain group communication, and provide expertise. The resources of religious personages and institutions include control over goods and services; organizational capabilities; social networks that are community-based but may also be global in scope; and various types of support for political personages, agendas, and programs. The resources of a particular religion are a direct result of its numbers, reputation, coherence, and willingness to mobilize for political/religious purposes.

Religion is an important power broker in human relationships. It helps define the attributes of a good and trustable person; prescribe rules concerning how individuals transact social, political, and economic business; and identify "friend" and "enemy" according to a set of traditional and legitimate factors. When states fail, or particular political personages are delegitimized, religious personages often help define whom, when, and under what conditions a new political leader will emerge. Most importantly, religious authorities are also assumed to be in touch with the power of a Supreme Being and therefore have special insight concerning social relations among God's children.

Religion provides for a common language and means of communication between members of a group. Religious leaders communicate with authority; generally have written and spoken expertise; have access to media; and know significant music, poetry, and art forms of nonverbal, symbolic communication. Historical languages often provide a sense of continuity and may be used in symbolic communication or to motivate. Religious personages and institutions are often deeply involved in the education of children and the training of future generations. Parents rely on religious educational and medical institutions when the state fails to provide those resources. Religious leaders are often accustomed to keeping confidences or secrets and are trusted for their discretion. Most importantly, religious leaders are often more *believable* in failed or fragile states than political leaders and therefore have power above and beyond the sheer strength of numbers or observable resources.

Religious authorities have expertise in many areas above and beyond that of the general population. They generally have in-depth knowledge of people, places, and communities. They know the sensitivities of the community. They know the personal history of leaders and their families. They move easily in a community and have access to areas off-limits to others. Quite literally, they know where the bodies are buried. In a very real sense, religious person-ages and communities know more about food, water, and health than others in the community. They are the individuals that people "go to" when all else fails.

Religious leaders, as force multipliers, have significant socio-cultural power and are able to affect war and peace more than is commonly recognized. Both on the "US" side and the "other" side, religious leaders must engage the topic of peace and use their inherent power to move toward a more peaceful world.

In summary, religion plays a significant role in contemporary conflict. It is both a cause when studied as "ideology" and a contributing factor when studied as "one of many factors of socio-cultural identity." In either case, the question remains as to why religion and religious warfare has been understudied and somewhat neglected in the public arena.

Why Is Religious Warfare a Significant Issue? Why Now?

Religion as a critical dimension of twenty-first-century warfare is a result of at least three principal factors: (1) the seeming failure of other ideologies and institutions, (2) the power of religion as ideology supporting social justice, and (3) the power of religion in society providing an ideological basis for social coherence and comprehensiveness.

In the twentieth century, as the world's problems became more complex and more visible, the solutions available in the ideologies and corresponding programs of Marxism, communism, fascism, nationalism, and materialism became less able to explain injustice or provide programs to ameliorate suffering. Even capitalism and democracy have had significant problems in explaining the ideal and the reality to peoples of the so-called third world. Democracy has succeeded in some places and failed in others. The important point is that much of the world believes that democracy, or the top-down institutionalization of democratic processes based on Western cultural assumptions and processes, will not work *for them*.[16] Many believe it works only in the Western context and even then is dependent on exploitative world capitalism. More sophisticated analysts also maintain that democracy (even a constitutional democracy) is the rule of the majority, and consequently not "moral and ethical." They contend that only the guidance and rules provided by a Supreme Being should guide the affairs of man. The Western, Christian world understands this argument only too well.

No one can disagree with the fact that the world remains horribly divided between rich and poor, haves and have-nots. The competing ideologies of the twentieth century that promised hope and a quick fix failed much of the world's population. Few who believe in a Supreme Being would disagree that it was meant to be that way, hence the entrance of religion as "default" ideology.

As human attempts are deemed inadequate, recourse to the supernatural power of a Supreme Being seems to be the only available strategy to ensure both temporal and spiritual security. Religion provides both rationale and modality for fighting against injustice and provides hope when all else has been "tried and failed." This is more than a passive default mechanism; religion is reemerging in a new, invigorated, and powerful force in global politics.[17]

FORMS OF RELIGIOUS WARFARE
AND RELATED RELIGIOUS FACTORS

One of the ways to analyze religious factors in conflict is to go directly to the form of violence and try to identify the specific religious content. In these cases, it is helpful to separate the motive, intent, capabilities, targeting, and effects.[18]

In a macro sense, religion is obviously a component of "motive and intent." Motive is supplied by the justification of violence against oppression and in support of social justice. Ideology (theology) provides intent in that it helps define reflective identity, that is, "who is responsible," thereby defining the enemy. Religious ideology also provides capability in that all of the resources of a religious community can be brought to bear in a religiously motivated conflict. (Examples include communication, money, places of refuge, and external support.) Religion also contributes to specific targeting of specific factors identified as symbolically "evil, dangerous, and threatening." These can be individual people or places and are strikingly clear in religious writing and reporting. The effect of religious violence, when assessed in terms of theology, is seen as "supernatural," that is, the purpose of religious violence is religious—therefore, the effect of justifiable violence is assessed in terms that God (or a Supreme Being) would understand and appreciate.

There are four forms of contemporary, nonstate violence that are particularly significant in relationship to modern lethality and the "fear factor": (1) terrorism, (2) ethnic conflict, (3) suicide martyrdom, and (4) genocide.

Terrorism

Religious terrorism, and the religious terrorist, differs from other forms of terrorism in very specific patterned ways. The single most important characteristic is that religious terrorists have God for an audience. The following characteristics of religious terrorism can be noted:[19]

- There is a grave social injustice that offends God
- There is an identifiable enemy that can be held responsible
- Individuals are required to obey God
- God needs earthly help to rectify evil and restore justice
- The battle is a cosmic battle that takes place on earth
- God approves of actions taken on His behalf and will reward the faithful

Timothy McVeigh provides a good example of this type of reasoning: social injustice perpetuated by the US government, the government's culpability, his individual responsibility to rectify wrong, his statements that he was responsible only to God, and the assumption that eventually all would agree that he was right and that God would approve of his bombing of the Oklahoma federal building.

The *London Times* quoted bin Laden as saying: "The Twin Towers were legitimate targets; they were supporting U.S. economic power. These events were great by all measurement. What was destroyed were not only the towers but the towers of morale in that country," and further that the hijackers were "blessed by Allah to destroy America's economic and military landmarks." (He has also pointed out that the Saudis were coconspirators because they did the bidding of the infidel. The Palestinian cause seemed to be an afterthought but fit the pattern of reasoning.)

For the religious terrorist, violence first and foremost is a sacramental act or divine duty executed in direct response to a theological imperative. Because the religious terrorist's goal is fulfillment of a divine cause, he will take the most effective measure possible. This may mean a complete rejection of any traditional or cultural norm. As the religious terrorist has few qualms about sacrificing his life for the sake of a divine cause, he is also willing to let the most harmless of individuals, young children, sacrifice their lives for the divine cause, assuming that the end justifies the sacrifice. This is in specific contradiction to major world religious practice where innocent children are to be protected and spared.

The religious terrorist is generally:

- middle-aged
- former military of mid-rank
- knowledgeable about weapons and low-level operations
- appearing subsequent to a failed military operation
- uncomfortable around women to the point of being a misogynist
- virulently homophobic, believing that homosexuals are evidence of weakness of the group
- extraordinary communicators (not necessarily good administrators)
- leadership qualities akin to the "messianic" or "charismatic"

The religious terrorist may not fit all of these criteria; however, most apply to some extent. Noticeably there is little evidence that the religious terrorist has significant formal religious teaching or training.[20] In addition, terrorists use religious factors, sometimes creatively applied, to justify repression and control within the society and violence against infidels and outsiders. The treatment of women is especially interesting. These men tend to like sexual violence but blame the "feminine" for taking the strength of the community and maintain that it is the way "God intended." The control of, persecution of, and violence against women in these groups are startling.

Ethnic Conflict

Religious factors in ethnic conflicts contribute to warfare and may be either causal or contributive. Religious factors in ethnic situations are never a single-factor explanation but are helpful in understanding the mind-set of an ethnic group and how religious power is mobilized in pursuit of social-economic-political goals.

In Sri Lanka, the Hindu Tamil and Buddhist Sinhalese have had a tragic civil war that seems particularly intransigent. Religion is used as an identity factor, some religious personages have contributed to the polarization of the communities, and places of worship have been destroyed or used as bases for guerrilla operations, and yet, no one would say that the Sri Lankan conflict is basically about theology. Ireland is another case in point: the protagonists are religiously identified and international journalists refer to the parties as "Catholic" and "Protestant."[21] Religious leaders have contributed to both war and peace, and religious institutions have been used as places of power and refuge. Clearly religion plays a role, but neither can claim that the mandate for violence comes from scripture. The Lord's Resistance Army (LRA) in Uganda, often defined as both tribal and ethnically based conflict, uses and abuses children in religious rites and practices prior to sending them into battle for causes unrelated to religion. In each of these cases, religious factors may contribute to definition, polarization, and escalation but are only a part of an explanation. Religion plays a role in ethnic violence because it typically is one of the major factors of group identification. In some societal contexts, it can undermine the state and thereby contribute to state failure when the leaders of the polity are not seen as "religious enough."[22]

Suicide Martyrdom

Religion is assumed to be a significant factor in suicide bombing and death squads as it is said to provide both "cause" and promise of "reward." Yet the number of instances seems low in comparison to the public perception and political reaction. According to the Future War Studies research provided by the US Army Warfare Center between 1981 and 2002, there were 274 apparent cases of suicide terror. Of the fifty-seven attacks in 2001–2002, twenty-nine were in Sri Lanka and conducted by the Tamil Tigers, twenty in Israel, three in Pakistan, and five "others." If the Palestinian-Israeli cases were assigned to "insurgency" or "reactive violence," the numbers of people killed, the number of groups involved, and the numbers of suicide terrorists would be virtually halved.

There is clear evidence that political pressures and opportunism effect defining "religious suicide terrorism." The cases of suicide terrorism in Israel are often related to definitions of substate conflict or ethno-religious conflict, the Russian Chechnya cases relegated to "insurgency" and ethnic nationalism, and one-of-a-kind incidents to those of "psychopathic or sociopathic" personalities. In other words, the definition (and related numbers) of suicide terrorist incidents reflects a political assessment of the "causes" as well as the strategy of destruction.

Most of the stereotypes of suicide terrorism are incorrect. It is commonly assumed that they are young, single, uneducated males who are Islamic fundamentalist fanatics. In fact, the profile is of individuals who are preteen to mid-sixties, both male and female, educated and uneducated, single and married, many with families, and not exclusively motivated by religion.

Often called "human bombers," the first suicide terrorist act in recent history that made it to the front page of the news occurred in Vietnam in 1963. A Buddhist nun, Nhat Chi Mai, stated that "I want to use my body as a torch . . . to dissipate the darkness . . . and to bring peace to Vietnam." She conducted a self-immolation in Saigon to protest the activities of the "Roman Catholic oppressive regime."

Most interestingly, female terrorists have the same profile as male terrorists. They do not differ from men in motive, intent, or capability. The response of the media is extraordinary: female terrorists are generally assumed to be "victims" and sacrificing themselves either because they are emotionally unstable or because they lost a male family member. The response of the viewing world is prejudiced by the gender of the suicide martyr.

Suicide terrorism results in death and should not be minimalized; however, the public response (fear) is out of proportion to the actual numbers and measurements of lethality. Religion is as important, but no more important, than other factors in explaining this form of violence.

Genocide

Genocide is a systematic policy of group extermination.[23] Although defined politically and legally, predicting genocide is both an art and a science.[24] The indicators of portending genocide are reasonably clear, but the contribution of religion and religious factors has not been rigorously examined until recently. The following indicators of the relationship between religion and genocide were extrapolated from research on the Rwandan genocide and are clearly applicable to other cases:[25]

- Historic reinforcement of religious differentiation in public policy
- Historic reinforcement of religious differentiation in private lives of leadership
- A close relationship between government leaders and church leaders
- Financial support from government institutions to religious institutions
- Educational policy based on religious differentiation
- Preferential law and policy of one religion over another
- Association of specific religious groups as a threat to state security and welfare of the larger group(s)
- Lack of control over small arms and a religiosity that does not proscribe individual use of violence
- Ethnic/religious differentiation in military force structure
- Implicit assumption of nonintervention of external forces—lack of visibility in the international community
- The historic participation of the church in reinforcing ethnocentric thought and behavior both in public life and in the church itself
- A close relationship enjoyed by leaders of churches and the government
- A traditional teaching of churches that scripture mandates submission to religious and governmental authority[26]

- Inability to control individuals and events after the inception of violence as a result of the "lack of authority"

CONCLUSION

Those responsible for US national security are increasingly convinced that religion and war must be addressed in new, comprehensive, and focused ways. Not only were the events of September 11, 2001, a tragic, if clarion call, but the wars in Afghanistan and Iraq were telling instances of the consequences of both "information overload" and "not knowing." Theory and analysis are needed to provide information that is timely, accurate, important, informative, and actionable.

However, all is not lost; all is not gloom and doom. The very ideological factors that support violence and the taking of life can be seen to protect peace and support life. Religious power can be used as leverage to enhance the possibilities of peaceful management and resolution of conflict.[27] The White House and Congress of the United States have shown enthusiasm for supporting faith-based nongovernmental organizations in aspects of homeland security, democratization, and stability and support operations. The Department of Defense demonstrates a keen, if belated, interest in religious factors relevant to the Middle East and other AORs. The Departments of State, Justice, and Homeland Security are engaged in learning about the "religious factor" as it applies to their responsibilities.

There is evidence that the countries of Europe, including Russia and the republics of the former Soviet Union, the People's Republic of China, and the government of India are readdressing religion and conflict not only in their respective countries, but also as a regional and global reality. The motivation may be a fear of state destabilization, nuclear annihilation, or religious terrorism, but the reality is a renewed global awareness of the religious factor in warfare both in aspects of support for violence and support for peace.

The complex configuration and interplay of economic, political, social, and religious factors as they relate to war and peace is of concern to all. The fear of ethno-religious wars, the incomprehensibility of religiously motivated terrorism, and the shadow of "clash of civilization" scenarios are on the forefront of world consciousness, and provide motivation for taking the subject of religion very seriously. Religion and warfare are two of the most difficult and important issues of our time. It is time to make a systematic and critical study of how religion impacts war and how war impacts religion.

NOTES

1. Fabio Petito and Pavlos Hatzopoulos, eds., *Religion in International Relations: The Return from Exile* (New York: Palgrave-Macmillan, 2003).

2. The use of the terms "conflict," "war," and "violence" in this essay are not mutually exclusive. Although it is recognized that professional literature has traditionally defined them in discrete terms, it may be more historically accurate, ethically mandated, and timely to bring the definitions into this century as related to contemporary reality.

3. Jonathan Fox's 2004 book, *Bringing Religion into International Relations* (New York: Palgrave Press), provides a thorough and exhaustive commentary on this dilemma.

4. In his recent volume *Terror in the Mind of God: The Global Rise of Religious Violence*, Mark Juergensmeyer provides information and analysis of six terrorist groups. His work provides clear evidence of both the global nature of the violence and the fact that all major "global" religions are somehow implicated.

5. There is a paucity of good research data and analysis possibly because scholars tend not to agree simply on how to define and tabulate statistics on (1) when religion is the primary factor and/or (2) when religion plays a role in the escalation and maintenance of conflict. Current research tends to be politically or religiously motivated and thus inherently biased.

6. "Area of Operations" is a US military term for the organization of areas of responsibility and includes AORs such as CENTCOM, PACOM, EUCOM, NORTHCOM, and SOUTHCOM.

7. Adherents.com has a compendium of some 4,443 named, organized religious groups.

8. See Jonathan Fox's *Ethnoreligious Conflict in the Late Twentieth Century* (Boston: Lexington Books, 2002) or his very fine article published by *Studies in Conflict and Terrorism*, "Do Religious Institutions Support Violence or the Status Quo?" (1999, pp. 119–39).

9. Not only has warfare changed, but the *jus bello* and *jus in bello* rules so familiar and comfortable for ethicists, theologians, and military scientists are outmoded, outdated, and in serious need of rethinking.

10. These statements represent the author's conclusions and are drawn from a number of different research projects that include religious, military, historical, and political sources.

11. Note Jonathan Fox's *Ethnoreligious Conflict in the Late Twentieth Century*.

12. Definitions are always subject to critique and these are offered only as a reference point for this essay.

13. Dr. Douglas Johnston, in *Religion: The Missing Dimension of Statecraft* (Oxford: Oxford University Press, 1994) and *Faith-Based Diplomacy: Trumping Realpolitik* (Oxford: Oxford University Press, 2002), makes the point that not the religious factor is regularly overlooked in the analysis of both war making and peacemaking.

14. It is always interesting to note that neither sociobiological nor sociopsychological explanations seem to be as much persuasive explanatory power in explaining suicide terrorists as religious beliefs and behaviors.

15. Many studies of religious groups and religious conflict pertain specifically to the beliefs and behaviors of a single in-group propensity to violence but neglect the conflict environment that would include not only contiguous groups but also international actors.

16. When democracy is defined in terms of individual and group choice and finds voices from indigenous cultures, it is more likely to succeed. See James G. March, *Democratic Governance* (New York: Free Press, 1995).

17. In *Ambivalence of the Sacred: Religion, Violence, and Reconciliation*, Scott R. Appleby coherently and cogently describes religious "power" to be both a factor in violence and in peacemaking.

18. These are standard terms used in the Department of Defense and Department of State when analyzing violence and terrorism.

19. These are in addition to the usual definitions and indicators of more traditional terrorism analysis. Although they may overlap, correspond, and relate to other political and social goals, the religious component provides additional predictive power.

20. Attendance at madrassas or religious schools is not a reliable indicator of an individual's future terrorist activities.

21. Popularly known, however, as "the troubles."

22. Assassination of religious leaders seen as "not quite religious enough" seems to be a recurring pattern in international affairs. Note the deaths of Anwar Sadat, Mohandas Gandhi, and Rajiv Gandhi at the hands of "fanatics." This is part of a polarization process that contributes to a definition of "us" and "them" or "friend" and "enemy."

23. United Nations General Assembly Convention on the Prevention and Punishment of the Crime of Genocide Adopted by Resolution 260 (III) A of the U.N. General Assembly on December 9, 1948: (G)enocide means any of the following acts committed with intent to destroy, in whole or in part, a national, ethical, racial or religious group, as such: (a) Killing members of the group; (b) Causing serious bodily or mental harm to members of the group; (c) Deliberately inflicting on the group conditions of life calculated to bring about its physical destruction in whole or in part; (d) Imposing measures intended to prevent births within the group; (e) Forcibly transferring children of the group to another group.

24. Basic indicators are listed by Israel Charny in *How Can We Commit the Unthinkable? Genocide, the Human Cancer* (Boulder, CO: Westview Press, 1992).

25. Carol Rittner, John K. Roth, and Wendy Whitworth, *Genocide in Rwanda: Complicity of the Churches?* (St. Paul, MN: Paragon House, 2004).

26. Derived from David P. Gushee's "Why the Churches Were Complicit," in *Genocide in Rwanda: Complicity of the Churches?* ed. Rittner et al.

27. See Douglas Johnson's books: *Religion: The Missing Dimension of Statecraft* and *Trumping Realpolitik*. Dr. Johnson is president of the International Center for Religion and Diplomacy, and his writings and public presentations provide a roadmap of religion that is an integral part of statecraft and peacemaking.

10

HOLY TERROR

Regina M. Schwartz

I n Osama Bin Laden's view, "the world is split into two camps: the camp of believers and the camp of infidels." His rhetoric of violence is filled with God: "God attacked America at its heart and filled the American people with fear." Rather than being the language of a deranged person, it is an invocation of an all too familiar monotheistic God of vengeance, a God who destroys his enemies and rejoices at their defeat, the God invoked at the Crusades to destroy Muslims, during the conquest of the New World to destroy Natives, during the Spanish Inquisition to expel the Jews, during ethnic cleansing in Bosnia, during the invasion of Iraq—and the list of religiously authorized violence goes on. How does this happen? What gives rise to such perversity? In theory, monotheism should be heir to the philosophical problem of the One and the Many. Parmenides, Plato, and Plotinus should be its companions. But in practice, monotheism was born and reared in a very different soil—the climate of group identity. The monotheistic God was first the God of a people; hence, from the start, there was a particularism built into monotheism. There may be only one God but he is not God for everyone: he is the God of a group. In its beginnings, belonging to the group was the focus of monotheism's energy. This belonging is a fraught: its condition is possession, and as I will show, that understanding of identity as belonging, as possession, is the wellspring of religious violence. The holy scriptures have not only inspired charity and hope, they have also been deployed as a weapon to degrade peoples who have been classified as infidels, pagans, and idolaters. When a people forges its identity negatively, against some "Other," too easily "Us as distinguished from Them" turns into "Us versus Them"—in religious parlance, believers versus infidels. This means that in their very process of defining and defending the borders of their religious identity, people often defy their religious ethics. I am not the first to say this and I won't be the last. Jeremiah stood on the steps of the Temple of Jerusalem when worshippers streamed past him, to warn them that their abuses of their fellow men denied them the divine favor they sought through ritual. Erasmus was impatient that monks worried too much about the color of their habits and not enough about feeding the poor. Matthew Arnold defined religion as heightened ethical sensibility, so genocide in the name of God makes no sense. So before we extol the exodus as a magnificent myth of liberation in contrast to many other foundational myths of conquests, we should also ask, "What about the Canaanites?"—the conquered Canaanites?

We can discern two poles of representation of monotheism in the Bible. One endorses generosity: God is depicted as infinitely charitable, infinitely giving, with blessings for all. In Exodus, the story of manna offers the image of a God who rains food from the heavens, enough for everyone. The notion that some would want to hoard, to take more than they needed, is addressed in a remarkable narrative that schools the Israelites in an equitable distribution of their resource.

"That," said Moses to them, "is the bread Yahweh gives you to eat. This is Yahweh's command: Everyone must gather enough of it for his needs." . . . When they measured in an omer of what they had gathered, the man who had gathered more had not too much, the man who had gathered less had not too little. Each found he had gathered what he needed. (Exod. 16:15–18)

But the Israelites' failure to accept this divinely ordained distribution of resources—each according to his needs—engenders greed. When they hoard their food, it rots and indicts them.

> "Moses said to them, "No one must keep any of it for tomorrow." But some would not listen and kept part of it for the following day, and it bred maggots and smelt foul; and Moses was angry with them. (Exod. 16:19–20)

Despite all evidence to the contrary—despite their starving in the wilderness—the Israelites are asked to trust in a God who will provide and they are asked to base their ethics on such a belief in divine generosity so that they will not hoard.

This vision of generosity and bounty recurs in the New Testament where Jesus miraculously multiplies the loaves and fishes to feed everyone. But even the meaning of these stunning visions of generosity can be twisted when the Bible is invoked to legitimize hatred of the other, as it so often is. In an Op-Ed about the Albanian refugees fleeing to Italy, a spokesman for the Italian Right wrote: "We can offer them a plate of pasta but not open the cafeterias. Even Jesus who multiplied bread and fishes did not open trattorias. He transformed water into wine, but, it seems to me, only once, and even then, for a wedding. Albania, like Bosnia, is not our problem, but the problem of Europe."

At the other end of the spectrum, monotheism is depicted as endorsing exclusion and intolerance. Here, divine favor and blessings are rendered as so scarce that they must be competed for, inspiring deadly rivalries like the first fratricide, the story of Cain and Abel.

While centuries of Christian theology have focused on the "original sin," I turned my attention to the next narrative in Genesis, the story of Cain and Abel, for here, the first brothers commit the first murder, and so long as we continue to murder our brothers, we are the heirs of Cain. Interestingly, the story depicts God as *implicated* in the problem of deadly rivalry rather than *solving* it.

The story depicts both brothers offering a sacrifice to God, Abel from the flock and Cain from the soil, but God inexplicably "looks with favor" upon Abel and his offering but does not "look with favor" upon Cain and his. Devastated, Cain murders Abel in a jealous rage.

As a thought experiment, we could wonder what would have happened if the story had described God accepting both of their sacrifices, thereby promoting cooperation between the sower and the shepherd instead of violent competition. This deeply troubling depiction of divinity is not unique to that story, for God is depicted as playing favorites repeatedly, with someone receiving his blessings at someone else's expense—some are blessed and some are cursed. As a drunken Cassio puts it in *Othello*, "God's above all, and there be souls that must be saved and there be souls must not be saved."

In the story of Jacob and Esau, after Jacob steals his elder brother's blessing, the unsuspecting Esau approaches his father to ask for his blessing only to learn that because his younger brother has already been blessed, there is no blessing left for him.

> When Esau heard his father's words, he burst out with a loud and bitter cry and said to his father, "Bless me—me too, my father!" But he said, "Your brother came deceitfully and took your blessing." . . . "Haven't you reserved any blessing for me?" Isaac answered Esau, "I have made him lord over you and have made all his relatives his servants and I have sustained him with grain and new wine. So what can I possibly do for you, my son?" (Gen. 27:30–37)

And then Esau asks a profound question, one that resonates throughout the history of religious strife: "Do you have only one blessing, my father? Bless me too, my father!" Then Esau wept aloud.

This ancestral myth of Jacob/Israel and Esau/Edom, with its terrible answer to Esau's pointed question, points to an interminable future of violence between peoples. There will be no blessed future for the Edomites, the enemies of ancient Israel (Gen. 27:30–37). Scarcity impels this pain: What if the authors had imagined the Edomites and Israelites enjoying equally blessed futures? What if there had been two blessings? Would the cultural legacy of the Bible have been a less violent one? Would it have been more difficult to use the Bible as a weapon to degrade those who have strayed from the one jealous God? Surely, we would still have had the Crusades, the Inquisition, the genocides of modernity motivated by religious identity, but would the perpetrators have had to look elsewhere in their cultural legacy, other than to representations of the will of God as recorded in his authorized text, to authorize their hate-crimes?

I believe that the role of biblical narratives in our understanding of collective identity, in the ways in which we imagine peoples, can hardly be overestimated. Encoding Western culture's central myth of collective identity, the Bible grounds it in belonging. In the narrative, a transcendent deity breaks into history with the demand that the people he constitutes obey the laws he institutes and first and foremost among those laws is the requirement that they pledge allegiance to him and to him alone: "Thou shalt have no other gods before me," as the familiar commandment puts it. In this story, a people who will be the ancient Israelites are forged by their worship of one deity, and what makes others the Other—Egyptian, Moabite, Ammonite, Canaanite, Perizzite, Hittite, or Hurrian—is their worship of other gods. When ancient Israel is forged negatively as a collective identity against the Other, that is also figured as against other deities, and so when Israel is threatened, it is not by the power of other peoples or other nations, but by the power and wrath of her own God because she has wavered in her exclusive loyalty to him. Inclinations toward polytheism are repeatedly figured as sexual infidelity: "I am a jealous God, you will have none but me"; and Israel is castigated for "whoring after" other gods, thereby imperiling her "purity": "so shameless was her whoring that at last she polluted the country." Jeremiah's kinky confusion of idolatry and adultery condemns Israel for "committing adultery with lumps of stone and pieces of wood."

These preoccupations with divine and sexual fidelity are part of an understanding of collective identity as a people set apart, with boundaries that could be mapped and ownership that could be titled; they are to be the exclusive possession of the deity—and none other—and they are to have exclusive allegiance to him, and to none other. Not only does God possess the people, but the people possess the land and men possess women. This possession is the dark side of monotheism. Delimiting identity as a possession is fraught with violence, both in history and in biblical narratives, which could also, by the way, be plausibly read more as a warning than a recommendation of such a doctrine of possession.

In the biblical discourse, the ownership of land and women is deeply homologous (Locke understood Adam's authority over the land as the same as his authority over Eve); both land and women are conquerable territory, both have borders that must be kept intact—with a host of purity laws expressing anxiety about bodily emissions and countless warnings about the foreigner's potential to make the land impure—and both, like any valuable property, must be defended against theft. But the violence that continually erupts around this ownership belies its hazards: exclusive rights to the people prove impossible, and their multiple allegiances are the grounds for exile and extinction. Ezekiel 16 offers an extended allegory of Israel as a whore, bringing into sharp relief the violence of possession and the nexus of adultery, defiled land, and idolatry. It tells the story of a child being born and growing up wild in the field, and when she matures into puberty, of her being owned, sexually and materially, by Yahweh.

> And I passed by you and I looked on you and behold, your time was the time of love. And I spread my skirt over you and I cov-

ered your nakedness. And I swore to you and I entered into a
covenant with you and you became Mine. (Ezek. 16:8)

She is now washed, anointed, dressed, wrapped, covered, and
adorned with silks, fine linen, gold and silver. But then young Israel
commits adultery with the nations: with Egypt, Assyria, Canaan,
Chaldea, not incidentally, with all of Israel's enemies.

> At every head of the highway you have built your high place and
> have made your beauty despised, and have parted your feet to all
> who passed by, and have multiplied your fornications. You have
> whored with the sons of Egypt. . . . You have whored with the
> sons of Assyria without being satisfied. You have multiplied your
> fornication in the land of Canaan. (Ezek. 16:26, 27)

The emphasis on property is underscored by her punishment: it
describes her being stripped of her wealth, of her luxurious gar-
ments, before being brutally stoned and stabbed to death.

> Because your lewdness was poured out and your nakedness was
> bared, . . . I will uncover your nakedness to them, and they will
> see all your nakedness.. They shall also strip you of your clothes
> and shall take your beautiful things and leave you naked and bare
> . . . and they shall stone you with stones and cut you with their
> swords. (Ezek.16:35)

The word for uncover, *gala*, also means "go into exile." No longer
covered, the adulteress is no longer owned from one point of view, no
longer protected from another. Israel has become a whore in exile.

The violence of possession is not just a metaphor. As Serbs took
over the territory inhabited by Muslims, murdering men, they systematically raped women, holding them in captivity during their
pregnancy in order to claim not only land but also progeny.

It is difficult to call attention to how impossible the notion of possession is, that we cannot really own anything. Not only can objects

of possession be taken away by others, they can defy being owned on their own accord—they can break, wither, and die, making persistent efforts to appropriate land, dwellings, women, and portable property futile. Territorial claims turn out to be squatter's rights, marriage contracts cannot command love, and even divine ownership of humankind fails. It seems we not only kill in order to own, but also we kill because we cannot own. In the biblical narrative, this violence erupts with the revelation of the covenant itself: when Moses comes down from the mountain with the tablets in his hand that create the people as the people possessed by the one God who must obey him, he discovers them worshipping another.

> "Whoever is for the Lord, come to me," he said, and all the Levites rallied to Him. This is what the Lord, the God of Israel says, "Gird on your sword, every man of you, and quarter the camp from gate to gate killing one his brother, another his friend, another his neighbor." The sons of Levi carried out the command of Moses and about three thousand people perished that day. (Exod. 32:26–28)

And the violent rhetoric permeates the Bible, with Hosea imagining God tearing the Israelites apart:

> I will be a lion to them a leopard lurking by the way
> Like a bear robbed of her cubs I will pounce on them
> and tear the flesh around their hearts
> the dogs shall eat their flesh and the wild beasts tear them to
>   pieces. (Hosea 13:4–8)

What is the alternative? The challenge is to imagine land, people, and women in particular, not as objects of possession, or as objects at all, but as expressions of infinite giving, and the religions of the Book offer resources for this, too. In Jean-Luc Marion's distinction between the idol and the icon, "The idol presents itself to man's gaze in order that representation, and hence knowledge, *can seize hold of it.*"[1] For many thinkers, biblical through Reformation through contemporary, "the invisible made visible" is the very definition of idolatry, claiming not only access to the divine, but also manipulation over it. But opening onto plenitude, the icon defies possession for it defies limits.

It is because of the real and palpable scarcities in the world that we are in danger of responding with competition and violence, and therefore that mode of apprehension must be put into question, to enable us to share goods and to circulate them rather than hoard them like the Israelites hoarded manna. The possession of objects must be contrasted with the love that knows no possession, a love presupposing an endless supply—even before the reality of dearth. The Israelites were asked to believe in plenty precisely when they had nothing to eat but manna, and the loaves and fishes multiplied precisely when there were not enough. These miracles are not a testimony that real dearth will disappear if we have enough faith; rather, they are a recommendation for generosity, to imitate divine generosity.

If, from an idolatrous perspective, monotheism depicts multiple loves as adulterating (as pollution, a base admixture), constituting faithlessness against God (an idolatry that pollutes the purity of the land and the people themselves, issuing in violence and exile), from another perspective monotheism offers a vision of love that is not reducible to possession, and that is not burdened by rules of obedience to one, that is not exclusive and abhorrent of the other. This love is not driven to violations of exclusivity that spawns violence. Monotheism also has a proliferating dimension in blessings to be fruitful and multiply, embracing pluralism, loving others as thyself, taking responsibility for the widow, orphan, and poor—a generous love that contrasts to the exclusivism of "obey me or lose all."

Kant puts the question of instrumentality at the center of his ethics, but even more than ethics, instrumentality is finally a question about love. Instrumentality may infect ethics, but it destroys love. Love begins precisely where instrumentality ends. You can do good and still be instrumental: you may want to secure the safety of a parent for your own well-being. But you cannot love and be instrumental, or possess. Possession is the absolute antithesis of love.

Infidelity is not the opposite of fides—of faith—for faith does not speak the language of possession, threatening with the demand of obedience. Faith, like Hosea's *hesed* or love, is unrequired, unrequited, and unconditional. "With love, it is about neither object nor appropriation, it is about, on the contrary, the other as such, irreducibly distinct and autonomous." Love has no interest in possessing the Other, whether epistemologically, ideologically, or materially, but in embracing the Other in full life instead of decreeing her objectification or death for possession.

Love does not speak the language of subjection, exile, terror, and murder.

"Where there are prophecies, they will fail; where there are tongues, they will cease; where there is knowledge, it will vanish away. Love never fails (1 Cor. 13:8). These sentiments are also biblical, Pauline, to be precise, but I am not able to go down a road of Christian triumphalism, of love over law.

The Hebrew Bible offers a vision of monotheism that is alien to idolatry, defined not against the idols of other peoples, but against the idol of possession. This is the monotheism of plenitude, of infinite giving, of love, that is described from the creation through the prophets.

Idolatry, then, is not only about the worship of images, of mistaking an image of God or a vehicle for the true god, nor is it only about the worship of false gods. It encompasses wider meanings than the idolatry of "replacement" wherein worship of the wrong object is substituted for worship of the right one. It also includes the radical understanding voiced succinctly by Wittgenstein: "All that philosophy can do is to destroy idols. And that means not making any new ones—say out of the 'absence of idols.'"[2] It is especially those who are sensitive to the limits of language, like Pseudo-Dionysius or Maimonides, like Marion or Levinas, who are also sensitive to erecting new idols. They, too, would distinguish between the object of worship—if it is false or misleading, leading to a false life, one devoted to the wrong pursuit, an unworthy cause—and the manner of worship, one that approaches the wrong in a troubling way. As Halbertal and Margalit remind us, the Hebrew term for idolatry—*avodah zarah*—literally means "strange worship" and that strangeness registers in two senses: as the worship of a strange thing, but also as a strange way of worshipping.

I have focused on a very strange way of worshipping—possessing—and noted the violent cost of that idolatry. When we imagine that we possess God, we can use him as an authorizing instrument for our violence. Such a God can authorize, for us, the slaughter of our enemies. But depicting God as intolerant of the traditions of other people, as slaughtering our enemies, strikes me as a deeply impoverished version of divinity, one that speaks more about human intolerance and violence than about God.

When we imagine that God possesses us, we can explain the terrors of history as his righteous wrath for our infidelity, and the possession and resulting violence trickle down. If I have been suspicious about the adequacy of narratives about God, it is not only because such narratives tend to be projections of human life, human desire, human possession, and human violence, but also because of the idolatry of any such description. To speak of representation as idolatry is not new: it is several thousand years old. But to speak of the idol not as a visual representation, a statue or a painting, but a verbal one, a narrative, seems to still be somewhat controversial. And yet it is our narrative idolatries that hold us in their grip.

NOTES

1. Jean-Luc Marion, *God Without Being*, trans. Thomas A. Carlson (Chicago: University of Chicago Press, 1991), p. 10.
2. Ludwig Wittgenstein, *The Big Typescript*, ed. and trans. C. Grant Luckhardt and Maximilian Aue (Malden, MA: Blackwell, 2005), MSS 213 and 413.

11

"IN VAIN HAVE I SMITTEN YOUR CHILDREN"

AUGUSTINE DEFINES JUST WAR

Joyce E. Salisbury

The coming of Christ did not bring peace to the world. Therefore, Christians then (and now) have had to come to grips with violence both as victims and perpetrators, and Christian thinkers have spent millennia trying to distinguish good violence from bad, that is, how to know if God is on one's side. I suggest that the whole question is flawed; there is no way to know in advance if any war is "just." I do not want to suggest that there are no "justifiable" wars, because there are a number of reasonable reasons to go to war, most obviously, in self-defense. However, justifiable reasons are different from ideas of a "just war" that suggest that an overall "justice" lies in a particular war, and most importantly that such justice can be ascertained in advance of the battles. Some wars that seemed justifiable can turn out badly, and we only know this in retrospect. (The Vietnam War is one such war that seemed justifiable at the beginning and unjust when it ended.) Since I propose that we cannot know in advance if a war is just, I suggest we can only hope for a just peace to come out of institutionalized violence. I further suggest that we can see this reality at the dawn of Christianity when Augustine, one of the greatest theologians of all time, developed criteria for Christians to predict the justice of their warfare.

The story of the relationship between Christians and war actually began in the earliest centuries of the Christian era, when decisions about the morality of warfare were made by individuals as each Christian facing war wrestled with his own conscience. Some Christians believed their faith to be incompatible with fighting in the armies of Rome. For example, the account of the martyr Maximilian describes his strong stand when he was told to enter the army: "I shall not serve. . . . You may cut off my head, I will not serve this world, but only my God."[1] While modern commentators often consider this to be the prototypical behavior of pacifist early Christians, more than likely this was the exception rather than the rule. Warfare in the armies of Rome was a job like any other, and even Christians had to work. By the 170s, for example, a large number of the soldiers in the so-called Thundering Legion (*Legio Fulminata*) were Christians.[2]

When Christian soldiers came into conflict with Rome, it was neither about killing enemies nor whether the required war was just. Instead, martyr accounts show that soldiers most often drew the line at military rituals that seemed idolatrous. For example, Julius was a veteran of many years service, and he proclaimed:

> In all the twenty-seven years in which I . . . served in the army, I was never brought before a magistrate either as a criminal or a trouble-maker. I went on seven military campaigns, and never hid behind anyone nor was I the inferior of any man in battle. My chief never found me at fault. . . . All of this time, I worshiped in fear the God who made heaven and earth, and even to this day show him my service.[3]

However, when this faithful soldier was told to light incense at the altar of the emperor, he refused and was martyred. This example shows that some Christians found warfare compatible with their faith.

All Christian soldiers were not even consistent on where they drew the line at compliance with military custom. For example, Dasius was willing to be martyred rather than participate in a celebration for Saturn, even though other Christians in his legion were happy to dress up in animal skins and participate in the festival.[4] Perhaps the most famous example of the differing opinions on how Christian soldiers should act was related by the North African church father Tertullian, who described the case in his tract "The Chaplet." In 211, at the death of the emperor Septimius Severus, his two sons followed the tradition of giving each soldier in the army a gift of money. When the gift was distributed, it was traditional for each soldier to wear a crown of laurel in celebration. One North African soldier refused to wear the crown, arguing that it was inconsistent with his Christian beliefs. He was arrested and prepared himself for martyrdom. Tertullian used the incident to argue not so much against pagans as against Christians who objected to the soldier's stance, saying,

> Why does he have to make so much trouble for the rest of us Christians over the trifling matter of dress? Why must he be so inconsiderate and rash and act as if he were anxious to die? Is he the only brave man, the only Christian among all his fellow soldiers?[5]

All these incidents show that there was no consistent policy on war during the earliest Christian centuries. The real problems were idolatry, not violence, and Christians struggled to determine where the lines lay between serving the emperor and serving God. There were no issues of a just war when all wars were secular and soldiers followed orders.

The emperor Constantine changed everything. In 313 he signed the Edict of Milan that proclaimed toleration of Christianity throughout the empire. For most Christians, this ended the holy war for the soul of the Roman Empire that had raged from the time of Nero's first persecution of Christians in 64 CE. That war was a dramatically unequal battle in which the formidable force of the state was brought against the consciences of individual believers, but faith had won. Now it seemed that the peace that had been promised by the birth of Jesus had come, and Constantine's historian, Eusebius, captures the euphoria of the age:

> Men had now lost all fear of their former oppressors; day after day they kept dazzling festival; light was everywhere, and men who once dared not look up greeted each other with smiling faces and shining eye. They danced and sang in city and country alike. . . .[6]

The alignment of church and state that Constantine brought about ended the age of the martyrs, but it did not end warfare. Instead it brought about new questions. Now there was no obvious reason for Christian soldiers to decline to fight; after all, the emperor for whom they fought was Christian, the symbols that led their forces were increasingly Christian, so surely their cause was just. It is in this context that Christian theologians first articulated the theory of "just war." These theologians linked the older idea of a just war with the newer idea of "holy war" since they believed all just wars were fought by divine command. (It is only in the early modern period that these two concepts will be separated. Now there are secular just wars as well as religious holy wars.) The problem for the medieval world (and the modern one as well) remained how you could tell which wars God supported.

The simplest definition of a just war for fourth-century theologians lay in the combatants. If Christians were fighting pagans, for example, God was on the side of Christians, so the battle was just. After all, even Constantine's acceptance of Christianity came about through God's aid in a battle. In 312, Constantine's forces were outnumbered about three to one by his rival Maxentius. On the evening before battle, Constantine saw a cross in the sky with the writing, in Greek, "By this sign, conquer." This was confirmed by a vision that night that told him to put the monogram for Christ on the armor of his troops. Miraculously—the Christians said—Constantine won the battle at Milvian Bridge, just north of Rome.[7] The precedent was set: God at times chose sides in war, giving the assurance of victory to the just.

Fourth-century Christians believed that God was clearly on their side in wars against pagans. The problem became more complex when Christians were fighting Christians. Ambrose, bishop of Milan, in 378 deepened the discussion by using biblical explanations to reassure Emperor Gratian about God's role in battle. Two years earlier, the Germanic Visigoths had defeated a Roman army in the devastating Battle of Adrianople. Did this mean that God was no longer on the side of the Christian Roman Empire? Ambrose explained this seeming paradox: The defeated emperor Valens had favored Arianism (a theological position that held that God the Father preexisted the Son). Ambrose argued that the defeat of Valens demonstrated the fallacy of Arianism; in a sense, God used war to show the truth of a theological position. Ambrose then reassured Gratian that God would thus be on Gratian's side in the emperor's forthcoming wars against the Arian Goths in the region of the Danube.[8]

Ambrose used biblical authority to demonstrate his point, thus giving further weight to his assurance that the war against the Goths was divinely sanctioned. Ambrose equated the Goths with "Gog," the peoples the prophet Ezekiel promised would be destroyed with divine help.[9] Thus, in the hands of the great bishop Ambrose, Gratian's battle was not simply one more of Rome's seemingly endless border wars, but it was a holy war—one more battle in the unfolding history of God and His chosen people. Gratian won, raising the credibility of both the Christian God and His bishop Ambrose.

Thus, here in the middle of the fourth century—at the beginning of the collaboration between Christian church and state—a bargain had seemed to be struck: God would help armies as long as they were Christian—and orthodox (for example, Catholic, not Arian). In 381 the Edict of Thessalonica made orthodox Christianity the official religion of the empire, and from this time on wars Christians believed to be just were fought not only against foes on the fringes of the Roman Empire.

At the end of the fourth century, Augustine, the most influential theologian in the West, detailed a description of a just war that became the basis for future discussions for at least the next one thousand years. Augustine wrote to justify a bloody war in North Africa that pitted Christian against Christian—orthodox against heretic—so the groundwork laid by Ambrose was directly relevant to his arguments. Before I explain Augustine's conclusions about what constitutes a just war, I will briefly introduce the Donatist conflict that stimulated his writings.

Christians in North Africa became polarized during the final great persecution of Christians that had taken place in 304. During this persecution, many Christians were martyred, many recanted, and some tried to hold a middle ground by turning over nonsacred Christian writings to be burnt. In 311 (two years before Constantine's Edict of Toleration) Caecelian, one of the Christians who had compromised, was named bishop. Purists who remembered the blood shed by the martyrs objected and ordained another bishop named Donatus in his place. The patronymic "Donatism" was given to the split in the African church caused by the rift between those who followed Caecelian and his successors and those who followed Donatus and his. The Donatists had separate church buildings, a separate hierarchy, and separate congregations.

Augustine returned to Africa from Milan and became bishop of Hippo. He found the African church profoundly split, but he failed to understand the depth of the passions that kept the two sides apart. The Catholic Church as he understood it was what we might call a "big tent" under which people possessing different degrees of piety and sin might dwell. What mattered was that all obey a unified hierarchy that could bring the blessings of peace so praised by Eusebius in the first glow of toleration. Augustine was sure this old division could be healed through persuasion, his eloquent preaching, and common sense; he was wrong. In the decades of violence that accompanied this schism, Augustine lost patience. He moved from preaching persuasion to justifying war, as he explained to a critic: "For originally my opinion was that no one should be coerced into the unity of Christ, that we must act only by words, fight only by arguments, and prevail by force of reason. . . . But this opinion of mine was overcome not by words. . . ."[10] Sadly mirroring modern events, terrorists drove Augustine to preaching violence.

At the heart of the matter, Donatists believed Constantine had led the church astray; they believed compromise and alignment with the state corrupted spiritual communities. This was the same attitude that had led some early Christians to be pacifists even to martyrdom. This antiestablishment stance led a fringe group of Donatists called the Circumcellions to challenge authority with violence. Some Circumcellions terrified local property owners, associating property with anti-Christian privilege. As a contemporary witness wrote,

> No man could rest secure in his possessions. . . . Very soon everyone lost what was owing to him—even to very large amounts, and held himself to have gained something in escaping from the violence of these men. Even journeys could not be made with perfect safety, for masters were often thrown out of their own chariots and forced to run, in servile fashion, in front of their own slaves, seated in their lord's place.[11]

Roman secular authorities viewed these people as no better than bandits, and Augustine shared their point of view. He dismissed the terrorists' religious claims and simply identified them as lunatics "inflamed by wine and madness."[12] Augustine was also shocked that they would assume the mantle of "martyr" in their search for a church of the pure. He wrote with disdain, "It was their daily sport to kill themselves, by throwing themselves over precipices, or into the water, or into the fire." In fact, he explained that these terrorists threatened Catholic travelers, forcing them to kill out of self-defense.

He continued, "If they could not find anyone whom they could ter-rify into slaying them with his sword, they threw themselves over the rocks, or committed themselves to the fire or the eddying pool."[13]

Here was Augustine's dilemma (which again has disconcerting modern parallels): what do you do with people who believe that their cause is divinely sanctioned and who are willing to kill and die violently for that cause? He deemed they were too "irrational" to listen to persuasive arguments, and he recommended violence. This was the context within which Augustine developed his ideas for a "just war" against the self-styled Donatist martyrs.

A man with a strong classical as well as a Christian education, Augustine had several previous models from which to draw his arguments for a just war. Here are the precedents in a nutshell: The Greeks believed that just wars were fought by the "just," which for them meant the Greeks. Aristotle coined the term "just war" and applied it to wars waged by Greeks against non-Greeks.[14] Aris-totle's definition would continue to be influential as Christians claimed their wars were just. The Romans governed a multiethnic empire that made it difficult to define just wars simply as "us against them," so they looked to *causes* to identify just wars. If the cause was just—for example, to fulfill a legal contract or to defend the state—then the war was just.[15]

Finally, Augustine drew from Scriptures—particularly the Old Testament Hebrew Scriptures—to identify just wars as those con-ducted with divine authority. For example, he told the Donatists the "repression and correction" they experienced were "ordained by God."[16] Throughout his works, he used Ambrose's method to apply biblical explanation to current events. Unlike modern thinkers who separate "just wars"—which might have fully secular justifications —from "holy wars," those divinely sanctioned, Augustine believed the two were combined: all just wars were divinely sanctioned. With these basic ideas, Augustine developed the following criteria for determining whether a war was just (and to justify violence against the Donatists).

For Augustine, just wars must adhere to three criteria: (1) they must have a just cause; (2) they must be waged with good intentions, that is, the expected outcome must benefit both parties in the conflict; and (3) they must be waged under the leadership of legitimate authority. (For Augustine, that meant the Christian emperor or his designated authority, rather than the leaders of Donatist ranks who had no officially sanctioned authority.)[17] How did these criteria apply to the Donatist conflict?

Augustine used the Roman definition of wars fought for a just cause in claiming that wars can be offensive or defensive as long as they were waged in "defense of the fatherland, its citizens and their property."[18] Augustine saw the attacks of the revolutionary Donatists as representing a perfect example of threats to property and authority. The test of authority was also easily met since the Christian emperors had decided that the Catholic, not the Donatist, was the legitimate church in North Africa. In fact, Augustine makes a stunningly strong departure from centuries of Christian persecution by Roman imperial authority by claiming "whosoever resisteth the power, resisteth the ordinance of God; for rulers are not a terror to good works, but a terror to the evil."[19] Emperors who were once perceived as the real enemy to the church were now the ones empowered to bring the sword in service of the church. Times had indeed changed; and Augustine's Donatist critics were quick to point out what they saw as the fundamental incongruity in the bishop's position. The Donatist Petilian cried out in horror: "What have you to do with the kings of this world, in whom Christianity has never found anything save envy towards her."[20] Augustine's support of Constantine's position of the emperor leading a Christian empire drove a further wedge between him and the Donatists; the heretics would never have supported the notion that authority yields a just war.

Augustine's test of "intention" as a measure of a just war seems a bit more of a stretch to the modern ear. Augustine wrote that coercion was the kindest way to save Donatists from their errors, so the intentions of the persecutors were pure. In one letter, he answered a critic writing, "You are of the opinion that no one should be compelled to follow righteousness . . . ,"[21] but the bishop argued it was kinder to punish first to get dissenters' attention. As he wrote, "many have found advantage . . . in being first compelled by fear or pain, so that they might afterwards be influenced by teaching. . . ."[22] Augustine argued that the greater good of having a unified community of the faithful justified the violence, so Catholic "intentions" were good even when they tortured the dissenters. He told his critics that to assess actions which are similar, like violence and torture, one had "to distinguish the intentions of the agents . . . and let us not . . . deal in groundless reproaches, and accuse those who seek men's welfare as if they did them wrong."[23] As you can imagine, the tortured were not persuaded by such logic.

Augustine raised the standard of good intentions even higher when he argued that soldiers had to wage war with "charity" and not hatred in their hearts.[24] How do soldiers kill dispassionately? Augustine explained that when they wage war through obedience to legitimate authority rather than through individual desire, soldiers can kill not only without sin, but also without hatred. Thus, only the intentions of the ruler who declared war mattered in the assessment of the conflict. For example, Augustine claimed that punishment of heretics (like the Donatists) was an act of charity,[25] and thus legitimate rulers had love in their hearts when they ordered their troops to the field. Each soldier did not have to love; he had only to obey a loving command. Augustine wrote that "it is better with severity to love, than with gentleness to deceive,"and the bishop followed with many biblical examples of famine and other hardships brought by God.[26] By these associations, Augustine justified the violence that was sweeping through North Africa.

Some modern analysts argue that in a just war efforts should be made to reduce innocent casualties, but this criteria did not trouble Augustine. He argued that sometimes God permits the innocent to suffer in this life along with the guilty, but in eternity the just will be rewarded.[27] In his perspective, the charitable intention of Christian soldiers who inflicted violence to achieve a good end was predominantly important. What mattered wasn't that some innocents died, but that they not die in vain. When he quoted the Book of Jeremiah in which the prophet lamented, "In vain have I smitten your children," Augustine emphasized the phrase "in vain" to indicate that in a just war the casualties were acceptable as long as the result was beneficial. In this, the church father departs most from modern analysts who strive to reduce "collateral damage." It did not seem to concern Augustine.[28] The bishop further explained that the best way to return heretics to the Catholic fold was through both fear and instruction; instruction alone would not work, and fear alone would be simply cruel.[29] Innocent suffering inspired the most fear, so was most effective in achieving a just resolution to a war.

In the fourth century, then, Christian armies fought in North Africa against dissenting Christians. Individuals on both sides fought and died for what they claimed was a righteous cause. Augustine's polemics written in the heat of this war shaped many future discussions on just wars, but how much impact did he have on this one? Not surprisingly, his opponents the Donatists did not support his explanation of how God was on the Catholic side. The Donatist Petilian wrote a series of letters to Augustine accusing the Catholics of behaving as badly as the pagan Romans before them. He wrote passionately, "Do you serve God in such wise that we should be murdered at your hand? You do err, you do err, if you are wretched enough to entertain such a belief as this. For God does not have butchers for his priests."[30]

Not only did Augustine's rhetoric in support of violence not persuade his opponents, the violence did not end the schism. Ultimately, the only thing that stanched the flow of blood let by these two groups of North African Christians was greater violence: The Arian Vandals invaded in the spring of 429 and Augustine died as the Vandals were besieging Hippo in the following year. He did not live to see the heretical Arians take over the churches he so vigor-

214   THE JUST WAR AND JIHAD

ously kept from the heretical Donatists. The invasion of the Muslims in the early seventh century finally ended the wars between Christians in North Africa. Augustine was wrong; justifying this war by religious reasoning did not make it a virtuous war, nor did it make it a successful war.

His criteria for evaluating whether a war is just are too general to work for the future as well. A war declared by a legitimate ruler for a good cause and conducted by good intentions can justify both sides of almost any war that has been fought ever since. We may be able to make rules to help some wars be less destructive than others, but as soon as we claim that God is supporting a war, it may make the conduct of the war easier, but it makes a compromised resolution of the war almost impossible. "Holy wars" are notoriously difficult to end.[31]

If the genius of a profound thinker like Augustine could not identify criteria that will allow us to determine in advance whether a war is just or not, I am persuaded that the enterprise itself is flawed. I suggest that Augustine and others have been wrong—we can judge whether a war is a "just" one only after it is over. We live life forward, but we understand it backward as history. Just wars are only identified in retrospect, not in advance. After all, what would poor Ambrose have said when Arian Goths conquered North Africa after he promised that God was not on their side? Even Aristotle was not able to distinguish a just war from a merely successful one.[32] We cannot hope for just wars; we can only strive for just peaces.

Our goal then as we struggle through this imperfect world is to fight wars only when absolutely necessary and conduct them with as much integrity as possible. Then when they are done and we look back to examine whether they were just or not, it is the resulting peace that will determine the justice of the battle. Only in retrospect can we say with certainty that our children were not "smitten in vain."

NOTES

1. "The Acts of Maximilian," in *Acts of the Christian Martyrs*, vol. 2, ed. H. Musurillo (Oxford: Clarendon Press, 1972), p. 245.

2. J. T. Johnson, "Historical Roots and Sources of the Just War Tradition in Western Culture," in *Just War and Jihad*, ed. J. Kelsay and J. T. Johnson (Westport, CT: Greenwood Press, 1991), p. 9.

3. "Martyrdom of Julius the Veteran," in Musurillo, *Acts of the Christian Martyrs*, pp. 262–63.

4. "Martyrdom of the Saintly Dasius," in ibid., pp. 273, 275.

5. Tertullian, "The Chaplet," in *Disciplinary, Moral and Ascetical Works*, trans. R. Arbesmann et al. (New York: Fathers of the Church, 1959), pp. 231–33.

6. Eusebius, *The History of the Church from Christ to Constantine*, trans. G. A. Williamson (Harmondsworth, England: Penguin, 1984), p. 413.

7. J. E. Salisbury, *The Blood of Martyrs* (New York: Routledge, 2004), p. 28.

8. Ambrose *De Fide Christiana* 16. http://www.newadvent.org/fathers/34042.htm (accessed November 2, 2004).

9. Ezekiel 38–39.

10. Augustine, "Letter XCIII" in *Nicene and Post-Nicene Fathers*, vol. 1, *Augustine: Prolegomena, Confessions, Letters*, ed. Philip Schaff (Peabody, MA: Hendrickson, 1995), p. 388.

11. Augustine, "The Correction of the Donatists," in ibid., vol. 4, *Augustine: The Writings against the Manichaens, and against the Donatists*, p. 637.

12. Augustine, " In Answer to the Letters of Petilian," in ibid., 4:537.

13. Augustine, "The Correction of the Donatists," in ibid., 4:641.

14. Frederick H. Russell, *Just War in the Middle Ages* (Cambridge: Cambridge University Press, 1975), pp. 3–4.

15. Ibid., pp. 4–6.

16. Augustine, "Letter XCIII," Schaff, *Nicene and Post-Nicene Fathers*, 1:382.

17. Russell, *Just War in the Middle Ages*, pp. 16–26; Salisbury, *The Blood of Martyrs*, pp. 160–61.

18. Augustine, *City of God III, 10*, trans. H. Bettenson (Harmondsworth, England: Penguin, 1972), pp. 97–99.

19. Augustine, "Letter XCIII," Schaff, *Nicene and Post-Nicene Fathers*, 1:389.

20. Augustine, "In Answer to the Letters of Petilian," ibid., 4:577.

21. Augustine, "Letter XCIII," ibid., 1:382.

22. Augustine, "The Correction of the Donatists," ibid., 4:641.

23. Augustine, "Letter XCIII," ibid., 1:384.

24. Russell, *Just War in the Middle Ages*, pp. 17–18.

25. Augustine, "Letter XCIII," Schaff, *Nicene and Post-Nicene Fathers*, 1:382, 384.

26. Ibid., p. 383.

27. Augustine *City of God* 1.9.16.

28. R. Hartigan, "Saint Augustine on War and Killing: The Problem of the Innocent," *Journal of the History of Ideas* 26 (1966): 195–204, for a full discussion of Augustine's willingness to sacrifice noncombatants.

29. Augustine, "Letter XCIII," Schaff, *Nicene and Post-Nicene Fathers*, 1:383.

30. Augustine, "The Letters of Petilian," ibid., 4:539.

31. Kelsay and Johnson, *Just War and Jihad*, p. 122.

32. Russell, *Just War in the Middle Ages*, p. 4.

12

SACRIFICIAL HEROICS

THE STORY OF ABRAHAM AND ITS USE IN THE JUSTIFICATION OF WAR

Carol Delaney

I would like to begin this essay with a poem. I will then provide some thoughts about how and why *this* story—the story told in Genesis 22 of the Hebrew Bible and in Sura 37 of the Qur'an—is used to legitimate or justify war (and to protest against it).

> So Abram rose, and clave the wood, and went,
> And took the fire with him, and a knife.
> And as they sojourned both of them together,
> Isaac the first-born spake and said, My Father,
> Behold the preparations, fire and iron,
> But where is the lamb, for this burnt-offering?
> Then Abram bound the youth with belts and straps,
> And builded parapets and trenches there,
> And stretched forth the knife to slay his son.
> When lo! an Angel called him out of heaven,
> Saying, Lay not thy hand upon the lad,
> Neither do anything to him, thy son.
> Behold! Caught in a thicket by its horns,
> A Ram.
> Offer the Ram of Pride instead.

But the old man would not so, and slew his son,
And half the seed of Europe, one by one.

That is "The Parable of the Old Man and the Young," one of Wilfred Owen's war poems written during the First World War. Because this biblical story has often been invoked in times of war, it is not surprising that it has also been used in protests against war as in Owen's poem. Some of you may also recall the Vietnam War–era songs by Leonard Cohen and Bob Dylan that explicitly referred to the Abraham story.

The poem told the story pretty well, except that in the Bible and the Qur'an the son is not slain. But is that difference major or only deceptively so? Think for a minute. It is not Abraham who prevents the slaughter, but God. Throughout history Abraham has been revered precisely for his *willingness* to go through with it. That is what makes him the "father of faith" at the foundation of the three monotheistic religions—Judaism, Christianity, and Islam.

Abraham showed his love of God by his willingness to sacrifice his son. But what about his love for his son? The message to humans, affirmed in all three religious traditions, is that love of God must come first. Christianity takes the story a step further: it is God the Father who allows the sacrifice of his only son. But what about his *love* for his son? Unlike Jesus, Isaac did not cry out: "Father, father why have you forsaken me?" Regardless, both are portrayed as being at one with the father, a complete submission of their will to the Father. Theological interpretations of "at-one-ment" abound; here I will focus on what I think is behind the story and the implications of this sacred model for human behavior and morality.

Abraham is thought to be heroic precisely because "he concedes nothing to the tie of relationship, but his whole weight is thrown into the scale on the side of acceptability with God . . . he did not incline partly to the boy and partly to piety, but devoted his whole soul through and through to holiness and disregarded the claims of their common blood" (Philo 1959, 97). Or take the lines from the prayer of supplication recited during the services of Rosh Hashanah where Abraham is extolled because he "suppressed his compassion in order to perform thy will with a perfect heart." Abraham is *the* model of a faithful man.

The faithful man is one whose faith in an abstract, transcendent *concept* takes precedence over his earthly emotional ties to his child. The unwritten message is that to be faithful, fathers ought to be willing to sacrifice their sons if God, or a surrogate transcendent authority, such as the state, demands. If Abraham was willing to sacrifice his son, so much more so should ordinary fathers be willing. It was especially disturbing to learn just before the conference (and the election) that President George W. Bush reads every morning from a devotional, inspirational book by a nineteenth-century minister, Oswald Chambers, who praises "Abraham for preparing to slay his son at God's command without . . . conferring with flesh and blood" (Wright 2004).

Emotional ties (with flesh and blood) have been seen as womanly, as impeding moral development; yet I would argue that psychological detachment is far more dangerous because it can lead to a devaluation of human life. To detach one from affective ties, to abjure ordinary human emotions are, however, the very qualities desired and instilled in soldiers. Those who have undergone military training have reported this. The model is authoritarian and hierarchal: as Abraham is obedient to God, so is the son to his father. It communicates a message to sons, and to putative sons— the soldiers. It is their duty to obey. They are not allowed to question: "Theirs not to make reply; Theirs not to reason why; Theirs but to do and die."[1] *Their* duty is to follow orders; obedience is perhaps the primary virtue and value in the military. Those who do not obey should be punished, for they threaten not only the authority of the fathers but also the system that supports them. The refusal of a group of soldiers in Iraq to obey a command is but one example.

The story has been used to justify war, especially when the war is seen as "holy" or against an evil one. All three religious traditions

have drawn upon it for this purpose. I have heard it used in sermons, in the news, and in fiction. If the references are not always
explicit, allusions make it obvious. Following are a few war stories
from each of the three religious traditions.

Renowned Talmudic scholar Adin Steinsaltz "tells us that if we
accept the fatherhood of God, we must obey His every command.
This vision is compelling enough to elicit the consent of hundreds of
millions of men and women of all nations and religions who are able,
on faith alone, to accept as the voice of God a command to sacrifice
their sons" (cited in Cohen 1990, 54).[2] In a story, "The Way of the
Wind," by Israeli novelist Amos Oz, a father purposely deceives his
wife—the boy's mother—and signs the paper that permits the son to
join the air force. The son wants to escape from the father, but cannot
escape from his father's desire that he prove himself a man and a
worthy son. The paternal desire leads to the son's death.

A similar story is told in Rev. Robert Herhold's play *Who Asked
Isaac?* set during the period of the Vietnam War. The father wants
the son to join the army and fight in Vietnam; *his* own honor
depends on it. The son didn't want to go but risked losing his
father's love and respect if he did not. The son says: "I thought the
first job of parents is to protect their children." The father
responded: "I'll love my son when he proves he's a man. How can
I love a wimp?" and acknowledged that he would be proud if his
son died in the army.

The "Sacrifice of Isaac" was the title also of the last chapter of
the novel *Fail-Safe* where the president of the United States makes
the decision to drop four nuclear bombs on New York City, thereby
sacrificing millions of his own countrymen including his wife and
children, in order to honor a "Gentleman's Agreement" he made
with another Father of State, the Russian premier.

An Iranian mullah led Islamic guards to the hiding place of his
eldest son who was a Marxist. The father eagerly assented as a
firing squad executed his son. He said: "Abraham didn't sacrifice
his son, but I did . . . even today, I don't regret it."

During an earlier phase of the Israeli-Palestinian conflict, Suha Arafat, Yasser Arafat's wife, was quoted in the *New York Times* as saying: "If I had a son, there would be no greater honor than to sacrifice him for the Palestinian cause."[3]

While the story of Abraham and the stories just briefly told are primarily about the relationship between fathers and sons, once it becomes *the* supreme model of faith, some women also adopt it, as in the case of Suha Arafat. And there is a midrash on Maccabees where a mother proudly says: "Go tell Father Abraham not to puff up his heart, if he made an Akedah of one son, I made an Akedah of seven" (Lam. Rab cited in Spiegel 1969,16).[4] But women who talk like that are seen as symbolic men. Regarding the woman in Maccabees it is written: "she took her womanly thoughts and fired them with manly spirit" (2 Macc.7:21). In short, the story has consistently been seen as related to manliness.

But it is much more than that, for this manliness is embedded in notions of fatherhood, authority, and obedience, and ultimately about a particular concept of God. Yet, these are not the usual foci of interpretation. Before turning to my interpretation, which delves into these issues, and which I discuss at length in my book *Abraham on Trial: The Social Legacy of Biblical Myth*, let me briefly outline (and dispose of) some of the more traditional interpretations.

Traditional exegeses proceed from the story, and move quickly to conventional contexts for interpretation, namely sacrifice and faith, contexts that predetermine the lines of interpretation. For example, when the story is viewed in the context of the theories and meanings of sacrifice, the questions put to it will be how and in what ways does it conform to, deviate from, or shed light on known sacrificial practices. This is the approach taken by Nancy Jay in her book *Throughout Their Generations Forever*. However, *theories* about sacrifice are relatively recent.

And why start there? There is hardly any mention of sacrificial practices in Genesis before this story and most of the theorizing has to do with much later practices, so it is anachronistic both narratively and chronologically.

Why not develop a theory of sacrifice through the story rather than interpret the story through theories of sacrifice?

Another question that often comes up in relation to this is whether the story represents the end of the supposed practice of child sacrifice and the substitution of animal sacrifice. A good example of this interpretation comes from the eminent scholar Shalom Spiegel: "The ancients can accept the rigors of sacrifice as they offer up their first born to the gods . . . it is only inch by inch that laws were mellowed and humanized. [The story of Abraham] is the remembrance of the transition *to* animal from human sacrifice—a religious and moral achievement which in folk memory was associated with Abraham's name, the father of the new faith" (Spiegel 1969, 63–64).

Such a thesis assumes a cultural evolutionary approach—that is, that the more ancient the people, the more barbaric they are and thus they must have been sacrificing their children—a hypothesis that is untenable anthropologically.[5] Such interpretations also assume that child sacrifice was practiced in that area before (the story of) Abraham. There is no evidence for such a practice in that early time. The only evidence—and it is hotly debated—for a practice of child sacrifice is from Carthage; regardless, it is much later than *any* estimates for the Abraham story.

Much more important, however, the story *itself* shows that animal sacrifice was presupposed.

The most poignant sentence in the whole story is "Father: Behold the fire and the wood: but where is the lamb for the burnt offering?" Even Isaac knew that the appropriate sacrifice was an animal. So, the story cannot be interpreted to indicate the substitution of an animal for child sacrifice. And if the story was really meant to put an end to the supposed rampant practice of child sacrifice, why is there no mention of such a practice in the earlier chapters of Genesis? If the intention was to stop it, God could simply have forbidden it. Or the biblical writers could have. As a prominent Jewish scholar has said: "A prohibition against child sacrifice, if that is what it was, is merely negative, rather than a positive construction of a new faith. The Akedah in its final form is not an attempt to combat existing practice, but is itself the product of a religious attitude."[6]

I agree. For don't forget: Abraham was *willing to go through with it*—that is the symbol of his faith. The story is also a performative in that it establishes a notion of the kind of God to whom such faith is owed. That is, I believe that the concept of God and the Abraham story are interdependent, indeed, that the Abraham story is necessary for the three faiths, which is why they all go back to it. This approach is very different from assuming that the notion of God existed first and is somehow independent from the story.[7]

Others, taking a cue from Maimonides, talk about the story as a trial or "a test case of the extreme limits of the love and fear of God."[8] Shlomo Riskin, formerly a rabbi in New York and now chief rabbi of Efrat and dean of the Ohr Torah institutions, said this means: "Abraham was asked to do what all subsequent generations of Jews . . . would be asked to do. . . . The paradox in Jewish history is that, had we not been willing to sacrifice our children for God, we would never have survived as a God-inspired and God-committed *nation*" (Riskin 1983, 31).

My question, echoed at least by a number of modern Israelis and others, is: Is nationhood worth more than one's children? That is the question we need to be thinking about. Young people are called upon to make the ultimate sacrifice—their lives—for what Benedict Anderson called "that invention of imagination," the nation. Perhaps it is time to imagine something different!

If the point of the story was to prove Abraham's faith and obedience, why not have him sacrifice himself? That would not be enough, says biblical scholar Nahum Sarna (1989, 393), because of course Abraham would be willing to sacrifice himself in order to save his son. But there is no evidence for that assumption. Still, if he had been willing to sacrifice himself why does he do nothing to try to save his son? Why doesn't he argue with God as he did when trying to save Ishmael from banishment and Sodom from destruction?

At the same time, and in seeming contradiction to that view, is the one where Abraham is extolled for being willing to give up the thing he loved most in the world. But giving up something is quite different from taking the life of another, for taking the life of one's own child. To equate them or to put them on the same continuum is entering on the slippery slope of the meanings of sacrifice. Even if Abraham loved his son more than anything else in the world, is the child *his* to sacrifice? This is the question that began to propel my thoughts in a very different direction. *Is the child his to sacrifice?*

At the very least, Isaac belonged also to the mother. Or did he? By what right did Abraham take his son without consulting with, and getting the consent of, the child's mother? One could say, "Well, God commanded him and thus he had to obey."

Not so fast!

Would an all-knowing God ask only one parent for a child when He surely knew that the child came from both and therefore belonged to both (or perhaps only to Him)? This has never come up in all the centuries of commentary. The Bible and the exegetes seem to assume that Isaac (or Ishmael) belonged to the father in a way he did not belong to the mother. Some say, "Well, it's because of patriarchy." But that just defers the question, since patriarchy means the power of fathers. So, my next question was: What is that power based on? Why fathers and not mothers? What is it about fatherhood that confers such power? Here is where anthropology and especially kinship theory came to the rescue. This is a complicated topic; here I can give only the barest of outlines.[9]

It may be difficult for many people to realize that the terms "father" and "mother" are not simply labels hung onto male and female parents; they are meaningful terms that derive from and embody a particular *theory* of procreation.[10] There are cultures in which there are no equivalents; this is not to deny that people everywhere live in domestic situations and that babies come from the bodies of women, but notions of how the process comes about and what are the necessary ingredients and actors vary considerably. So do the kinship terms. For the purposes of this discussion, however, "father" and "mother" derive from a theory of procreation that I have called a *monogenetic* theory (Delaney 1986, 1991). It is monogenetic because the principle of creation was believed to come only from one source—the male. In the Bible, men *beget* while women *bear*. Symbolically, the monogenetic theory is the human analogue of divine, monotheistic creation. The life-giving abilities attributed to men allied them with God, while women became associated with what was created by God, namely the earth. The theory is encapsulated by the word *seed*. Men were thought to provide the seed (which was also thought to convey the soul). Women, in contrast, were imagined as the nurturing medium, like the earth, in which the seed is planted; they foster its growth and bring it forth, but do not provide its essential identity. "Mother" and "father" are *not* cocreators. The child belongs to the father because he *is* his seed. In this theory, paternity has not meant just the recognition of a biological relationship between a man and a specific child; it has meant the *primary, creative, engendering role*. The very notion of paternity, therefore, already embodies *author*ity. As God is imagined as author/creator of the world so, too, were men imagined as the authors/creators—with God's help, of course—of children. At the same time a man does not have to become a father to partake of the power; it is potential in all males, it is part of the definition of what it means to be a man.

The story of Abraham is all about his seed. Commentators discuss *who* is the true seed of Abraham and thus who will inherit the patrimony, the promises. Is it Isaac and thus all Jews, is it Ishmael, the firstborn, and thus all Muslims? Or is it Jesus and thus all Christians? Some Christian Bibles capitalize the word *seed* when it is believed to refer to Jesus, but in many revised editions the word *seed* is changed to *child* or *progeny*. This is one instance where I feel strongly that inclusive language distorts the message. Children and progeny were imagined as the products of seed, and seed was thought to come only from the male. Commentators discuss *who* is seed, but never once *what* is seed and what are the implications.

In this theory, then, the son does belong to the father in a way he does not belong to the mother; indeed, in a very important sense, *father and son are one*[11]—the son is his father's seed, he is of the same essence as his father, thus, he belongs to him. His father has authority over him. Of course, traditionally, he has also had power over daughters but the way it works out in practice is different. In either case, what is at stake is the family name, honor, or, to put it more crudely, the purity of the seed line. It is only sons who can perpetuate it. To be a good son has meant to be an obedient son, to carry out the father's orders or wishes.

Abraham is obedient to God, Isaac is obedient to Abraham; the story sets up a hierarchy of command, a hierarchy of authority. Isaac's thoughts, desires, and will are not considered; indeed, most commentators say his will was identical with the father's—as that of Jesus was supposedly "at-one" with God the Father's. In the Qur'anic version it is notable that Abraham tells his son—who, by the way, is not named—what he is about to do. And the son replies: "O my father! Do that which thou are commanded. God willing, thou shalt find me of the steadfast" (Sura 37:102). Already he has been constructed as the obedient son, the willing victim.

*   *   *

Let me now return to the relation between this story and justifications for war. Some of the stories cited at the beginning perpetuate the idea of fathers wanting their sons to be courageous, to join the military, to fight the nation's wars, to be a hero. Military service has always been a major issue in presidential campaigns and elections. Who is the most heroic, most courageous, most qualified to lead the nation? Who is willing to ask the young people to die for the nation? It is the Fathers of State who make the decisions to go to war—without consulting the very people who will do the fighting and the dying. In substate groups such as al Qaeda or Hamas, it is the older men, the leaders, who recruit the suicide bombers, or "martyrs" as they are known, and the latter obey their decision about when it is their turn to perform a mission. These young people are told they will be transported directly to Paradise where the men will have up to seventy virginal maidens awaiting them. It is not said what awaits the young women who volunteer.

The rhetoric of war is glory, heroism, and sacrifice, yet any soldier who survives knows that war is hell. We have some presidents who think they can read the will of God, that God is on our side. Some Jews in Israel and Muslims in Iraq and Palestine believe the same thing.

Personally, I think the wars between these groups will be interminable because these *sibling* faiths are like three sons fighting over the patrimony—who has the right to inherit the promises given in the beginning to Abraham? Really, it is about who has the right concept of God, and who has the right understanding of the kind of society He wants. The fighting will be interminable because even though these religious traditions share many concepts and stories, they are constructed in mutually exclusive worldviews. The fighting will continue until there is a widespread critique of the story of Abraham and the kind of faith it extols and the patriarchal social organization it has spawned.

Note, too, how the story of Abraham and the internecine fighting is all about men—a male-imaged God, a father and a son. This is not accidental but an essential feature in the establishment of a patriarchal *theosocial* order. These religious traditions are, I believe, inherently exclusive, inherently violent, and inherently patriarchal; they haven't even glimpsed the gender violence—the way in which women were left out of the foundation story and out of the concept of God.

I don't mean to suggest that we need to insert women into it.

Instead, we need to change the stories. We also need different notions of the sacred, of faith, of gender, of family, of authority. We need to imagine something beyond, or at least different from, monotheism. Rather than putting love of God first, I think we need to love our children and one another first. Rather than waiting for salvation (for the chosen or the elect) in the next world, I think we need to focus on making this world a haven for everyone. Rather than focus on authority and obedience, I think we need to think more about responsibility—to and for each other. I think we need to rethink and revalue the emotional ties that link us to one another, that help us realize our common humanity.

Finally, I ask you to consider how our world would look had protection of the child been at the foundation of faith instead of the willingness to sacrifice him.

NOTES

1. Alfred Lord Tennyson, "The Charge of the Light Brigade," 1854.

2. It is unclear to me what "all nations and religions" means since this command is only found in the Abrahamic religions.

3. I might also note that chapter 2 in my book discusses an actual trial of a man who sacrificed his child because God told him to. It took place in the 1990s. I attended the trial and interviewed all the participants; the Abraham story became part of the discussion.

4. In Jewish tradition, *Akedah* refers to the story of Abraham in Genesis 22.

5. As a cultural anthropologist I also reject theories that tend to reduce cultural specifics to some human universal propensities, even less to genetics. This kind of approach is taken by René Girard in his *Violence and the Sacred*. Nor, in that book, did he account for the differentials in gender in sacrificial rituals; that is, if it is only males who participate in blood sacrifice it cannot be considered a *human* universal or propensity! As will become clear, I think there is nothing natural or inherent in males that promotes their violence, even less a propensity to sacrifice children.

Rather, these things come about in relation to definitions of gender and gender roles and numerous other associations in a specific culture.

6. Nahum Sarna, *Understanding Genesis* (New York: McGraw Hill, 1966), p. 162.

7. It is my belief that this is the foundational story and that the earlier ones—Cain and Abel, Noah and the Flood, and others—have been borrowed from the ancient Near Eastern traditions and reworked within the monotheistic ideology to provide a framework for the story of Abraham.

8. This is from Maimonides' *Guide to the Perplexed* but is cited in the *Encyclopedia Judaica*.

9. See Delaney 1986, 1991, 1998 for discussion of anthropological theories of kinship and gender including matriarchy and the non-appropriateness of the term and concept. These issues came up during the conference.

10. One can get an understanding of the differences between male and female gender definitions from a comparison of the terms *paternity* versus *maternity* or *patrimony* versus *matrimony*.

11. It should be clear that I think the theological concept of God is intimately related to notions of human pro-*creation*. Denaturalized male generativity is used symbolically to describe God's creativity; conversely, God's creative power is naturalized in notions of male generativity. In Christianity, not only is God considered Father and Creator, but also father and son are one. Mary is merely the vehicle to bring him into the world, to provide human flesh. The theory is portrayed in some paintings where a *whole* baby Jesus is seen descending on heavenly rays and enters Mary's ear. There is clearly no notion that male and female provide equally to the genetic constitution of a child (and in addition, of course, women also bear).

REFERENCES

Burdick, Eugene, and Harvey Wheeler. *Fail-Safe*. New York: McGraw Hill, 1962.

Cohen, Jack. "Is This the Meaning of My Life? Israelis Rethink the *Akedah*." *Conservative Judaism* 43, no. 1 (1990): 50–60.

Delaney, Carol. *Abraham on Trial: The Social Legacy of Biblical Myth.* Princeton, NJ: Princeton University Press, 1998.

———. "The Meaning of Paternity and the Virgin Birth Debate." *Man* 21, no. 3 (1986): 494–513.

———. *The Seed and the Soil: Gender and Cosmology in Turkish Village Society.* Berkeley: University of California Press, 1991.

Encyclopedia Judaica. Jerusalem: Keter Publishing House, 1971.

Girard, René. *Violence and the Sacred.* Baltimore: Johns Hopkins University Press, 1972.

Herhold, Robert M. "Who Asked Isaac?" Unpublished play performed October 27, 1995, University Lutheran Church, Palo Alto, CA.

Jay, Nancy. *Throughout Your Generations Forever: Sacrifice, Religion, and Paternity.* Chicago: University of Chicago Press, 1992.

Oz, Amos. "The Way of the Wind." In *Where the Jackals Howl and Other Stories,* 39–60. 1965. Reprint, New York: Harcourt Brace Jovanovich, 1973.

Philo of Alexandria. *De Abrahamo.* Translated by F. H. Colson. Cambridge, MA: Loeb Classical Library, Harvard University Press, 1959.

Riskin, Shlomo. "The Akeda: A Lesson in Martyrdom." *Jerusalem Post,* October 21, 1994.

Sarna, Nahum, ed. *The JPS Torah Commentary: Genesis.* Philadelphia: Jewish Publication Society, 1989.

Spiegel, Shalom. *The Last Trial.* Translated by Judah Goldin. New York: Schocken Books, 1969.

Wright, Robert. "Faith, Hope and Clarity." *New York Times,* October 28, 2004, Op-Ed page.

13

RELIGION AND VIOLENCE

WAR, TYRANNICIDE, TERRORISM

Gabriel Palmer-Fernandez

T o focus the discussion, consider the following two events.

In 1905 a young man, a member of a successor group to the Russian Narodnaya Volya, was tasked with assassinating a tsarist official, Grand Duke Serge Alexandrovich, for his involvement in the repression of revolutionary activity. The group had learned the route the duke would take on a particular day. As the duke's carriage came into view, the young man carrying a bomb approached it, ready to deliver the deadly parcel. But he noticed that the duke was accompanied by his two children and decided to abort the mission. "Even in destruction," Albert Camus would later write of this incident, "there's a right way and a wrong way—there are limits."[1] The duke was assassinated at a later date.

In 1994 Dr. Baruch Goldstein, a disciple of the ultranationalist Rabbi Meir Kahane, entered the Ibrahim Mosque in Jerusalem and opened fire on Muslim worshipers who had gathered there for Friday prayers. Using an M-16 assault rifle, he quickly fired 119 rounds into the crowd, killing 29 and wounding 150 before he was beaten to death. Like Kahane, Goldstein firmly believed that any "land for peace" program agreed to by the Israeli government would amount to a betrayal of what God has ordained. The mission, he believed, would redeem Israel's biblical birthright and ensure the coming of the Messiah.

The differences between these events illustrate some of the issues before us: the object and motivation of violence; the relation between religion, the state and war; and the recent emergence of contemporary religious terrorism. In what follows I document some of the ways in which religion and violence are, or have been, related. In the first two sections I briefly explore two forms of religiously sanctioned violence, the Christian doctrines of the just war and of tyrannicide. In the third part, I look more generally at the relation between religion and violence, giving particular attention to religiously motivated terrorism and why it has become so prevalent today. I conclude with the suggestion that religion does not stand alone in the generation of violence. Rather, the source of recent religiously motivated violence lies in a competition between secular and religious ideologies as the basis of legitimacy of the nation-state.

THE CHRISTIAN DOCTRINE OF JUST WAR

From its beginnings in Augustine in the fifth century, the Christian doctrine of the just war was conservative in character and designed to meet the needs of the state. It assumed that the right to war belongs only to the sovereign authority of a particular kind of community—a city, commonwealth, or empire—marked by a defined and reasonably permanent territory, an organized government, and a degree of independence from any foreign power. One can, of course, acknowledge other types of communities based on race, religion, ethnicity, or common interests as, say, a corporation, civic group, or a gang of thieves, but so long as these do not possess some, if not all, of those features they do not count as states and so lack the right to war. For Augustine the relevant political community was the Roman Empire, whose citizens had a positive duty to protect. For example, as Rome was on the verge of attack by Vandals, Augustine wrote the following to his friend Boniface, who having lost his wife desired to retire and become a monk:

> Not now. . . . Monks indeed occupy a higher place before God, but you should not aspire to their blessedness before the proper time. You must first be exercised in patience in your calling. The monks will pray for you against your visible enemies. You must fight for them against the barbarians, their visible foes.[2]

The counsel to Boniface, that a Christian should take up arms for defense of the state, was a radical departure from received doctrine. Christians of the first centuries had lived within Roman society but had accepted little responsibility for its protection. Theologians of the time held doctrines that deprecated service to the state and devalued the political order, often pronouncing that government service was perilous to the soul. St. Martin of Tours, for example, asked to be released from military service because he was already a soldier of Christ. But for Augustine the state plays a positive, constructive role in human affairs. In a condition marked by avarice, self-interest, pride, and lust individuals would destroy each other in their competition for power and advantage. Much like Thomas Hobbes centuries later, Augustine was aware of the need for a power strong enough to restrain the countless appetites and ceaseless conflicts of the earthly city, lest order and peace be rent apart by unending civil strife. To minimize destruction, to punish wrongdoers, and to insure order the state has the important task of maintaining the external conditions requisite for the "acquisition of the necessaries of life."[3]

For Augustine, the essential function of the state is corrective— a remedy for the confusion and disorder sin has brought upon the world. Like private property, slavery, the law of the family, the regulation of the sex life, the state and its sovereign, for Augustine, are ordained by God as a painful and humiliating penalty of the Fall and, at the same time, as a remedy for sin.[4] Augustine writes:

> Surely it is not without purpose that we have the institution of the power of kings, the death penalty of the judge, the barbed hooks of the executioner, the weapons of the soldier, the right of punishment of the overlord, even the severity of the good father. All these things have their methods, their causes, their reasons, and their practical benefits. While these things are feared, the wicked are kept within their bounds, and the good live more peacefully among the wicked.[5]

Along similar lines, Thomas Aquinas required as a necessary condition for war that it be waged by the king or sovereign of the political community, an idea much of which was taken from what Aristotle called a *polis* (*Politics* 1.1; NE 1.2). Such political units Aquinas often called "perfect communities" as they were sufficient to meet all of a citizen's earthly needs. These communities would have a supreme ruler or prince charged with promoting the common good of the subjects and protecting their welfare, including protection from internal threats (e.g., crime and sedition) and those of foreign enemies. To do so, the sovereign and only he possessed "perfect coercive power"[6] to "put evildoers to death."[7] Aquinas writes:

> [T]he ruler under whom the war is to be fought must have authority to do so. A private person does not have the right to make war since he can pursue his rights by appealing to his superior. In addition a private person does not have the right to mobilize the people as must be done in war. But since the responsibility for the commonwealth has been entrusted to rulers it is their responsibility to defend the city or kingdom or province subject to them. And just as it is legitimate for them to use the material sword to punish criminals in order to defend it against internal distur-

bances . . . so they have also the right to use the sword of war to defend the commonwealth against external enemies.[8]

Later just war theorists Francisco de Vitoria, Francisco Suárez, and Hugo Grotius followed Aquinas in using the language of "perfect communities" and according the right to war only to heads of states. Suárez, for example, writes: "External hostilities that are opposed to peace are properly called war, when undertaken between sovereigns or between states. . . . By natural right the sovereign, without temporal superior, holds legitimate power to declare war, or the republic which reserves a similar jurisdiction for itself."[9]

An important difference between war and other forms of political violence emerges from these remarks. War is a condition of armed hostility between states under the power of a sovereign and the right to war belongs only to them. Accordingly, a group that fails to meet those conditions lacks the right to war, and should it engage in armed hostilities commits not acts of war, but of terror. So conceived, the principle of sovereignty or legitimate authority captures the core of the just war tradition. It might even turn out that sovereignty is the necessary and sufficient condition for war.[10] Even if only necessary, the principle favors states over secessionist, resistance, and revolutionary movements and suggests the essentially conservative character of the just war tradition. As the tradition developed in medieval Catholic theology (Aquinas) and was then gradually secularized in the early modern period with the Spanish Catholic writers (Vitoria, Suárez) and the Dutch Protestant jurists (Grotius), it sought to preserve an international system of independent nation-states with established customs and laws. For that tradition, war is always a condition between states, a kind of public institution serving a common, political purpose, and never a private adventure.

THE CHRISTIAN DOCTRINE OF TYRANNICIDE

But the just war is not the only doctrine of justifiable lethal force developed by Christian theologians. Alongside it, there is a second independent, parallel doctrine on the just use of force. It concerns not violence between states, but by private persons or a group for a common, political objective: the overthrow of the unjust sovereign of their own or another's state.[11]

John of Salisbury introduced the doctrine into medieval Catholicism in the twelfth century in the latter chapters of his book *Policratus*. A prince, that is, a legitimate ruler, John states, is one who "rules in accordance with the laws," which are from God (as John puts it: law is "the gift of God, the model of equity, a standard of justice, a likeness of the divine will, the guarding of well-being."). So, the prince by obeying the law shows reverence and obedience to God (is, John writes, "a kind of likeness of divinity").[12] But a tyrant is a ruler who does not obey the law, "who oppresses the people by rulership based upon force," and in his disobedience is the "likeness of wickedness" and assails God who "in a sense is challenged to battle."[13] So the tyrant "is generally to be even killed."[14] "It has always been," John declares, "an honorable thing to slay them if they can be curbed in no other way" and "even priests of God repute the killing of tyrants as a pious act."[15] Tyrants, he writes, are "always punished by the Lord," who sometimes uses a "human hand . . . [as] a weapon wherewith to administer punishment to the unrighteous."[16]

Aquinas agreed. Borrowing the ancient distinction between two types of tyrants, by illegitimate acquisition (*tyrannos in titulo*) or by abuse of power (*tyrannos in regimine*), the former, Aquinas says, may be killed "by any one [to] resist such dominion. . . . For in that case he who kills the tyrant for the liberation of his country is praised and receives a reward."[17] While here Aquinas affirms teachings of earlier writers, notably John of Salisbury, in later writings he grew hesitant in upholding the right of private persons to kill a king who degenerates into a tyrant, that is, a *tyrannos in regimine*, for unless the tyranny is "excessive it would be more expedient to endure [it], rather than bring about many dangers graver than the tyranny itself." The right to remove this kind of tyrant, however, is transferred to the community: "if a given community has the right to appoint a ruler it is not unjust for the community to depose the king or restrict his power if he abuses it by becoming a tyrant."[18]

Most other medieval writers emphasized the right of the individual to kill the tyrant, agreeing with John of Salisbury, rather than the more cautious view requiring some kind of public deliberation and community decision, as with Aquinas. Either way, the discussions were mainly academic and seldom, if ever, a dominant theme of medieval political thought. They were essentially logical developments of the deeply held belief that the king had an objective purpose instituted by God. Its neglect could well forfeit the king's authority. But in the later Middle Ages the doctrine became a very practical issue.

In November 1407 the Duke of Orléans, brother of the king of France, was killed. His cousin John the Fearless, the Duke of Burgundy, was suspected of complicity in the act. Jean Petit, a French cleric at the University of Paris, justified the killing: "It is lawful for any subject, without any order or command, according to moral, divine, and natural law, to kill or cause to be killed a traitor and disloyal tyrant. It is not only lawful, but honorable and meritorious, especially when he is in such great power that justice cannot well be done by the sovereign."[19] Several years later, Jean Gerson, chancellor of the University of Paris, denounced Petit's teaching and instructed his contemporaries on the correct interpretation of those authorities, especially Aquinas, whom Petit had employed in his justification. Gerson had earlier supported the doctrine in a sermon preached before Charles VI of France, but it required, as with Aquinas, a public authority: "wise philosophers, expert jurists, legists, theologians, men of good life, of good natural prudence, and of great experience should be consulted and confidence should be placed on them."[20]

At two subsequent church councils, the Council of the Faith held in Paris in 1414 and then at the General Council of the Church convened in Constance in 1415, Gerson's condemnation of Petit's teaching on tyrannicide was approved. Although Petit's name was never mentioned at either council, the following proposition was declared heretical: "It is lawful and even meritorious for any vassal or subject to kill any tyrant; he may even resort to ambushes, subtle flattery or adulation, may disregard any oath or pact made with the tyrant and need not wait for the opinion or order of any judge."[21] A tyrant could still be killed if he is not just "any tyrant" but sufficiently wicked, with the approval of the proper authorities, and without ambush or ruse. Aquinas seems to have won the debate. For the remainder of the Middle Ages, almost all theologians affirmed the council's condemnation of Petit's justification. But the condemnation did not to extend to the killing of a tyrant who had gained power by force (i.e., a *tyrannus in titulo*). The killing of such a tyrant could be justified by an individual's natural right of self-defense as a means to liberate the community.

During the Counter-Reformation period, Suárez argued that the condemnation of tyrannicide issued at the Council of Constance does not say that "no tyrant may be slain [but that] not every tyrant may be slain before sentence has been pronounced against him . . . [for] a private individual who slays a tyrant . . . is acting by the authority of a tacitly consenting state, and by the authority of God, Who has granted to every man, through the natural law, the right to defend himself and his state from the violence inflicted by such a tyrant. . . . For he who . . . slays a tyrant, in order to liberate his country, is accorded praise and given a reward."[22] Suárez then adds a novel feature to the doctrine that arises from his particular historical setting. A heretical king (that is, a Protestant), he argues, may be deposed by the pope in virtue of his temporal authority. Once dethroned and after sentence has been pronounced, he may be killed as a *tyrannos in titulo* by any private individual, whether subject to that king or not. Such a king, by reason of his heresy, is "deprived of his dominion [which] is to pass to his lawful Catholic successor."[23]

The last Catholic theologian to write on the doctrine was Juan de Mariana. In 1599 Mariana published his major work titled *The King and the Education of the King*. Chapter 6 of that work considers "Whether it is Right to Destroy a Tyrant." It begins by recounting the story of a young Dominican monk, Jacques Clement, who in 1589 assassinated Henry III, king of France, as he laid siege to the city of Paris. Clement had received instruction from his ecclesial superiors on the great medieval Catholic theologians. "He was told by the theologians," Mariana writes, "whom he had consulted, that a tyrant may be killed legally."[24] Because a tyrant is a "public enemy," Mariana continues, "he may be removed by any means and gotten rid of by as much violence as he used in seizing power. . . . [Tyrants] can be killed not only justly but with praise and glory."[25] Although the assassin himself might die for his deed, as Clement did, whoever takes the "lead in killing tyrants [is] held in great honor."[26] So, Clement, Mariana concludes, is to be considered an "eternal honor to France [in whom] a greater power strengthened his normal power and spirit."[27]

In the nineteenth century, at a time of great social ferment, a form of violence begins to emerge that has a strong family resemblance to tyrannicide—the use of violence by private persons for a common, political objective. In Europe, especially in Russia and Germany, but also in the Balkans, Turkey, Italy, Egypt, and the United States, the emergence of anarchist and revolutionary movements employed violence, dubbed terrorism by the revolutionaries themselves, to bring about political change, reaching its zenith in the immediate post–World War II disintegration of European empires. Terrorism in this period referred to a way of fighting restricted to the assassination of highly placed political figures, by bomb, dagger, or poison, as either vengeance or punishment, coupled with a "propagandistic effect." As the anarchist Johann Most put it:

What is important is not solely these actions [assassinations] . . . but the propagandistic effect they are able to achieve. Hence, we preach not only action in and for itself, but also action as propaganda. . . . The great thing about anarchist vengeance is that it proclaims loud and clear for everyone to hear, that: this man or that man must die for this and this reason; and that at the first opportunity which presents itself for the realization of such a threat, the rascal in question is really and truly dispatched to the other world.[28]

There was during this period hardly a trace of indiscriminate violence or the desire to intimidate and create fear in a civilian population for a political objective. On the contrary, a crucial feature of anarchist or revolutionary terrorism during this period, the "propaganda by deed," was the attempt to arouse the spirit of revolt among the masses by highly selective violence and assassinations. Although a few civilians might die, as in any armed struggle, terrorism directed "its blows against the real perpetrators of evil."[29] Nor was the terrorist negatively described as either a criminal or psychopath, as some contemporary sources assert. Instead, he was seen along the lines of ancient and medieval doctrines of the tyrannicide as a virtuous killer. "The terrorist is noble . . . [and] combines in himself the two sublimities of human grandeur: the martyr and the hero."[30]

CONTEMPORARY RELIGIOUS TERRORISM

Much of contemporary terrorism departs in at least one very significant way from its immediate precursor in European anarchist or revolutionary terrorism. In what is clearly a trend over the past two decades, its nature is predominantly religious, giving violence more the character of a sacramental act or religious duty than a means to a strategic political objective. In this regard, it has the look of premodern forms of violence, particularly of religiously sanctioned doctrines of tyrannicide. Osama bin Laden's declaration in 1988 illustrates this trend:

> All those crimes and calamities are an explicit declaration by the Americans of war on Allah, His Prophet, and Muslims. . . . Based upon this and in order to obey the Almighty, we hereby give Muslims the following judgment: The judgment to kill and fight Americans and their allies, whether civilians or military, is an obligation for every Muslim who is able to do so in any country.[31]

Aside from the important juridical question whether bin Laden has religious authority to declare such an obligation, his declaration raises at least two questions: What is the relation between religion and this kind of violence? And why is it so prevalent today?

Relation between Religion and Violence

Two responses are readily available. Both, I think, are mistaken. One denies any real connection between religion, violence, and war; the other dismisses the connection through the use of various psychological categories. The first response—call it the *denial of religion view*—is made clear in a recent study titled "God and War: An Audit and an Exploration," commissioned by the British Broadcasting Corporation for its program "What the World Thinks of God."[32] The study begins by citing some remarks I made in the introduction to the *Encyclopedia of Religion and War*. "There is a view," its authors write, "that the number of groups involved in conflicts with significant religious dimensions has increased dramatically in the more than half-century since the end of World War II: from 26 between 1945 and 1949 to 70 in the 1990s, with the greatest increase in the 1960s and 1970s. The author of that view," they say, "postulated that 'by the 1980s militant religious sects accounted for one-quarter of all armed rebellions.' He cited Martin van Creveld: 'There appears every prospect that religious attitudes, beliefs, and fanaticism will play a larger role in the motivation of armed conflict than it has, in the West at any rate, for the past 300 years."[33] It concludes that "at a philosophical level, the main religious traditions have little truck with war or violence. All advocate peace as the norm and see *genuine* spirituality as involving a disavowal of violence."[34]

I agree that the main religious traditions advocate peace, and say as much near the end of my introduction to the *Encyclopedia*. But it is factually not the case that *genuine* spirituality involves a disavowal of violence or that religion has no truck with violence. Examples abound. "Perhaps the most troubling war ideology in the Hebrew Bible is that of the ban, or *herem*, a term rooted in the sacrificial meaning 'devote to destruction,'" Susan Niditch writes. Such wars are "imagined to be commanded by God and require that all human enemy and sometimes also their animals be slaughtered [as] a whole burnt offering to God."[35] Deuteronomy 7:2 reads: "and when the Lord your God gives them over to you and you defeat them, then you must utterly destroy them." The ancient Hindu code *The Law of Manu* reads: "Those kings who, seeking to slay each other, fight with the utmost exertion and do not turn back, go to heaven."[36] "The Lord said: Look to your law and do not waver, for there is nothing more salutary for a baron than a war that is lawful. It is an open door to heaven, happily happened upon; and blessed are the warriors, Partha, who find a war like that. . . . Therefore rise up . . . resolved upon battle!" reads the Bhagavadgita.[37] D. T. Suzuki, one of the most important modern apologists for Japanese Buddhism, wrote: "A good fighter is generally an ascetic, or stoic, which means he has an iron will. This, when needed, Zen can supply."[38] And Harada Sogaku, Zen master, wrote:

> It is necessary for all one hundred million subjects [of the emperor] to be prepared to die with honor. . . . If you see the enemy you must kill him; you must destroy the false and establish the true—these are the cardinal points of Zen. It is said that if you kill someone it is fitting that you see his blood. It is further said that if you are riding a powerful horse nothing is beyond

your reach. Isn't the purpose of the [Zen] meditation we have
done in the past to be of assistance in an emergency like this?[39]

How is this not trucking with war and violence? In what sense is
Hebrew sacrifice and Zen meditation not "genuine spirituality"?

I do think the authors of this study are correct when they state
that there have been "few genuinely religious wars," if by that they
mean wars or other forms of political violence that occurred solely
on account of religion or of a particular religion, that is, that it
would otherwise not have occurred. The role of religion in war and
political violence is, I think, second order. Religion does not itself
generate war, but comes instead to justify and sanctify war subsequent to material causes and lifts them to a transmaterial level in
which killing in war often takes the form of a religious duty.

Religion has a constructive, though not necessarily causal, role
in the generation of violence. It provides an interpretive framework
through a system of narratives and symbols that make possible
extreme violence. Such a framework is not particular to Islam,
Judaism, and Christianity, to Japanese Zen or ancient Manichean-
ism. Killing in the name of God, as sacrifice and worship, as an act
expressive of religious devotion, is one of the most enduring and
universal features of religion. Near the core of religion lies a grand,
cosmic battle between order, equated with all that is righteous and
good, and chaos, equated with all that is evil, sinful, and bad, along
with heroes, martyrs, and holy warriors who maim, kill, and die
fighting the foes of the cherished divinities and receive vast and
eternal rewards.

The second response—call it the *dismissal of religion* view—
has its greatest currency in popular and media accounts of religious
violence, but scholars are hardly resistant to its appeal. It is evident
in accounts and analyses of extraordinary events such as the mass
suicide-murder of 914 Americans in Jonestown, Guyana, in 1978
and of 74 women, children, and men in April 1993 in the compound
called Mount Carmel outside Waco, Texas. Much of the interpretive

framework brought to bear upon both events dismissed them as genuine religious phenomena. Waco was "a place where . . . powerless individuals, broken of their will, were subjected to the whims of a megalomaniac who orchestrated their deaths in a 'mass suicide' that was really an elaborate murder."[40] Media accounts, popular as well as many scholarly, of Waco reflected the narratives of Jonestown and its leader, Jim Jones, who was described as, among other things, "a self-proclaimed messiah," "a man who played god," "full of hokum . . . and carnival stuff," "one who mesmerized," "fanatical," "a foul paranoid," "one vulnerable to forces in his own mind," "gifted with a strange power," and "victim of darker forces."[41] Jonestown and Waco, Jim Jones and David Koresh. They are always other: bizarre, nightmarish, lustful, and belonging, as Foucalt observes, in the prison or the asylum. Either way, never among us. Ultimately, such narratives are employed as a political strategy meant to reinforce the normative boundaries of the dominant culture, much like René Girard argues in his book *Violence and the Sacred* that sacrificial violence preserves or restores social order.

Yet this kind of violence as a religious phenomenon is not new. "We all wish to die in the old faith," declared members of the Russian Orthodox church known as the Old Believers in a formal petition of September 15, 1667. This language expressed not only resistance to liturgical changes, which, by their account, would deprive Old Believers of the traditional rituals. It was also declaratory of their intent to self-impose martyrdom. Rather than die a less than fully human death, they would commit mass suicide. In 1665 and the following year, small groups of Old Believers burned themselves to death. In 1687 some twenty-seven hundred followers seized a monastery, locked themselves inside, and set the building on fire. By the early eighteenth century, nearly twenty thousand Old Believers had died in mass suicides.

The strategy of dismissal is most evident today in many discussions on suicide bombers. "Those who would commit suicide in their assaults on the free world are not rational and are not deterred by rational concepts," Senator John Warner said to the *Washington Post*.[42] "Terrorists are extreme maniacs," claims a publication by the Unitarian Universalist Association of Congregations.[43] Two leading experts on the psychological profiles of suicide bombers characterize them as single men in their late teens from broken families, socially marginal, drawn to terrorist violence because they are drawn to violence itself.[44] Like the followers of Jim Jones or David Koresh, suicide bombers are weak-willed individuals under the power of a charismatic fanatic who distorts and hijacks religion leading them to beliefs and actions that no sane, rational person would even contemplate. But more recent studies strongly suggest the opposite: "suicide bombers exhibit no socially dysfunctional attributes . . . or suicidal symptoms."[45] We now know that suicide bombers range in age from late teens to mid-forties; many have attained professional degrees; while some are unemployed and poor, others are middle class; a significant number are women; and over 40 percent of all suicide bombings between 1980 and 2001, or 86 out of 188, had no ties to any religious organization. Indeed, the leading organization in suicide bombings is the Liberation Tigers of Tamil Eelam, whose ideology is secular and nationalistic with little, if any, explicitly religious ideas.[46]

But Why Now?

One historically accurate response is that the connection between religion and terrorism is not new. They share a long history. There are the Zealots and Sacarii of first-century Judea. The latter were named for the type of dagger they used, often in daylight, against Jewish officials who collaborated with Roman occupation authorities. There are the Islamic Fedayeen of the Shi'a Ismaili sect of the eleventh and twelfth century commonly known as the Assassins, who opposed Christian crusaders and Sunni rulers of the Abbasid dynasty. The most noteworthy group is the ancient Hindu Thugees,

perhaps the ideal type of religious terrorist insofar as their act of
killing had no discernible political purpose. Over their thousand-
year history, the Thugs may have killed, at least by one estimate,
some one million individuals. Plundering the possession of their
victims and then burying their corpses, mostly travelers with whom
they would go a long distance, killing for them was a religious duty,
always done in rigidly prescribed rites, offering a portion of the loot
to their cherished divinity, Kali, the goddess of destruction and
recipient of blood sacrifices. She is usually represented as a beau-
tiful dancer surrounded by skulls, corpses, and jackals; her tongue
dripping with blood; a garland of human heads hanging on her neck
and on her waist a girdle of human hands.[47] The following quotation illustrates the kind of devotion that can be inspired by Kali:

> Ever art thou dancing in battle, Mother. Never was beauty like
> thine, as, with thy hair flowing about thee, thou dost ever dance,
> a naked warrior on the breast of Shiva.

> Heads of thy sons, daily freshly killed, hang as a garland around
> thy neck. How is thy waist adorned with human hands! Little
> children are thy ear-rings. Faultless are thy lovely lips; thy teeth
> are as fair as the jasmine in full bloom. Thy face is bright as the
> lotus-flower, and terrible is its constant smiling. Beautiful as the
> rain-clouds is thy form; all blood-stained are thy feet.[48]

This historical connection between religion and terrorism has
led a number of writers, following David Rapoport's 1984 seminal
study, to argue that prior to the nineteenth century, religion provided the only justification for terrorism. Secular political terrorism
emerged with the anarchist movements throughout Europe and the
United States, followed in the immediate postcolonial period by
revolutionary, separatists, and nationalist violence.[49] So, religious
terrorism is not new. Still, why now?

Since the Iranian Revolution so much has been written about
Islam and violence that old stereotypes rather than being dispelled

by close scholarly work have been reinforced. "The image of Muslim armies converting as they advance," G. H. Jansen wrote some twenty-five years ago, "has sunk so deeply into the Western mind that no amount of repetition of the truth is likely to dislodge it."[50] Accordingly, many have looked to Islam for an explanation of violence and not to the particular characteristics of the evolution, or the conditions, of Muslim societies. Islam has provided the ideological framework for social and cultural developments with significant political and economic dimensions throughout the Middle East and other parts of the world. Yet these have been passed over by the old stereotype and the focus has largely been on the violent means of a militant fringe. Such emphasis of focus has led several authors to argue that Islamic terrorism is a symptom of a failed civilization. Hamas, Hezbollah, Islamic Jihad, al Qaeda, and so on have been kindled by the realization that Islamic culture has failed and Muslims are consequently motivated by a desire to destroy the successful civilizations of the West by producing an Armageddon-type war between the two. Ralph Peters, for example, writes:

> A religio-social society that restricts the flow of information, prefers myth to reality, oppresses women, makes family, clan, or ethnic identity the basis for social and economic relations, subverts the rule of secular law, undervalues scientific and liberal education, discourages independent thought, and believes that ancient religious law should govern all human relations has no hope whatsoever of competing with America and the vibrant, creative states of the West and the Pacific Rim. We are succeeding, the Islamic world is failing, and they hate us for it.[51]

James Klurfield, in very similar language, writes that the attacks of September 11, 2001:

> came from a religious sect lashing out at modernity and the leading exponent of modernity, the United States. Osama bin Laden is the product of a failure, a failed culture that is being left

behind by the rest of the world. He and his followers are lashing out because they cannot cope with the modern world. . . . Bin Ladenism and other forms of Islamic fundamentalism are attempts to deal with the Arab world's inability to cope with modernity.[52]

If this view were true, we should explore what is particular to the Arabic experience to identify the conditions that are productive of this type of violence—widespread poverty, social and political breakdown, tyrannical governments, inequality of women, high illiteracy, decrepit infrastructures, for example. But the view fails to convince for two reasons: first, many if not all of those conditions exist in many parts of the non-Arab world—Thailand, Bangladesh, Zimbabwe, Guatemala, Haiti, Appalachia. Second, contemporary religious terrorism is not limited to Arabs or Muslims. Instead, we find it in the bombing of an abortion clinic in Atlanta, Georgia; in the neo-Nazi Christian Identity group the Covenant, Sword, and Arm of the Lord in Mountain Home, Arkansas, where nearly one hundred women, children, and men were stockpiling weapons, including cyanide, in preparation for a war that would usher in God's rule; in the bombing of the Murrah Federal Building in Oklahoma City; in a Sarin gas attack on the Tokyo subway, among so many other places. Contemporary religious terrorism knows no denominational or geographical boundaries, no demographic or class differences, no distinction between advanced and developing nations. It is global and endemic to our time.

There might, however, be a core of truth in the argument advanced by Peters, Klurfield, and others, that there is a failed project or at least one that is being challenged. I suggest it is the modern project of the secular nation-state. The challenge was perhaps first announced by the ethnopolitical conflicts that began to emerge after World War II among peoples under colonial rule in West Africa, India, the Middle East, and Sri Lanka, for example. They foretold of the increasing erosion of the secular state as the protector of good order and the purveyor of a common identity of a people. The revival of religion as a public, political force and the resurgence of religiously motivated violence suggest that what Jurgen Habermas and others have called the project of modernity may have come to a close; that the secular state no longer holds a monopoly over violence; and that its ideology no longer entices loyalty and those other deep commitments from which we draw a sense of identity.

A clear trend is, I think, discernable here: the displacement of secular forms of social control by a religiosity that asserts itself as the only legitimate basis for social order.[53] Nation-states are artificial creations—a kind of fiction like the corporation—and are also a modern invention. In the West, they have been the dominant international actor for some three centuries. Much of the non-Western world did not know them until the colonial and postcolonial periods of the nineteenth and twentieth centuries. In both the emergence of the state was the product of particular historical forces. Other forces now come into play, challenging the old order. Ultimately, those new forces might prevail, eroding and perhaps dissolving the secular nation-state as other forms of political association establish themselves. The new forms are likely to have some resemblance to the old, for example, a centralized bureaucracy, a reasonably defined territory, and a high degree of political sovereignty. They could be much like the nation-states of today. But their ideology, founding ideas, and the sense of identity created for their citizens might have little, if anything, in common with the old—think of a Christian America, an Islamic Iran, a Buddhist Sri Lanka.

It is, of course, enormously difficult to predict what will occur, what new forms of order will emerge. But I suggest that to understand religiously motivated violence by Christians, Jews, Muslims, Hindus, Buddhists, and others we look not only to the violence that is endemic to religion, but also to that other social institution which has for a few centuries enjoyed at least a *de jure* monopoly of violence, the secular nation-state. My very strong hunch is that the cause of religious violence we see today emerges from a competition between two kinds of order, secular and religious—a competition not only for land and other material resources but also for our souls as well.

ACKNOWLEDGMENTS

An earlier version of this paper was presented at Hampshire College under the title "Religion, Terror, Justice." I am very grateful to Mary Russo and Dan Warner for their invitation to Hampshire and to a wonderful group of students and faculty who pushed me to get things right. My colleagues Mustansir Mir, Thomas Shipka, and Bruce Waller, and my spouse, Sarah Verrill Lown, gave me very helpful comments on earlier drafts and corrected several embarrassing mistakes. Those that remain are entirely mine.

NOTES

1. Albert Camus, "The Just Assassins," in *Caligula and Three Other Plays*, trans. Stuart Gilbert (New York: Knopf, 1958), p. 258.

2. Quoted in Roland H. Bainton, *Christian Attitudes Toward War and Peace* (Nashville, TN: Abingdon, 1960), p. 93.

3. Augustine, *City of God*, trans. Henry Bettenson (New York: Penguin, 1972), 19.17.

4. See R. A. Markus, "Two Conceptions of Political Authority," *Journal of Theological Studies*, n.s., 16 (1965).

5. Augustine, *Select Letters*, trans. James Houston Baxter (Cambridge, MA: Harvard University Press, 1993), 153.6.16.

6. Thomas Aquinas, *Summa Theologica* (New York: Benzinger, 1948), 2.65.2 ad 2; 67.4.

7. Aquinas *Summa* 2.64.3.

8. Aquinas *Summa* 2.2.40.

9. Francisco Suárez, *Guerra, Intervencion, Paz Internacional* (Madrid: Espasa-Calpe, 1956), pp. 47, 69. My translation.

10. Laurie Calhoun, "The Metaethical Paradox of Just War Theory," *Ethical Theory and Moral Practice* 4 (2001): 41–58.

11. Much of this section depends on my "Tyrannicide, Medieval Catholic Conceptions of," in *Encyclopedia of Religion and War*, ed. G. Palmer-Fernandez (New York: Routledge, 2004).

12. John of Salisbury, *Policratus*, trans. John Dickenson (New York: Russell & Russell, 1963), p. 335.

13. Ibid.

14. Ibid., p. 336.

15. Ibid., p. 370.

16. Ibid., p. 375. In his defense of tyrannicide, John appeals not only to classical writers, but also to Hebrew scriptures. For example, he quotes the Book of Judith 9:12–15: "Bring to pass, Lord, that by his own sword his pride may be cut off. . . . Grant to me the constancy of soul that I may despise him, and fortitude that I may destroy him . . . [as] a glorious monument of Thy name" (p. 371). Similarly, he cites the Book of Judges 4:17–21 and 5:24–26 recounting the story of Jael who killed the tyrant Sisera with a tent peg and a hammer, crushing then his head and piercing his temple. In these and other instances John stresses that God can and does employ the killing of tyrant as one weapon against wicked rulers.

17. Thomas Aquinas, *Scripturum in IV Libros Sententiarum*, ed. P. Mandonnet and M. F. Moos (Paris: A. Cattier, 1929–47), II, di. 44, q. 2, a. 2. My translation.

18. Thomas Aquinas, *On Kingship*, trans. G. H. Phelam (Toronto: Pontifical Institute of Medieval Studies, 1982), 1.6.

19. Quoted in Oscar Jászi and John D. Lewis, *Against the Tyrant* (Glencoe, IL: Free Press, 1957), p. 29; see also Franklin L. Ford, *Political Murder* (Cambridge, MA: Harvard University Pres, 1985), p. 132.

20. Quoted in Jászi and Lewis, *Against the Tyrant*, p. 31.

21. Quoted in G. Lewy, "A Secret Papal Brief on Tyrannicide During the Counterreformation," *Church History* 26, no. 4 (1957): 319.

22. Francisco Suárez, *A Defense of the Catholic and Apostolic Faith*, trans. G. Williams and J. Waldron (New York: Oceana, 1964), p. 714.

23. Ibid., p. 717.

24. Juan de Mariana, *The King and the Education of the King*, trans. G. A. Moore (Washington, DC: Country Dollar Press, 1948), p. 143.

25. Ibid., p. 147.

26. Ibid., p. 146.

27. Ibid., p. 144.

28. Johann Most, "Advice for Terrorists," in *The Terrorism Reader: A Historical Anthology*, ed. Walter A. Laqueur and Yonah Alexander (New York: New American Library, 1987), pp. 105–106.

29. G. Tarnovski, "Terrorism and Routine," in ibid., p. 81.

30. Serge Stepniak-Kravchinski, "Underground Russia," in ibid., p. 85.

31. Quoted in Peter L. Bergen, *Holy War, Inc.: Inside the Secret World of Osama bin Laden* (New York: Free Press, 2001), p. 105.

32. Greg Austin, Todd Kranock, and Thom Oommen, "God and War: An Audit and an Exploration," http://news.bbc.co.uk/1/shared/spl/hi/world/04/War_audit_pdf/war_audit.pdf (accessed May 12, 2004).

33. Ibid., p. 1.

34. Ibid. Emphasis mine.

35. Susan Nidith, "Judaism: Biblical Period," in *Encyclopedia of Religion and War*, ed. G. Palmer-Fernandez (New York: Routledge, 2004), p. 240.

36. Max Muller, ed., *The Laws of Manu*, (Delhi: Motilal Banarsidass, 1982), 7:89.

37. *The Bhagavadgita*, trans. J. A. B. van Buitenen (Chicago: University of Chicago Press, 1981), p. 77.

38. D. T. Suzuki, *Zen and Japanese Culture* (Princeton, NJ: Princeton University Press, 1959), p. 62.

39. Quoted in Brian Danzei Victoria, "Zen and Japanese Buddhism," in Palmer-Fernandez, *Encyclopedia of Religion and War*, p. 459.

40. John R. Hall, "Public Narratives and the Apocalyptic Sect," in *Armageddon in Waco*, ed. Stuart A. Wright (Chicago: University of Chicago Press, 1995), p. 206.

41. Quoted in Jonathan Z. Smith, *Imagining Religion: From Babylon to Jonestown* (Chicago: University of Chicago Press, 1982), p. 109.

42. *Washington Post*, October 7, 2002, p. A1.

43. "Confronting Anti-Arab or Anti-Muslim Sentiments," http://www.uua.org/uuawo/issues/respond/confront.html (accessed October 24, 2005).

44. Jerrold M. Post, "Terrorist Psycho-logic: Terrorist Behavior as a Product of Psychological Forces" and Ariel Merari, "The Readiness to

Kill and Die: Suicide Terrorism in the Middle East," in *Origins of Terrorism*, ed. Walter Reich (Boulder, CO: Westview, 1990).

45. Scott Atran, "Genesis of Suicide Terrorism," *Science* 299 (March 7, 2003): 1537.

46. Robert A. Pape, "The Strategic Logic of Suicide Terrorism," *American Political Science Review* 97, no. 3 (August 2003): 343–61.

47. Quoted in R. C. Zaehner, *Hinduism* (Oxford: Oxford University Press, 1984), p. 146.

48. Quoted in ibid.

49. David Rapoport, "Fear and Trembling: Terrorism in Three Religious Traditions," *American Political Science Review* 78, no. 3 (September 1984): 668–72. See also his earlier study, *Assassination* (Toronto: CBC Learning Systems, 1971), pp. 3–11.

50. G. H. Jansen, *Militant Islam* (New York: Harper & Row, 1979), p. 29. Quoted in Mustansir Mir, "Jihad in Islam," in *The Jihad and Its Time: Dedicated to Andrew Stefan Enrenkreutz*, ed. Hadia Dajani-Shakeel and Ronald A. Messier (Ann Arbor, MI: Center for Near Eastern North African Studies, 1991), p. 113.

51. Ralph Peter, *Beyond Terror* (Mechanicsburg, PA: Stackpole Books, 2002), p. 46.

52. James Klurfield, "Bin Laden Is No Match for the Modern World," *Long Island Newsday*, July 11, 2002. See also Daniel Benjamin and Steve Simon, *The Age of Sacred Terror* (New York: Random House, 2002), pp. 54–55, and Bernard Lewis, *What Went Wrong? Western Impact and Middle East Response* (New York: Oxford University Press, 2002), p. 159.

53. See, for example, Susanne Hoeber Rudolph and Lloyd I. Rudolph, "Modern Hate," *New Republic* 208, no. 12 (March 22, 2003): 24.

14

VITORIA'S JUST WAR THEORY

STILL RELEVANT TODAY?

Laura Purdy

INTRODUCTION

F rancisco de Vitoria, a distinguished sixteenth-century Spanish theologian, wrote the first extensive just war theory. This work was intended to show that the Spanish treatment of the Indians—which he defined as war—was unjustified.[1]

Vitoria's chief works were a commentary on the *Summa Theologiae* of Aquinas[2] and a series of twelve lectures, known as the *Relectiones Theologicae*, on subjects as diverse as simony and magic.[3] *De Indis Recenter Inventis*,[4] the subject of this essay, was one of those lectures, although three others, *De Iure Belli*,[5] *De Potestate Civili*,[6] and *De Potestate Ecclesiae*,[7] are also relevant to his views. None of Vitoria's works were published during his lifetime; however, notes of his lectures were preserved and later published.

Vitoria had long been interested in the Indian problem, and the lecture he gave in 1539 was the culmination of his thoughts on the matter,[8] but he had written letters as early as 1534 deploring the treatment of the Indians.[9]

What contemporary relevance does a just war theory like

Vitoria's have? After all, in principle, international law now appears to prohibit most wars altogether.[10] But it has more in common with just war theories than might be thought at first.

Since the 1928 adoption of the Kellogg-Briand Pact,[11] later incorporated into the United Nations Charter,[12] only defensive wars have been legal. Instead pacific means are to be employed when enforcing claims against other states.[13] But this position does not, of course, totally prohibit war: the law says when it is justifiable to go to war and when it is not. Thus a country may fight if attacked, but not otherwise, no matter how great the injury. But this is a just war theory. It differs from traditional ones only in the particular conditions it picks out as grounds for just war.

This fact has been underlined by recent developments. In the last half of the twentieth century, this doctrine has been eroded by claims that there are other justified uses of force in conflicts initiated by individual nations without permission from the United Nations. De facto, both wars of liberation from colonial powers and armed intervention on behalf of anticommunists have slipped into this category of accepted actions, primarily because the powerful states supporting them could not be opposed even by coalitions of weaker states. Certainly, in 2002, the United States claimed a right to engage in preemptive war against an alleged threat.[14]

Thus it appears that, de facto, international law is shifting from a policy of self-defense only to the use of war by individual nations to prosecute causes they claim are just. This development emphasizes our dependence upon the old notion of a just war theory. Hence there is still a need to examine its philosophical underpinnings.

Although such theories can be traced back to Aristotle,[15] at least, they remain thin and philosophically unsatisfactory until the Renaissance. Aquinas summarized traditional wisdom in the following three conditions: (1) war must be waged under a legitimate sovereign; (2) there must be a just cause for war; and (3) the actors must intend to do good and avoid evil.[16] This position is based on Augustine, who had developed these principles some nine hundred years before.[17] But until the sixteenth century, there was no attempt to find a home for these principles in a coherent, detailed theory, or to apply them to particular cases.

Two issues have obscured the relevance of Vitoria's work. Vitoria was both a theologian and a natural law philosopher, and contemporary philosophers have tended to ignore work in these traditions. It is true that Vitoria refers frequently to scripture, and he acknowledges the validity of positive divine law. But more importantly, while affirming the importance of religion, Vitoria repudiates attempts to undermine respect for secular authority. Although his natural law foundations may create problems for his theory as a whole, his particular claims can, for the most part, be evaluated independently of them.

De Indis Recenter Inventis is comprised of three sections. In section I, he examines the nature of the international community. In section II, he considers and rejects the Spanish attempts to justify war on the Indians. And in section III, he contemplates other possible grounds for war. Although he discusses both religious and nonreligious justifications for war, this essay will focus primarily on the former.

SECTION I: THE INTERNATIONAL COMMUNITY

Vitoria sees the international community as comprised of interdependent states.[18] This view is to be distinguished from two competing ones. The traditional medieval view emphasizes the international community, governed both by religious and secular authorities. The other more modern view focuses solely on independent states, pursuing only what they see as their own interests.

Students of Vitoria find the theoretical basis for his claim that states have rights and duties toward one another in his substitution of *ius inter gentes* for *ius inter homines*.[19] It is by this subtle change that Vitoria is thought to have indicated his realization that states exist and have rights and duties distinct from those of the individual human beings composing them. Vitoria recognized throughout his work the legitimacy of differences among peoples, justifying a conception of the international realm as a community of states rather than a world empire. Furthermore, he saw the necessity of setting up a body of laws to govern the relations of such states.

In Vitoria's *Commentarium in Primam Secundae*, he argues that the aim of every law is the common good.[20] Therefore international law (the "law of nations") must also aim at the common good. But what is the common good, and what does it require in particular cases? Vitoria gives no positive answer to these questions; we know only that war harms the common good.

Vitoria's recognition of the need for limiting egoism—both national and personal—is shown by his rejection of some attempts to defend war. For example, he denies that empire building justifies war because if it did, then both sides could be in the right. But then both sides would also be innocent, so no killing could be legal. For Vitoria, a war could be just on both sides only when, because of invincible ignorance, those on one side believe erroneously that they are in the right when they are not.[21]

However, the key reason empire building is wrong is because it is usually undertaken to benefit those who govern, not for the common good. Because all laws should aim at the common good, so should laws relating to war. And, as rulers derive their authority from the state, they ought to use it for the good of the state. Moreover, rulers ought to value the personal and financial welfare of their subjects more than their own interests. Only tyrants do otherwise: it is wrong to compel one's subjects to contribute their lives or their money for campaigns aimed at one's own benefit, for as Aristotle says, to do this is to treat them like slaves. To be a slave means that one may be used as an instrument and that one has no legitimate ends of one's own. But citizens are not slaves.

In short, a selfish reason cannot be a just cause for war. In fact, the only cause for war is a wrong received.[22] Vitoria provides three arguments for this claim.

He first explains that the proper goal of an offensive war is to avenge injustice; but this requires some preceding wrong and fault.[23] Vitoria's second argument is that rulers may not deal violently with their own subjects unless they have done some wrong. But they have no more authority over foreigners than over their own subjects, so they cannot deal violently with them either unless they commit some wrong. Natural law confirms this: it is forbidden to kill innocent persons except in special cases; but innocent persons are killed in war. Vitoria's last argument is an appeal to authority: Augustine, Aquinas, and "all the doctors" say that only a wrong received is a just cause of war.[24]

Without an effective world authority, no impartial party is available to settle disputes. In that case, the world community delegates rulers of some states to judge the actions of other rulers. So when a ruler commits a serious injustice, the ruler of any other state has the authority to try to remedy the wrong and punish the offender. Despite its evils, war is thus permitted when there are no other means of achieving this goal.

Vitoria argues that believing we are in the right is not sufficient for making us so. If this were true, then most wars would be just on both sides.[25] As we saw before, all belligerents would be innocent, and so no killing would be lawful. Domestic decisions must be carefully scrutinized, and so, given the much more far-reaching consequences of international decisions, they must be still more closely scrutinized.

Vitoria's key underlying assumption is that Indian communities must be treated like nations, just like Spain or France or Germany. This position follows from the doctrine of separate secular and religious spheres, and means that the Spanish must follow the same rules when they deal with the Indians as they would for France or Germany. In other words, they cannot make war on the Indians unless they themselves or a third party have suffered injury at Indian hands.[26]

What is the doctrine of separate spheres? It can be derived from positions Vitoria outlines in *De Potestate Civili* and *De Potestate Ecclesiae*. According to him, human life has two aspects, secular and religious. These constitute two "republics," with different origins, types of power, and goals.[27]

The secular, political republic has its roots in the social nature of humanity. The goal of society is the preservation and well-being of humans. Societies require rulers to protect them against internal and external enemies, and would fall apart in their absence.

Secular power is apparently separate and independent of the religious realm: humans have interests not directly linked with any religious end, and they are protected by the secular state. Thus, even non-Christian rulers have a legitimate function (*DI* 2.5). In short, Vitoria attempts to accord substantial autonomy to secular interests. The pope could have no legitimate reason for interfering with matters of sovereignty, since he has no role in adjudicating disputes between rulers about laws or sovereignty. Thus, humans have interests not directly linked with any religious end. They are protected by the secular state, and even non-Christian rulers have a legitimate function.

The religious republic focuses on humans' religious destiny. Its goal is to ensure everyone heavenly bliss in the afterlife. The pope, whose authority comes from God via positive divine law, is in charge of realizing this goal. Although he has no purely secular power, he can influence secular affairs if they interfere with religious ones because the religious goal is higher than the secular ones.[28] Thus worldly happiness is a stepping-stone to religious happiness. This last premise is seriously problematic, as we will see shortly.

SECTION II: REJECTION OF THE SPANISH WAR ON THE INDIANS

In section II Vitoria develops the implications of the position just sketched. That leads him to reject several religiously based attempts to deny the Indians sovereignty. The most important of these are the claims that they are sinners (no. 6) and that they refuse to accept Christianity (no. 7).

"Sin" here means alleged sins against nature, like cannibalism, and sexual intercourse with mothers, sisters, males, or animals. Of course, it is hardly clear that the Indians were guilty of any such activities, so this attempt to justify war was, in any case, simply a rationalization.

Vitoria makes several sensible observations about this supposed ground for war. The pope, he says, cannot even make war on Christian sinners, who are still more culpable than the Indians, because they know they are doing wrong. Nor could the pope make war on Indian communities just because their rulers are sinners. Societies need rulers, even if some of their acts are bad or if the source of their authority is dubious.[29]

Much more important, Vitoria here rejects the claim that the Indians' refusal to accept Christianity constitutes grounds for war against them. The case for war is based on three arguments (nos. 8–15). The first is that to reject the faith is to do evil, and doing evil is something that other rulers may curb. But the pope is a religious ruler, and can therefore compel the Indians to cease doing evil. The second argument is that since the king of Spain may force French subjects to obey the French sovereign should they rebel, Christian princes may force Indians to obey God (no. 15). The third argument is that Indian blasphemy would be, by itself, grounds for war; but unbelief is a greater sin than blasphemy; therefore the Indians can be compelled by war to cease being pagans.

Vitoria quite reasonably responds that paganism caused by invincible ignorance is not punishable, for no one is bound to believe in Christianity without evidence. Furthermore, invincible ignorance is not necessarily destroyed by preaching, so that the Spanish have no cause for war even if they have preached to the Indians but failed to convert them.

Vitoria supports this conclusion with three further arguments.

First, victory in war is no argument for the truth of the Christian religion. Second, even victory would produce only feigned belief anyway, which is "monstrous and a sacrilege." Last, Christian rulers have never made war on other non-Christians, so why would it be defensible to fight the Indians for this reason (no. 16)?

In general, why might the Indians' paganism fail to destroy their sovereignty? First, heretics (who are clearly worse than mere unbelievers) may keep their property until condemned. Second, sovereignty rests either on natural law or human law. Paganism is not a ground for loss of rights in either of these spheres.

Centrally at issue here is the claim that the Spanish are not seriously injured if the Indians refuse to become Christians. By taking this stand, Vitoria clearly rejects the Augustinian view that when any law is broken, God is injured. Foreshadowing Grotius, Vitoria, by focusing on war's ineffectiveness, is relying on God to deal with the pagans in his own way, and hence no human action is required.[30]

So much for the first and third arguments. The second argument (that since the king of Spain may force French subjects to obey the French sovereign should they rebel, Christian princes may force Indians to obey God) (no. 15) requires deeper examination—one that reveals serious potential theoretical problems with Vitoria's position.

First, Vitoria concentrates on arguments against a pope's right to make war on the Indians, whereas he really needs to show that *no* authority has grounds for war on them. Otherwise, the Spanish war on them might be justified. This is because any sovereign may become the judge of any other when possible injury is at issue.[31]

The reason is that injury within a community is dealt with by the ruler of the community. Injury that cannot be dealt with this way, either because the ruler himself is involved, as in cases of tyranny, or because the injury somehow involves two nations, ought to be dealt with by the international community. But since there is no international ruler, that task is delegated to rulers of other nations. The real reason why the pope cannot make war on the Indians for their sins must therefore be that no one ought to do so, not that the pope does not have jurisdiction over the Indians. Thus what Vitoria needs is a demonstration that there is something about the alleged sins in question that precludes them from being injuries.

Second, despite Vitoria's position that the religious and secular realms are independent, there is sufficient ambiguity in his arguments to fuel worries that it might, in the end, be impossible to deny the pope some jurisdiction over the latter after all.[32] This difficulty arises from the flawed Thomist synthesis of Aristotle and Christianity that ultimately subjects the secular realm to the religious one.

However, these are relatively remote theoretical issues. They show that it may be impossible to base contemporary just war theory on Thomism. The important point here is that Vitoria tried to use it to demonstrate how unjustified the Spanish war was, when some of his colleagues were trying to do exactly the reverse.

SECTION III: HYPOTHETICAL GROUNDS FOR WAR

In section III, Vitoria considers hypothetical reasons for war against the Indians. He comes up with seven scenarios, a majority of which involve secular injuries, such as restricting travel or trade.

However, three are religiously based. One asserts that the Spanish have a right to preach Christianity to the Indians. The other two involve protection and support of converts.

The right to preach Christianity is based on both religious and natural law (no. 9). According to them, the Indians injure the Spanish if they prevent them from preaching.

However, even here, Vitoria's pragmatic streak emerges when he points out that intrinsically defensible actions (preaching) may become indefensible because of their consequences:

> . . . it may be that these wars and massacres will hinder rather than procure and further the conversion of the Indians. Accordingly, the prime consideration is that no obstacle be placed in the way of the

Gospel, and if any be so placed, this method of evangelization must be abandoned and another one sought for. . . . (no. 12)

Vitoria's second religiously based justification for war is based on the alleged right to protect Christian converts or potential converts by replacing an intolerant ruler with a tolerant one, even at the cost of war (no. 13). There are two grounds for this: the first is religious (although he fails to show what these are); the second is based on rights and duties connected with the need for human friendship and alliance. He asserts that "native converts to Christianity have become friends and allies of Christians and we are under an obligation to do 'good unto all men, especially unto such as are of the household of faith'" (no. 13).

Vitoria's third religiously based ground for war also involves converts. He asserts that either the pope or the Spanish ruler could, for "reasonable cause," unilaterally replace a pagan ruler with a Christian one (no. 14). Reasonable cause might either be fear that converts would be harassed by the ruler or else lapse from the faith. This position is based only on positive divine law, which says that Christian slaves can be freed from their pagan masters by the church, so it is clear that subjects have at least this same protection. It also says that a Christian wife can be freed from a non-Christian husband. Therefore the church may free all Christians from pagan lords, provided that this can be done without too much trouble.

How reasonable are these justifications for war against the Indians? We have seen that Vitoria thinks two separate kinds of injuries might furnish the Spanish with a just cause of war against the Indians. One is that the Indians might deny the Spanish right to preach; the other is that Indian converts or potential converts might be mistreated by other Indians. Vitoria passes rather quickly over this last type of justification for war. But I think that it is worthwhile to analyze the possible cases here. One is where some Indians prevent others from hearing the Gospel. The other is where no Indians want to hear it. Vitoria maintains that the Spanish have the right to preach in both cases. Only the latter case will be dealt with here since the former seems to constitute an oppressive limitation of individual rights. Vitoria presents two basic arguments for his claim that the Spanish have the right to propagate Christianity. One is based on the secular rights of natural society and fellowship, which imply rights to travel and trade (3.1–4). These, in turn, imply a right of communication, and preaching Christianity is just an instantiation of that right. This explanation raises two potential problems. First, how is the right to communicate related to the right to trade? And must the two rights always be connected? One can certainly imagine situations where having one would be beneficial, but having the other would be harmful.

The second argument in favor of making war on the Indians if they prevent the Spanish from attempting to propagate Christianity is derived from positive divine law and natural law. Since the precepts of positive divine law are theological, not philosophical, they will be ignored here insofar as they do not coincide with those of natural law.

Natural law requires both "brotherly" love and "brotherly correction," from the Spanish toward the Indians, since they are, like all humans, neighbors. Because as pagans the Indians are outside of salvation, brotherly love and correction coincide, and it is up to the Spanish to try to save them. Therefore the Spanish must preach to them in hopes of saving their souls.

Before going any further, however, it is necessary to try to get clear about what, exactly, "preaching" means here. Vitoria links the right to preach with the right to trade, perhaps interpreting the right to trade as a right to offer to exchange goods. Then, the right to preach becomes analogous with the right to offer to exchange ideas. But the claim that one has the right to offer to exchange ideas seems weaker than what Vitoria probably had in mind when he asserted a Spanish right to preach Christianity. For the right to offer to exchange ideas could be satisfied by quite minimal efforts like distributing religious leaflets.

Potential problems with this notion can be made somewhat clearer by the following questions and considerations. The paradigm case of preaching is presumably a missionary holding forth in the village square. But suppose Indian tradition prevents this. Suppose that only the village speaker is permitted to speak in the square. Suppose that there is a rule against talking more than ten minutes in the square. Or suppose that no one is permitted to speak during certain hours of the day. Or that only "madmen" speak in the square. If people are denied the right to preach on the basis of such customs, or if they are not taken seriously, are they denied the right to preach?

Or suppose that there is no village and no square. But door-to-door preaching may be regarded as a serious invasion of privacy. And does the right to preach include the right to interrupt someone working in the fields or stalking a rabbit?

How long must one listen to people before their right to preach is satisfied? Who decides this, and on what grounds? May preachers bribe little children with trinkets to listen? May they require school-age children to listen to them? What about language barriers? Must non-Spanish-speaking peoples learn Spanish so they can understand the Gospel? Must they tolerate preaching in a foreign language? Can they oblige foreigners to learn their language before preaching?

Vitoria considers none of these problems, perhaps because his main concern was to find grounds for war less outrageously imperialistic than the ones being advanced by the most aggressive factions of his day. And, in any case, many intellectual and moral assumptions are now radically different than they were in his day. In the Anglo-American world in particular, it is expected that individual rights will play a much larger role in social and political decision making than in Vitoria's Spain. So attempting to apply Vitoria's guidelines to modern problems requires significant reconceptualizations. It is not obvious what Vitoria's reaction to this point would be. Perhaps he would maintain that no legitimate custom could exist which would preclude the application of his notion of preaching. But that would clearly fail to reflect Vitoria's generally humane and liberal attitudes.

However, there are other grounds for rejecting the claim that being denied the right to preach ought to be considered a legitimate justification for war: this conclusion need not depend entirely upon the doubts raised by the preceding discussion.

The problem is this: Vitoria thinks that one has the right to preach Christianity. This means that one is wronged if not allowed to preach. But what is the injury here? On a Christian view, the Indians are injured, naturally, but it seems unreasonable to go to war to avenge an injury inflicted by injured persons upon themselves. Also, Vitoria argues that there is no cause for war if the Indians refuse to accept the faith. But the injury to them is the same in both cases: the Indians burn in hell. So why may one make war if denied the right to preach, but not if the Indians refuse to convert?

The answer to all these questions must be that someone other than the Indians is injured. I speculated earlier that Vitoria's position is that we need not concern ourselves with injuries to God. Therefore, the injured party must be the Spanish.

Now, to be injured is to be deprived of some good that one deserves. Hence if the Indians prevent the Spanish from preaching, the Spanish are deprived of some good that they deserve. And this deprivation must be serious because wars should only be fought in the name of serious injury.

What then are the Spanish deprived of if the Indians deny them the right to preach? The only plausible answer is that they are deprived of the opportunity to win God's approval for trying to save Indian souls. But this is a peculiar and selfish reason to fight a war. After all, the Spanish can always try to get God's approval some other way. Given the evils of war, and the fact—that Vitoria has already conceded—that nothing would be gained by war, it would surely be preferable to seek another way to please God. And, if there is a God, surely he or she appreciates the Spanish intention to save the Indians. So they should get full credit for faith and righteousness, even if, in the end, they do not succeed either in preaching or converting them. Since intention and effort, not success, are the grounds for praise or blame, the Spanish lose nothing by writing the Indians off as a lost cause, and retiring peaceably with many prayers for their souls.

This point may be clearer if one keeps in mind the difference between asking people to believe X and asking them to listen to X. In the latter case, individuals have only to listen, an act apparently well within the capacity of any normal adult human being. In the former case, though, listeners are also required to believe something. But belief is not voluntary: it is something that happens when there is sufficient evidence for concluding that X is true. Of course, some people have more demanding standards of evidence than others. Hence the Indians, for example, might not necessarily accept Christianity, because they believe the evidence is insufficient. If threatened they may feign belief in order to avoid war. But feigned conversion achieves nothing since an all-knowing God can differentiate between opportunists and true Christians. In short, since it is not possible to force anybody to convert, there is no point in going to war to try to do this. So much is clear. But it is also true that one cannot force anybody to hear what one is telling them, even if one has just fought a war to enforce one's right to speak.

Unwilling listeners might find a preacher's material uninteresting, senseless, or frightening. They might not listen to it unless they appreciate the importance of having an open mind, or are convinced that their present beliefs are unsatisfactory, or that the material being presented is in some way worthwhile. Without such assumptions, they would not even listen unless forcibly detained. In fact, it might be necessary to threaten and/or punish them to force them to listen. Nor would there be any guarantee that the listeners even understood the material. This shows that listening long enough to gain any understanding depends on prior beliefs just as much as does conversion. So making war to achieve this end makes no more sense than making war to gain converts—which Vitoria admits makes no sense at all. Both enterprises are a waste of life and property.

CONCLUSION

Vitoria rejects all the religiously based claims that the Spanish war on the Indians in America is justifiable. He denies the pope any significant authority over Indian affairs, he denies any right to force the Indians to convert to Christianity, and he denies any right to punish the Indians for their alleged sins. Although these claims appear to involve some theoretical inconsistencies with Vitoria's earlier work, I believe that they should be taken at face value.

However, he does argue that the Spanish would have a right to make war on the Indians if they resisted Spanish attempts to preach Christianity. This claim is, in my view, an attempt to fill the perceived political void left by his denial of the claim that the Spanish could seek to convert Indians, even at the cost of war. Compared to this more extreme claim by writers such as Juan Ginés de Sepúlveda, his position must have seemed quite modest. But there are, nonetheless, good reasons for denying its legitimacy. Vitoria assumes that the Spanish, along with the Indians themselves, and God, would be seriously harmed by any denial of the right to preach, but this assumption is ill-founded. If there truly were an all-knowing and good God, then it's hard to see why the Spanish would be injured if they could not attempt to save the Indians' souls, and therefore why they might reasonably have recourse to war. Only this judgment is compatible with Vitoria's section II of *De Indis*, where he discusses what he takes to be illegitimate justifications for war.

In short, the negative part of Vitoria's theory is sound, but the affirmative part is dubious. Not only is the affirmative part incompatible with some of his negative claims, but also I would urge that war could harm individuals and nations in ways that Vitoria did not foresee because of his limited experience of international affairs.

This is especially true today because of the awesome power of contemporary weapons.

Does this conclusion mean that Vitoria's work should be left to gather dust in some archive? No. Although part of his work now looks inadequate, it nonetheless is a definite step forward in the theory of international relations. Moreover, despite what many now see as untenable justifications for war, I believe that he should be honored for, what was for his time, a remarkable concern for indigenous or less "developed" peoples, a concern that we would do well to emulate.

Vitoria's relevance is also striking in another way. In 1973–74, when I first started working on this subject, the prospect of religiously based wars seemed remote. So remote that I felt compelled to argue that the value of this part of his work would become obvious were we to substitute "ideology" for "religion," and "capitalist-democracy" or "communism" for "Christianity." For at the time, the world had tottered for at least thirty years on the brink of destruction because of fanatical and self-righteous political ideologies. And thus it seemed that nothing Vitoria said about religious grounds for war would have been of the slightest interest, as it was at the time almost unthinkable that religion could once again be taken seriously enough to motivate large-scale war. However, with the collapse of the Soviet Union, overt political ideology no longer plays anything like the same role in international affairs, despite the unrelenting US hostility toward anything less than thoroughly capitalist-friendly governments. And sadly, religious differences once again play a significant role in international hostility.

Serious objections have been raised against the overall framework of just war theory. Full consideration of them will have to await another day, but I will briefly consider three of them here. First, is just war theory realistic? After all, there is no necessary connection between the justice of one's cause and one's ability to win a war in pursuit of it. Second, does just war theory simply perpetuate a bellicose status quo by normalizing war? And third, is it even possible to judge whether any given war is just or not?

J. L. Brierly raises the first question:

> It is only a plausible theory of the nature of war if we assume, firstly, that in every war there is one party that is a violator and one that is a champion of the law, and secondly, that it is the champion of the law that will be the victor and therefore in a position to fulfill the functions of a judge. Unfortunately, there is no firm foundation for either of these assumptions in the history of war.[33]

It is true that there may be justice (or injustice) on all sides in war, and that this state of affairs is probably most often the case. But this should not deter us from trying to determine which side should be helped if it is not possible to prevent war or stay neutral.

Addressing the core issue here would be possible only by strengthening the United Nations and insulating it more from the self-interested pressures from sovereign nations. Only this approach offers any hope that parties suffering from unjust aggression can muster the resources to defend themselves. Moreover, a strong organization could apply pressures—such as economic sanctions—short of war, preventing unnecessary bloodshed and destruction. The hope would be that such measures could eliminate war altogether, but even if not, just war theory would still be needed to flesh out and justify the international laws of war embedded in the UN Charter.

Equally important, does just war theory undermine pacifist efforts to eradicate war altogether by suggesting that war can be justifiable or that there are morally better or worse wars? The answer to this question depends on whether one believes that war can be eliminated. In principle, war could be eliminated once all those who choose war are convinced that it is in no one's interest. Achieving that state of affairs requires publics who realize that, on balance, war is always harmful, and leaders willing to forego the benefits they see in war. Obviously, antiwar activists need to continue their efforts to achieve these goals. Unfortunately, until they are achieved, more wars are inevitable. In the meantime, just war theory can provide opponents of war with grounds for dissent. By ruling that some weapons or strategies are morally untenable, it can also provide a wedge for arguing against specific policies. Such policies include the indiscriminate killing of civilians, especially women and children, and the use of weapons like depleted uranium, which poisons the environment for thousands of years.

Last, and not least, is it possible to make judgments about the justice of any given war before or during the war? J. Salisbury argues that "if a profound thinker like Augustine could not identify criteria that will allow us to determine in advance whether a war is just or not, I am persuaded that the enterprise itself is flawed."[34] She concludes that only retrospectively is it possible to determine where justice lies. Her point is well taken insofar as poor information, weak reasoning skills, and perceived self-interest can delude us about any given state of affairs. And certainly governments deeply implicated in particular bellicose policies will never acknowledge moral error nor tolerate dissent; instead, they engage in ever more transparent cover-ups to avoid having to take responsibility for wrongful policies. But thoughtful and well-informed observers may still be quite able to make well-founded judgments about particular wars. For instance, the 2001 attack on Afghanistan in retaliation for the September 11 attack on the World Trade Center has by now been entered on the roster of just wars, even by many of those who are skeptical about the subsequent attack on Iraq. Yet there were excellent grounds for observers to conclude from the beginning that the war was unjust.

The official story is that the ruling Taliban knowingly harbored Osama bin Laden, who was responsible for that attack. But apparently forgotten by all but those with elephantine memories are the Taliban's repeated offers to make bin Laden available—even before the United States started bombing the country.[35] Also forgotten are the careless military policies that led to unnecessary civilian deaths and the use of depleted uranium, which undoubtedly constitute war crimes. Thus there is reason to think that the war itself could have been prevented, and that it could, in any case, have been conducted by means more consonant with the Geneva Conventions on the moral conduct of war.[36]And those are judgments easily made, even before raising the question whether it was reasonable to make war on Afghanistan at all only because an alleged terrorist was sheltered there.

All this suggests that just war theory can be a viable framework for judging contemporary wars. An updated version of Vitoria's theory would also suggest that recent wars motivated in part by religious dogmatism fail to meet the criteria for just wars. Proponents of both Christianity and Islam would do well to take note of this conclusion. Compared with typical contemporary hawks (represented by figures such as Ann Coulter ["we should invade their countries, kill their leaders and convert them to Christianity"]),[37] Vitoria seems the very model of restraint.

NOTES

1. My grateful thanks to Jules Weiss, without whom this paper would never have seen the light of day.

2. Francisco de Vitoria, *Comentarios a la Secunda Secundae de Santo Tomás*, ed. R. P. Vicente Beltrán de Heredia, 6 vols. (Salamanca: Biblioteca de Teologos Españoles, 1932–52).

3. Teófilo Urdanoz, *Obras de Francisco de Vitoria: Relecciones Teologicas* (Madrid: Biblioteca de Autores Cristianos, 1960). Henceforth abbreviated as OFV. A *relectio* was a public lecture required of university professors at Salamanca, according to the Introduction (p. iv) of *Francisco de Vitoria: Relectio de Indis, o Libertad de Indis,* ed. Luciano Perena and J. M. Perez Prendes, Corpus Hispanorum de Pace, vol. 5 (Madrid: Consejo Superior de Investigaciones Cientificas, 1967).

4. Franciscus de Victoria, *De Indis et de Ivre Belli*, ed. Ernest Nys, trans. John Pawley Bates, vol. 7 of *The Classics of International Law*, ed. James Brown Scott (Washington, DC: Carnegie Institution of Washington, 1917). This volume contains *De Indis* and *De Iure Belli* in English, in Latin, and in facsimile, and is the text used in this work.

Henceforth the two lectures will be abbreviated as *DI* and *DIB*, respectively. I will retain "Indian," despite the more recent and respectful appellations such as "Native Americans" and "indigenous peoples."

5. Ibid.

6. This *relectio* (*DPC*) is in OFV.

7. This *relectio* (*DPE*) is also in OFV.

8. This date is from Vicente Beltrán de Heredia, in his article "Personalidad del Maestro Francisco de Vitoria y Transcendencia de su Obra Doctrinal," in Pereña and Perez Prendes, *Francisco de Vitoria*, p. xxviii.

9. James Brown Scott, *The Spanish Origin of International Law: Francisco de Vitoria and His Law of Nations* (Oxford: Clarendon Press, 1934), pp. 78ff.

10. See http://www.un.org/aboutun/charter/ (accessed May 16, 2005).

11. See the Columbia Encyclopedia, 6th ed. (2001), accessible at http://www.bartleby.com/65/ke/KelloggB.html (accessed May 16, 2005).

12. See http://www.un.org/aboutun/charter/ (accessed May 16, 2005).

13. Telford Taylor, *Nuremberg and Vietnam: An American Tragedy* (New York: Bantam Books, 1970), pp. 69–74.

14. For a thoughtful response to this doctrine, see Ivo H. Daalder, "The Preemptive-War Doctrine Has Met an Early Death in Iraq," *Los Angeles Times*, May 30, 2004; available on the Web at http://www.brookings.edu/views/op-ed/daalder/20040530.htm (accessed May 16, 2005).

15. *Politics* 4.15.1334. All references to Aristotle are based on Richard McKeon's edition (New York: Random House, 1941), titled *The Basic Works of Aristotle*. Plato also mentions war, but he appears to be concerned only with ways of waging war, not reasons for war. (See *Laws*.)

16. Albert Marrin, *War and the Christian Conscience* (Chicago: Regnery, 1971), p. 68.

17. See his *City of God*, bk. 19, *Basic Writings of Saint Augustine*, ed. Whitney J. Oates (NewYork: Random House, 1948).

18. J. Barthelemy, "François de Vitoria," *Les Fondateurs du Droit International*, ed. A. Pillet (Paris: Giard et Briere, 1904), p. 7.

19. Teófilo Urdanoz, "Sintesis Teologico-Juridica de la Doctrina de Vitoria," in Perena and Perez Prendes, *Francisco de Vitoria*, p. cxxi.

20. Vitoria, Comentario al *Tratado de la Ley*, ed. R. P. Vicente Beltrán de Heredia (Madrid: Consejo Superior de Investigaciones Cientificas, Instituto Francisco de Vitoria, 1952), qu. 90 a. 2.

21. In practice having such an excuse would be the same as having a just cause. But the two must be distinguished in theory, or else Vitoria cannot maintain as he does that only one opponent can have justice on his side.

22. Vitoria does not specify to whom the wrong must be done. It appears that the wrong may be done to a person or nation. The person or nation may attempt to remedy the injury with or without the help of others. A person may fight a defensive war without consulting his sovereign if necessary, but he cannot fight an offensive war without doing so.

23. Unfortunately, this argument appears to depend on definitions in such a way as to render it circular.

24. This third argument is of some interest, since it shows how deceptive such an appeal can be. For it is true that Augustine thought it just to fight to avenge injuries. However, either this was not the only reason one might fight, or else Augustine's conception of "injury" was so different from that which it is plausible to believe Vitoria held, as to render dangerously misleading Vitoria's reliance upon him. In fact, his view of injury was so broad that it would justify precisely those wars that Vitoria prohibits. Augustine's opinion seems clear: ". . . even wars should be waged by the good, in order to curb licentious passions by destroying those vices which should have been rooted out and suppressed by the rightful government" (*CG*, XII, III, *Basic Writings of Saint Augustine*, ed. Whitney J. Oates [New York: Random House, 1948]). Vitoria therefore does ill to cite him since he disagrees with him about when it is right to go to war. This also shows that the general claim that it is just to go to war only if one has been wronged is quite meaningless unless one goes on to discuss what is meant by "injury."

25. Vitoria, *DIB* (no. 20).

26. J. L. Brierly, "Vitoria and the International Law," *Dublin Review* 117 (1947–48): 440–44.

27. *DPC*, nos. 2–8.

28. *DPE*, nos. 10–19.

29. A propos of this point, Thomas Gilby writes: "All power I of God, yet when as a theologian he comes down to its derived forms he

attends to the actual working of existing institutions, not to their origins; they were to be accepted as long as they were not manifestly wicked." (appendix 5, in the Blackfriars edition of Thomas Aquinas's *Summa Theologiae*, vol. 28).

30. Hugo Grotius, *The Rights of War and Peace*, trans. A. Campbell (New York: M. Walter Dunne, 1901), p. 249. This line of reasoning immediately raises the question of what distinguishes those injuries that can be left for God to deal with from those that humans may avenge.

31. Vitoria, *DIB*, no. 5.

32. Ibid.

33. Brierly, "Vitoria and the International Law," p. 15.

34. J. E. Salisbury, "In Vain Have I Smitten Your Children: Augustine's Definition of Just War," *Free Inquiry* (April/May 2005): 38.

35. L. Macquaig, "Lawlessness Hurting America's 'War on Terror,'" *Toronto Star*, September 19, 2004 (cited December 4, 2004; available at www.thestar.com/NASApp/cs/ContentServer?pagename=thestar/Layout/ Article_Type1&cid=1095459009236&call-pageid=970599109774&col =Columnist1022182710415.

36. For full information on the Geneva Conventions, see http://www .genevaconventions.org/ (accessed May 16, 2005).

37. Ann Coulter, "This Is War," http://www.anncoulter.org/columns/ 2001/091301.htm (accessed April 14, 2005).

15

CSER PROTOCOL ON RELIGION, WARFARE, AND VIOLENCE

The Committee for the Scientific Examination of Religion, meeting November 5–7, 2004, at Cornell University, has approved the following statement concerning "Just War and Jihad: Religion and Violence in the Monotheistic Tradition."

- **A Failure of Education:** The Fellows of the Committee recognize significant work in the determination of the causes of violence and warfare in the modern world. They are particularly sensitive to the long association of violence and war with religious traditions in general and the Abrahamic traditions in particular. The Committee regrets that neither Church, Mosque, nor Synagogue has exerted an educational responsibility with regard to illuminating the sources of religious violence within particular confessional frameworks. Similarly, church and public schools in the United States have failed to acquaint themselves with the growing body of literature and theory which identifies religious texts, imagery, and practice as an elemental source of violence and belligerence on the world stage. Students and congregations taught to believe that religion is inherently a force for good will unavoidably conclude that violence is a permissible means to achieve the good. The protection of religion from critical public scrutiny contributes to a general illiteracy about the darker side of religious history and mythology. In conservative and "fundamentalist" circles especially, religious teachers have often encouraged anti-intellectualism as a means of maintaining authority and influence. The political consequences of such illiteracy are visible not just among the populations of villages and cities, but in world capitals and the halls of government.

- **Rejection of "Divine Authority":** The Fellows of the Committee reject the idea of transcendent or supernatural authorization for warfare and violence in the modern world. In this rejection, they reflect the nearly unanimous view of world scholarship that scriptural images of divinely authorized combat express ancient conceptions of divine kingship, sovereignty, judgment, wrath and punishment. These images, especially in the monotheistic traditions, range from poetic descriptions of God's justice to gratuitous descriptions of God's cruelty and power. Such images have been used reciprocally by all religions as vehicles of exclusion, conquest, and subjugation. They have supported colonialism, imperialism, and theocracy. Equally, they have fostered and continue to sustain cultures of violence, the abuse and subjugation of women and children, glorification of combat rather than reasoned discourse as a means of achieving resolution of conflict, slavery, and intimidation of dissenters and intellectuals.

- **The Inappropriateness of Just War Theory:** The Committee rejects the use of the religiously based logic of late antiquity and the Middle Ages in determining the causes and justification for war. In particular, it maintains that the so-called principle of double effect, the principle of "lesser evil," the right of the nation-state to determine the permissibility of preemptive action, the concept of "proportionality," and the various scholastic configurations of "justice in war," and "justification for war," are inappropriate in the light of the modern understanding and experience of warfare. The Committee cautions that the use of the scholastic trajectory from Augustine to Grotius is based on the principle of the defensibility of violence in a *specifically* Christian context (the "breaking of the peace of Christendom") and is hence inapplicable to wars waged by secular states for nonreligious, especially economic, purposes. Furthermore the Committee urges that the nature of modern warfare calls for a new calculus of war to be decided at the international level and having the status of international law without exemption. The Committee notes with regret the tendency of modern nations, the United States among them, to employ a religious calculus based on metaphysical constructs of "good" nations and "evil" nations in its decisions concerning the right to declare war. The Committee also notes the weight assigned to the biblical doctrine of *lex talionis* in wars of reprisal now being pursued by the United States, Israel, and a number of African states. The Fellows note with sobriety the growing list of nations affected by some form of religious violence.

- **The Danger of Jihadist Logic:** The Committee rejects, by the same logic, the right of the Muslim religion to wage aggressive wars in defense of its metaphysics. It encourages careful and critical examination of the Qur'anic tradition, education in the sources and application of the sunnah and sharia concerning war, and a higher intellectual commitment to critical desconstruction of the supernaturalist and eschatological tendencies which seduce and mislead the younger adherents of the Islamic tradition to commit acts of suicide and murder. The committee rejects the exceptionalism of the view that the sacred texts of the Islamic tradition are exempt from the critical examination and literary and historical criticism that have revealed the texts of the Judaeo-Christian tradition to be a product of their time and culture. The Fellows accept the view that such exceptionalism, whatever its theological grounding, has had disastrous intellectual consequences and nurtures an uncritical mind-set that obscures the distinction between historical descriptions of violence and the situation of Islam in the modern world, creating a siege mentality among many young Muslims. The same methods of inquiry that have shown the Bible as an artifact of late antiquity and its world-views should be applied consistently and courageously to the sources of Islamic teaching. The Committee further acknowl-edges that the understanding of contemporary religious violence cannot be addressed without recognizing tendencies inherently violent in a revivalist Islam, especially its intemperate suspicion of "materialism," "philosophical naturalism," "infidels," "ene-mies of God," and secular values. It acknowledges the compati-bility of humanist values and religious values only when the latter have been critically examined and determined by an under-standing of the sources of religious ideas and images, the myths and texts that support them, and the modes of behavior which they evoke. Lacking the development of a self-critical intellec-tual tradition in the Muslim world, the Committee feels the temp-tation to martyrdom and cruelty towards the "enemies" will con-tinue to be the determinant of the Islamic appraisal of the West.

- **The Sources of Religious Violence:** The sources of religious violence are not texts but persons. It is the failure to recognize the origin of religious texts and symbols in *human* experience that accounts for the disproportionate influence of these texts on human behavior. Social anthropology and comparative religion have shown that the origins of religion are to be located not in "revelation," but in primal experiences of insecurity, distrust, scarcity, and fear. The rituals developed to deal with these condi-tions emerge gradually, first in oral and then in written form (mythology). Sacred texts are thus the embodiment of strong feelings and emotions, reflecting the human need for compassion and mercy as well as the human propensity for vengeance and conquest. The Committee does not believe that the way forward is through a process of selection or "excision" of toxic texts and negative images, since texts exist in a cultural totality and can be adequately understood only as reflections of that totality. The

Fellows of CSER believe that the textual culture of the monotheistic traditions extends from the second millennium BCE to the first millennium CE and that the sacred books express patterns of social thought and organization that are of historical and literary interest only. Despite their undeniable influence over patterns in legal reasoning, these texts cannot be used uncritically as sourcebooks for ethics and law. We feel that universities must do more to illuminate the historical context of the biblical and Qur'anic worlds and to stress the human character of the text. This task must be undertaken thoughtfully and systematically, not as a Nietzschean rage at the ignorance of the masses, but with the conviction that the world cannot continue to be divided between science and superstition, or between those whose cosmology and political vision is trapped in the metaphysics of the past as they try to make sense of the present, and those who accept the world as a present reality to be discovered and interpreted using the methods of inquiry developed after the Middle Ages.

The Fellows of CSER see not a clash of civilizations but a conflict of belief systems at the heart of the present crisis: a conflict between those who believe the world is best understood as the work of a divine being who reveals his "will" in sacred writings, and those who believe these writings to be products of the human imagination.

To recognize the human imagination as the source of violent images and actions is to take the first step to limit and control their power.

FELLOWS OF THE COMMITTEE

Mona Abousena (Ain-Shams University, Cairo)
Robert Alley (University of Richmond)
Karen Armstrong (Author, UK)
Peter Atkins (Lincoln College, Oxford)

Scott Atran (University of Michigan)
Hector Avalos (Iowa State University)
Aziz al-Azmeh (Budapest)
Nadia al-Baghdadi (Central European University)
J. A. Barnhart (University of North Texas)
Clinton Bennett (Cambridge, UK)
Susan Blackmore (Science writer, UK)
Laurence A. Brown (Monash University, Australia)
Vern Bullough (University of Southern California)
Margaret Chatterjee (Oxford University)
Bill Cooke (SUNY and Center for Inquiry, Amherst)
John Dominic Crossan (DePaul University)
Don Cupitt (Emmanuel College, Cambridge)
Austin Dacey (SUNY and Center for Inquiry, Amherst)
Carol Delaney (Stanford University)
Hermann Detering (Editor, Radikalkritik, Berlin)
Arthur Droge (University of California, San Diego)
Robert Eisenman (California State University, Long Beach)
J. Harold Ellens (University of Michigan)
Alvar Ellgard (University of Goteburg, Sweden)
Reuven Firestone (Hebrew Union College)
Antony Flew (University of Reading, UK)
Robin Lane Fox (New College, Oxford)
Michael Goulder (University of Birmingham, UK)
Stuart Guthrie (Fordham University)
Samira Haj (City University of New York)
Van A. Harvey (Stanford University)
R. Joseph Hoffmann, *Chair*
Wendy Kaminer (Associate Editor, Atlantic Monthly)
Paul Kurtz (SUNY and Center for Inquiry, Amherst)
Amy Jill Levine (Vanderbilt University)
Judith Lichtenberg (University of Maryland)
Gerd Lüdemann (University of Göttingen)
Daniel Maguire (Marquette University)

Irshad Manjit (University of Toronto)
Michael Martin (Boston University)
Justin Meggitt (Cambridge University)
David Nash (Oxford-Brookes University, UK)
Pauletta Otis (Pew Trust for Religion in Public Life)
Gabriel Palmer-Fernandez (Youngstown State University)
Katha Pollitt (Contributing Editor, *The Nation*)
Robert Price (Editor, *Journal of Higher Criticism*)
Philip Pullman (Writer, Oxford)
Rosemary Radford Reuther (Pacific School of Religion)
Betsy Reed (Contributing Editor, *The Nation*)
James M. Robinson (Claremont Graduate University)
Richard E. Rubenstein (George Mason University)
Alan Ryan (New College, Oxford)
Joyce E. Salisbury (University of Wisconsin, Green Bay)
Regina Schwartz (Northwestern University)
Robert B. Tapp (University of Minnesota)
Joseph Tyson (Southern Methodist University)
Ibn Warraq (Writer, Paris)

RELIGION AND VIOLENCE

A BIBLIOGRAPHY

Compiled by Charles K. Bellinger

(This is an expanded version of a bibliography published in *The Hedgehog Review* 6, no. 1 [2004]: 111–19.)

Social Science Perspectives

The books listed here are primarily analyses of violence written by psychologists, anthropologists, and sociologists. Becker's work develops a theory of "death denial" as the root of violence. Alford's book is an updated version of Becker. Bauman argues that Nazism was the logical outcome of modern technological advances and concern for efficiency. The set of four volumes edited by Ellens is a major contribution to this topic, presenting essays by an impressive gathering of scholars in various fields. Volume 3 of Stout's collection of essays is similar. Jung is a widely read shaper of contemporary psychological thought.

Library of Congress Subject Headings

Genocide—Psychological aspects (21)
Good and evil—Psychological aspects (23)
Psychopathology (328)
Religion and Psychology (203)
Shame (99)
Violence—Psychological aspects (138)
War—Psychological aspects (80)

Aho, James Alfred. *This Thing of Darkness: A Sociology of the Enemy.* Seattle: University of Washington Press, 1994.
Alford, C. Fred. *What Evil Means to Us.* Ithaca, NY: Cornell University Press, 1997.
Bartov, Omer, and Phyllis Mack, eds. *In God's Name: Genocide and Religion in the Twentieth Century.* New York: Berghahn, 2001.
Bauman, Zygmunt. *Modernity and the Holocaust.* Ithaca, NY: Cornell University Press, 1989.
Baumeister, Roy F. *Evil: Inside Human Violence and Cruelty.* New York: W. H. Freeman, 1999.
Becker, Ernest. *Escape from Evil.* New York: Free Press, 1975.
Bromley, David G., and J. Gordon Melton, eds. *Cults, Religion, and Violence.* New York: Cambridge University Press, 2002.
Carter, Jeffrey, ed. *Understanding Religious Sacrifice: A Reader.* New York: Continuum, 2003.
Diamond, Stephen A. *Anger, Madness, and the Daimonic: The Psychological Genesis of Violence, Evil, and Creativity.* Albany, NY: State University of New York Press, 1996.
Ehrenreich, Barbara. *Blood Rites: Origins and History of the Passions of War.* New York: Metropolitan Books, 1997.
Ellens, J. Harold, ed. *The Destructive Power of Religion: Violence in Judaism, Christianity, and Islam.* 4 vols. Westport, CT: Praeger, 2004.
Gilligan, James. *Violence: Reflections on a National Epidemic.* New York: Vintage Books, 1997.
Goldberg, Carl. *Speaking with the Devil: A Dialogue with Evil.* New York: Viking, 1996.

Good, Jeanette Anderson. *Shame, Images of God, and the Cycle of Violence in Adults Who Experienced Childhood Corporal Punishment.* Lanham, MD: University Press of America, 1999.

Grossman, Dave. *On Killing: The Psychological Cost of Learning to Kill in War and Society.* Boston: Little, Brown, 1995.

Jones, James William. *Terror and Transformation: The Ambiguity of Religion in Psychoanalytic Perspective.* New York: Brunner-Routledge, 2002.

Jung, C. G. *Jung on Evil.* Edited by Murray Stein. Princeton, NJ: Princeton University Press, 1995.

Lifton, Robert Jay. *Destroying the World to Save It: Aum Shinrikyo, Apocalyptic Violence, and the New Global Terrorism.* New York: Metropolitan Books, 1999.

———. *Superpower Syndrome: America's Apocalyptic Confrontation with the World.* New York: Thunder's Mouth Press, 2003.

Martin, David. *Does Christianity Cause War?* New York: Oxford University Press, 1997.

Miller, Alice. *For Your Own Good: Hidden Cruelty in Child-rearing and the Roots of Violence.* New York: Farrar, Straus, Giroux, 1983.

Oppenheimer, Paul. *Evil and the Demonic: A New Theory of Monstrous Behavior.* New York: New York University Press, 1996.

Peck, M. Scott. *People of the Lie: The Hope for Healing Human Evil.* New York: Simon & Schuster, 1998.

Reich, Walter, ed. *Origins of Terrorism: Psychologies, Ideologies, Theologies, States of Mind.* New York: Woodrow Wilson International Center for Scholars, 1990.

Selengut, Charles. *Sacred Fury: Understanding Religious Violence.* Walnut Creek, CA: Altamira, 2003.

Stout, Chris, ed. *The Psychology of Terrorism.* Vol. 3. Westport, CT: Praeger, 2002.

Waller, James. *Becoming Evil: How Ordinary People Commit Genocide and Mass Killing.* New York: Oxford University Press, 2002.

Weinberg, Leonard, and Ami Pedahzur, eds. *Religious Fundamentalism and Political Extremism.* Portland, OR: Frank Cass, 2004.

Humanities and Religious Studies Perspectives

The books included in this section are written from the perspectives of religious studies, or philosophy, history, literature, or journalism that includes attention to religious traditions. Appleby, Juergensmeyer, and Kimball have offered widely read commentaries on the various ways in which religion and violence are related to each other in the contemporary world. The Chase and Jacobs volume contains papers given at a major conference on Christianity and violence, including a lively debate between Stanley Hauerwas and John Milbank on the ethics of violence. The Jewett and Lawrence book criticizes the tendency of Americans to simplistically identify themselves with good and their enemies with evil. The Marty and Appleby book is part of an important five-volume series analyzing fundamentalism. There is also a growing strand of books on cults, new religious movements, and the like, in relation to violence.

Library of Congress Subject Headings

Social conflict—Religious aspects (11)
Violence—Religious aspects (124)
War—Religious aspects (151)

Adams, Carol J., and Marie M. Fortune. *Violence Against Women and Children: A Christian Theological Sourcebook.* New York: Continuum, 1995.

Appleby, R. Scott. *The Ambivalence of the Sacred: Religion, Violence, and Reconciliation.* Lanham, MD: Rowman & Littlefield Publishers, 2000.

Beuken, Wim, and Karl-Josef Kuschel, eds. *Religion as a Source of Violence.* London: SCM Press; Maryknoll, NY: Orbis Books, 1997.

Candland, Christopher. *The Spirit of Violence: An Interdisciplinary Bibliography of Religion and Violence.* New York: Harry Frank Guggenheim Foundation, 1992.

Chase, Kenneth R., and Alan Jacobs, eds. *Must Christianity Be Violent?*

Reflections on History, Practice, and Theology. Grand Rapids, MI: Brazos Press, 2003.

de Vries, Hent. *Religion and Violence: Philosophical Perspectives from Kant to Derrida.* Baltimore: Johns Hopkins University Press, 2002.

Delaney, Carol Lowery. *Abraham on Trial: The Social Legacy of Biblical Myth.* Princeton, NJ: Princeton University Press, 1998.

Docherty, Jayne Seminare. *Learning Lessons from Waco: When the Parties Bring Their Gods to the Negotiation Table.* Syracuse, NY: Syracuse University Press, 2001.

Ellis, Marc H. *Unholy Alliance: Religion and Atrocity in Our Time.* Minneapolis: Fortress Press, 1997.

Erickson, Victoria Lee, and Michelle Lim Jones, eds. *Surviving Terror: Hope and Justice in a World of Violence.* Grand Rapids, MI: Brazos Press, 2002.

Fields, Rona M., ed. *Martyrdom: The Psychology, Theology, and Politics of Self-sacrifice.* Westport, CT: Praeger, 2004.

Gourevitch, Philip. *We Wish to Inform You That Tomorrow We Will Be Killed with Our Families: Stories from Rwanda.* New York: Farrar, Straus, and Giroux, 1998.

Gushee, David P. *The Righteous Gentiles of the Holocaust: A Christian Interpretation.* Minneapolis: Fortress Press, 1994.

Hall, John R., Philip Daniel Schuyler, and Sylvaine Trinh. *Apocalypse Observed: Religious Movements, and Violence in North America, Europe, and Japan.* London and New York: Routledge, 2000.

Hashmi, Sohail H., and Steven Lee, eds. *Ethics and Weapons of Mass Destruction: Religious and Secular Perspectives.* New York: Cambridge University Press, 2004.

Hedges, Chris. *War Is a Force That Gives Us Meaning.* New York: PublicAffairs, 2002.

Houben, Jan E. M., and Karel R. van Kooij, eds. *Violence Denied: Violence, Non-Violence and the Rationalization of Violence in South Asian Cultural History.* Leiden, The Netherlands: Brill, 1999.

Ignatieff, Michael. *The Warrior's Honor: Ethnic War and the Modern Conscience.* New York: Metropolitan Books, 1998.

Jewett, Robert, and John Shelton Lawrence. *Captain America and the Crusade Against Evil: The Dilemma of Zealous Nationalism.* Grand Rapids, MI: Eerdmans, 2003.

Juergensmeyer, Mark. *Terror in the Mind of God: The Global Rise of Religious Violence.* Berkeley: University of California Press, 2000.

Kakar, Sudhir. *The Colors of Violence: Cultural Identities, Religion, and Conflict.* Chicago: University of Chicago Press, 1996.

Kimball, Charles. *When Religion Becomes Evil.* San Francisco: Harper-SanFrancisco, 2002.

Kirk-Duggan, Cheryl A. *Refiner's Fire: A Religious Engagement with Violence.* Minneapolis: Fortress Press, 2001.

Lannstrom, Anna, ed. *Promise and Peril: The Paradox of Religion as Resource and Threat.* Notre Dame, IN: University of Notre Dame Press, 2003.

Levi, Ken. *Violence and Religious Commitment: Implications of Jim Jones's People's Temple Movement.* University Park: Pennsylvania State University Press, 1982.

Lincoln, Bruce. *Death, War, and Sacrifice: Studies in Ideology and Practice.* Chicago: University of Chicago Press, 1991.

Lorca, Ernesto. *One God: The Political and Moral Philosophy of Western Civilization.* Montreal: Black Rose Books, 2003.

Markham, Ian, and Ibrahim M. Abu-Rabi, eds. *11 September: Religious Perspectives on the Causes and Consequences.* Oxford: Oneworld, 2002.

Marty, Martin E., and F. Scott Appleby, eds. *Fundamentalisms and the State: Remaking Polities, Economies, and Militance.* Chicago: University of Chicago Press, 1993.

May, John D'Arcy. *Transcendence and Violence: The Encounter of Buddhist, Christian, and Primal Traditions.* New York: Continuum, 2003.

McTernan, Oliver. *Violence in God's Name: Religion in an Age of Conflict.* Maryknoll, NY: Orbis Books, 2003.

Milbank, John. *Theology and Social Theory: Beyond Secular Reason.* Cambridge, MA: Blackwell, 1991.

Palmer-Fernandez, Gabriel, ed. *The Encyclopedia of Religion and War.* New York: Routledge, 2004.

Perica, Vjekoslav. *Balkan Idols: Religion and Nationalism in Yugoslav States.* New York: Oxford University Press, 2002.

Reuter, Christoph. *My Life Is a Weapon: A Modern History of Suicide Bombing.* Princeton, NJ: Princeton University Press, 2004.

Rittner, Carol, John K. Roth, and Wendy Whitworth, eds. *Genocide in Rwanda: Complicity of the Churches?* St. Paul, MN: Aegis, 2004.

Robbins, Thomas, and Susan J. Palmer. *Millennium, Messiahs, and Mayhem: Contemporary Apocalyptic Movements.* New York: Routledge, 1997.

Rosenbaum, Ron. *Explaining Hitler: The Search for the Origins of His Evil.* New York: Random House, 1998.

Schwartz, Regina M. *The Curse of Cain: The Violent Legacy of Monotheism.* Chicago: University of Chicago Press, 1997.

Snow, Robert L. *Deadly Cults: The Crimes of True Believers.* Westport, CT: Praeger, 2003.

Steffen, Lloyd. *The Demonic Turn: The Power of Religion to Inspire or Restrain Violence.* Cleveland: Pilgrim Press, 2003.

Suchocki, Marjorie. *The Fall to Violence: Original Sin in Relational Theology.* New York: Continuum, 1994.

Voegelin, Eric. *Modernity Without Restraint: The Political Religions, The New Science of Politics and Science, Politics, and Gnosticism.* Columbia: University of Missouri Press, 2000.

Wessinger, Catherine Lowman. *How the Millennium Comes Violently: From Jonestown to Heaven's Gate.* New York: Seven Bridges Press, 2000.

René Girard, His Followers, and Critics

If there is one voice that stands out in the realm of reflections on religion and violence, it is certainly that of René Girard. His religiously framed and interdisciplinary theory of human psychology and cultural formation through violence has already spawned a large secondary literature of response and critical commentary. Many of these works take Girard's ideas and restate, popularize, or apply them to specific topics, and are written from the perspective of an admiring follower. My contribution, *The Genealogy of Violence*, brings Girard's ideas into conversation with the insights into human behavior that are present in Kierkegaard's thought.

In my opinion, Girard ought to be nominated for the Nobel

Prize for Literature (or Peace), but it is doubtful that he is even on the radar screen of the nominating committee. If that prize can be given to Sartre and Churchill, it could certainly be given to an author whose ideas are likely to make a significant contribution to any substantive improvement in human self-understanding that may occur in the twenty-first century.

A significant database of information on primary and secondary works relating to Girard is located on the Web site of the Colloquium on Violence and Religion, http://theol.uibk.ac.at/cover/

Library of Congress Subject Headings

Girard, René, 1923– (20)
Sacrifice (96)
Scapegoat (16)
Violence—Religious aspects—Christianity (56)

Alison, James. *Raising Abel: The Recovery of Eschatological Imagination.* New York: Crossroad, 1996.
Bailie, Gil. *Violence Unveiled: Humanity at the Crossroads.* New York: Crossroad, 1995.
Bartlett, Anthony W. *Cross Purposes: The Violent Grammar of Christian Atonement.* Harrisburg, PA: Trinity Press International, 2001.
Bellinger, Charles K. *The Genealogy of Violence: Reflections on Creation, Freedom, and Evil.* New York: Oxford University Press, 2001.
Girard, René. *The Girard Reader.* Edited by James G. Williams. New York: Crossroad, 1996.
———. *I See Satan Fall Like Lightning.* Maryknoll, NY: Orbis Books, 2001.
———. *The Scapegoat.* Baltimore: Johns Hopkins University Press, 1986.
———. *Violence and the Sacred.* Baltimore: Johns Hopkins University Press, 1977.
Girard, René, Jean-Michel Oughourlian, and Guy Lefort. *Things Hidden since the Foundation of the World.* Stanford, CA: Stanford University Press, 1987.

Hamerton-Kelly, Robert. *Sacred Violence: Paul's Hermeneutic of the Cross.* Minneapolis: Fortress Press, 1992.

Juergensmeyer, Mark, ed. *Violence and the Sacred in the Modern World.* London: Frank Cass, 1992.

Lefebure, Leo D. *Revelation, the Religions, and Violence.* Maryknoll, NY: Orbis Books, 2000.

Reineke, Martha Jane. *Sacrificed Lives: Kristeva on Women and Violence.* Bloomington: Indiana University Press, 1997.

Schwager, Raymund. *Must There Be Scapegoats? Violence and Redemption in the Bible.* San Francisco: Harper & Row, 1987.

Swartley, Willard M., ed. *Violence Renounced: René Girard, Biblical Studies, and Peacemaking.* Telford, PA: Pandora Press, 2000.

Wallace, Mark I. *Fragments of the Spirit: Nature, Violence, and the Renewal of Creation.* New York: Continuum, 1996.

Wallace, Mark I., and Theophus Harold Smith, eds. *Curing Violence.* Sonoma, CA: Polebridge Press, 1994.

Webb, Eugene. *Philosophers of Consciousness: Polanyi, Lonergan, Voegelin, Ricoeur, Girard, Kierkegaard.* Seattle: University of Washington Press, 1988.

Williams, James G. *The Bible, Violence, and the Sacred: Liberation from the Myth of Sanctioned Violence.* San Francisco: HarperSanFrancisco, 1992.

Commentaries on Islam, Violence, and Terrorism

This is a sampling of the many works that were published before the September 11 attacks, and some since then, that consider the relationship between Islam and violence. Many of these works have the conscious intention of providing a counterbalance to the distorted views of Islam that are unfortunately widespread in the West. Huntington's work describing the "bloody borders of Islam" has provoked much discussion and critique in academic circles (including the book by Jonathan Sacks listed in the "Peacemaking and Conflict Resolution" section below). James Turner Johnson, Bruce B. Lawrence, and Bernard Lewis are widely recognized as "deans" of this field of study.

Library of Congress Subject Headings

Islamic Fundamentalism (146)
Jihad (54)
Terrorism—Psychological aspects (37)
Terrorism—Religious aspects (99)
War—Religious aspects—Islam (17)

Akbar, M. J. *The Shade of Swords: Jihad and the Conflict Between Islam and Christianity.* New York: Routledge, 2002.

Davis, Joyce. *Martyrs: Innocence, Vengeance, and Despair in the Middle East.* New York: Palgrave, 2003.

Easwaran, Eknath. *Nonviolent Soldier of Islam: Badshah Khan, A Man to Match His Mountains.* Tomales, CA: Nilgiri Press, 1999.

Firestone, Reuven. *Jihad: The Origin of Holy War in Islam.* New York: Oxford University Press, 1999.

Huband, Mark. *Warriors of the Prophet: The Struggle for Islam.* Boulder, CO: Westview Press, 1998.

Huntington, Samuel P. *The Clash of Civilizations and the Remaking of World Order.* New York: Simon & Schuster, 1998.

Johnson, James Turner. *The Holy War Idea in Western and Islamic Traditions.* University Park: Pennsylvania State University Press, 1997.

Johnson, James Turner, and John Kelsay. *Cross, Crescent, and Sword: The Justification and Limitation of War in Western and Islamic Tradition.* New York: Greenwood Press, 1990.

Kepel, Gilles. *Jihad: The Trail of Political Islam.* Cambridge, MA: Harvard University Press, 2002.

Lawrence, Bruce B. *Shattering the Myth: Islam Beyond Violence.* Princeton, NJ: Princeton University Press, 1998.

Lewis, Bernard. *What Went Wrong? Western Impact and Middle Eastern Response.* New York: Oxford University Press, 2002.

Meddeb, Abdelwahab. *The Malady of Islam.* New York: Basic Books, 2003.

Mozaffari, Mehdi. *Fatwa: Violence & Discourtesy.* Aarhus, Denmark: Aarhus University Press, 1998.

Nelson-Pallmeyer, Jack. *Is Religion Killing Us? Violence in the Bible and the Quran.* Harrisburg, PA: Trinity Press International, 2003.

Partner, Peter. *God of Battles: Holy Wars of Christianity and Islam.* London: HarperCollins, 1997.

Reuter, Christoph. *My Life Is a Weapon: A Modern History of Suicide Bombing.* Princeton, NJ: Princeton University Press, 2004.

Victor, Barbara. *Army of Roses: Inside the World of Palestinian Women Suicide Bombers.* Emmaus, PA: Rodale, 2003.

Responses to 9/11

If you are imagining that there has been a flood of books written about the terrorist attacks of September 11, 2001, you are right. This is a very selective listing of some of them. The current archbishop of Canterbury, Rowan Williams, who happened to have been in Manhattan on the day of the attacks, has offered thoughtful reflections on how the West ought to work through its emotional and political/ethical response to terrorism. Cooper draws on the philosophy of Eric Voegelin. Esposito, Lewis, Stern, and Lincoln are experts on Islam with important insights to offer from their years of study.

Library of Congress Subject Headings

September 11 Terrorist Attacks, 2001 (392)

Benjamin, Daniel, and Steven Simon. *The Age of Sacred Terror.* New York: Random House, 2002.

Berquist, Jon L., ed. *Strike Terror No More: Theology, Ethics, and the New War.* St. Louis: Chalice Press, 2002.

Cooper, Barry. *New Political Religions, or an Analysis of Modern Terrorism.* Columbia: University of Missouri Press, 2004.

Esposito, John L. *Unholy War: Terror in the Name of Islam.* New York: Oxford University Press, 2002.

Heyward, Carter. *God in the Balance: Christian Spirituality in Times of Terror.* Cleveland: Pilgrim Press, 2002.

Ignatieff, Michael. *The Lesser Evil: Political Ethics in an Age of Terror.* Princeton, NJ: Princeton University Press, 2004.

Langford, James R., and Leroy S. Rouner, eds. *Walking with God in a Fragile World*. Lanham, MD: Rowman & Littlefield, 2003.

Lewis, Bernard. *The Crisis of Islam: Holy War and Unholy Terror*. New York: Modern Library, 2003.

Lincoln, Bruce. *Holy Terrors: Thinking About Religion after September 11*. Chicago: University of Chicago Press, 2003.

Pyszczynski, Thomas A., Sheldon Solomon, and Jeff Greenberg. *In the Wake of 9/11: The Psychology of Terror*. Washington, DC: American Psychological Association, 2003.

Scruton, Roger. *The West and the Rest: Globalization and the Terrorist Threat*. Wilmington, DE: ISI Books, 2002.

Stern, Jessica. *Terror in the Name of God: Why Religious Militants Kill*. New York: Ecco, 2003.

Williams, Rowan. *Writing in the Dust: After September 11*. Grand Rapids, MI: Eerdmans, 2002.

Sermons

Church, Forrest, ed. *Restoring Faith: America's Religious Leaders Answer Terror with Hope*. New York: Walker, 2001.

Kraybill, Donald B., and Linda Gehman Peachey, eds. *Where Was God on September 11? Seeds of Faith and Hope*. Scottdale, PA: Herald Press, 2002.

Polk, David P., ed. *Shaken Foundations: Sermons from America's Pulpits after the Terrorist Attacks*. St. Louis: Chalice Press, 2001.

Simmons, Martha J., and Frank A. Thomas, eds. *9.11.01: African American Leaders Respond to an American Tragedy*. Valley Forge, PA: Judson Press, 2001.

Willimon, William H., ed. *The Sunday after Tuesday: College Pulpits Respond to 9/11*. Nashville: Abingdon Press, 2002.

Peacemaking and Conflict Resolution

Out of the immense literature on peacemaking in general, I have selected some of the works that specifically focus on religious aspects of the problem. Lederach and Stassen are leaders in the area of conflict resolution strategizing. The Easwaran book tells the fascinating story of Badshah Khan, a Muslim associate of Gandhi. The Chappell, Goleman, and Nhât Hanh books present Buddhist perspectives on peace. Gopin is a Jewish scholar deeply involved in issues of interreligious dialogue between Jews, Christians, and Muslims in the Middle East. Volf, Wink, and Yoder are significant contributors to theological discussions of peacemaking in Christian circles. I haven't listed any of the immense literature by and about Gandhi simply because that could be a book unto itself.

Library of Congress Subject Headings

Conflict management—Religious aspects (41)
Nonviolence—Biblical teaching (10)
Peace—Moral and ethical aspects (22)
Peace—Religious aspects (280)

Abu-Nimer, Mohammed. *Nonviolence and Peace Building in Islam: Theory and Practice*. Gainesville: University Press of Florida, 2003.
Ariarajah, S. Wesley. *Axis of Peace: Christian Faith in Times of Violence and War*. Geneva: WCC Publications, 2004.
Arinze, Francis A. *Religions for Peace: A Call for Solidarity to the Religions of the World*. New York: Doubleday, 2002.
Barbé, Dominique. *A Theology of Conflict and Other Writings on Nonviolence*. Maryknoll, NY: Orbis Books, 1989.
Burns, J. Patout, ed. *War and Its Discontents: Pacifism and Quietism in the Abrahamic Traditions*. Washington, DC: Georgetown University Press, 1996.
Campbell, Charles L. *The Word Before the Powers: An Ethic of Preaching*. Louisville, KY: Westminster John Knox Press, 2002.
Carmody, Denise Lardner, and John Carmody. *Peace and Justice in the Scriptures of the World Religions: Reflections on Non-Christian Scriptures*. New York: Paulist Press, 1988.
Chappell, David W., ed. *Buddhist Peacework: Creating Cultures of Peace*. Somerville, MA: Wisdom Publications, 1999.
Coffey, Joseph I., and Charles T. Mathewes, eds. *Religion, Law, and the*

Role of Force: A Study of Their Influence on Conflict and on Conflict Resolution. Ardsley, NY: Transnational Publishers, 2002.

Coward, Harold, and Gordon S. Smith, eds. *Religion and Peacebuilding.* Albany: State University of New York Press, 2004.

Easwaran, Eknath. *Nonviolent Soldier of Islam: Badshah Khan, A Man to Match His Mountains.* Tomales, CA: Nilgiri, 1999.

Frost, J. William. *A History of Christian, Jewish, Hindu, Buddhist, and Muslim Perspectives on War and Peace.* 2 vols. Lewiston, NY: Edwin Mellen Press, 2004.

Goleman, Daniel. *Destructive Emotions: How Can We Overcome Them? A Scientific Dialogue with the Dalai Lama.* New York: Bantam Books, 2003.

Gopin, Marc. *Between Eden and Armageddon: The Future of World Religions, Violence, and Peacemaking.* New York: Oxford University Press, 2000.

———. *Holy War, Holy Peace: How Religion Can Bring Peace to the Middle East.* New York: Oxford University Press, 2002.

Gordon, Hayim, and Leonard Grob, eds. *Education for Peace: Testimonies from World Religions.* Maryknoll, NY: Orbis Books, 1987.

Johnson, David M., ed. *Justice and Peace Education: Models for College and University Faculty.* Maryknoll, NY: Orbis Books, 1986.

Johnson, James Turner. *The Quest for Peace: Three Moral Traditions in Western Cultural History.* Princeton, NJ: Princeton University Press, 1987.

Küng, Hans. *Global Responsibility: In Search of a New World Ethic.* New York: Crossroad, 1991.

Lederach, John Paul. *The Journey Toward Reconciliation.* Scottdale, PA: Herald Press, 1999.

———. *Preparing for Peace: Conflict Transformation Across Cultures.* Syracuse, NY: Syracuse University Press, 1995.

Nardin, Terry, ed. *The Ethics of War and Peace: Religious and Secular Perspectives.* Princeton, NJ: Princeton University Press, 1996.

Nhât Hanh, Thích. *Creating True Peace: Ending Violence in Yourself, Your Family, Your Community, and the World.* New York: Free Press, 2003.

Peck, M. Scott. *The Different Drum: Community-Making and Peace.* New York: Simon and Schuster, 1987.

Rouner, Leroy S., ed. *Religion, Politics, and Peace.* Notre Dame, IN: University of Notre Dame Press, 1999.

Sacks, Jonathan. *The Dignity of Difference: How to Avoid the Clash of Civilizations*. New York: Continuum, 2002.

Said, Abdul Aziz, Nathan C. Funk, and Ayse S. Kadayifci, eds. *Peace and Conflict Resolution in Islam: Precept and Practice*. Lanham, MD: University Press of America, 2001.

Sampson, Cynthia, and John Paul Lederach, eds. *From the Ground Up: Mennonite Contributions to International Peacebuilding*. New York: Oxford University Press, 2000.

Schmookler, Andrew Bard. *Out of Weakness: Healing the Wounds That Drive Us to War*. New York: Bantam Books, 1988.

Schrock-Shenk, Carolyn, and Lawrence Ressler. *Making Peace with Conflict: Practical Skills for Conflict Transformation*. Scottdale, PA: Herald Press, 1999.

Smith-Christopher, Daniel L., ed. *Subverting Hatred: The Challenge of Nonviolence in Religious Traditions*. New York: Orbis Books, 2000.

Smock, David R. *Perspectives on Pacifism: Christian, Jewish, and Muslim Views on Nonviolence and International Conflict*. Washington, DC: United States Institute of Peace Press, 1995.

Stassen, Glen. *Just Peacemaking: Transforming Initiatives for Justice and Peace*. Louisville, KY: Westminster John Knox, 1992.

Stassen, Glen, ed. *Just Peacemaking: Ten Practices for Abolishing War*. Cleveland: Pilgrim Press, 1998.

Volf, Miroslav. *Exclusion and Embrace: A Theological Exploration of Identity, Otherness, and Reconciliation*. Nashville: Abingdon Press, 1996.

Wink, Walter. *The Powers That Be: Theology for a New Millennium*. New York: Doubleday, 1998.

Yoder, John Howard. *Nevertheless: Varieties of Religious Pacifism*. Scottdale, PA: Herald Press, 1992.

CONTRIBUTORS

Hector Avalos is associate professor of religious studies at Iowa State University. He is the author of *Health Care and the Rise of Christianity* and *Fighting Words: The Origins of Religious Violence.*

Charles K. Bellinger is professor of religious studies at Brite Divinity School, Texas Christian University. A distinguished bibliographer in the field of religious violence, he is the author of *The Genealogy of Violence: Reflections on Creation, Freedom, and Evil.*

Bahar Davary, University of San Diego, is a specialist in gender in Islam, Islam and the political order, and interreligious dialogue.

Carol Delaney, a Stanford University sociologist, was winner of the Galler Prize and was formerly associate director of the Harvard Center for the Study of World Religions.

J. Harold Ellens is a practicing psychologist and research lecturer at the University of Michigan. He is the editor of the distinguished four-volume work *The Destructive Power of Religion: Violence in Christianity, Judaism and Islam.*

Reuven Firestone is professor of medieval Judaism and Islam at Hebrew Union College, Los Angeles, where he directs the Mangin School of Graduate Studies. He is the author of *Jihad: The Origin of Holy War in Islam, Children of Abraham: An Introduction to Judaism for Muslims*, and many other titles.

R. Joseph Hoffmann is Campbell Professor of Religion and Human Values at Wells College and a specialist in the social history of early Christianity. He is the author of a number of books in the history of the church and translator/compiler of *Celsus: On True Doctrine* and *Julian's Against the Galileans*.

Judith Lichtenberg is a philosopher at the University of Maryland and author of "Preemption and Exceptionalism in US Foreign Policy" and "Judging Soldiers Whose Cause Is Unjust."

Pauletta Otis is Senior Fellow at the Pew Forum on Religion and Public Life in Washington, DC. An expert on cultural and religious violence in the global context, she is the author of *Conflict Prevention: Path to Peace or Grand Illusion?* and *Ethnic Conflict: What Kind of War?*

Gabriel Palmer-Fernandez, professor of religion and philosophy at Youngstown State University, is the editor of the *Routledge Encyclopaedia of Religion and War*.

Laura Purdy is Koch Professor of Humanities at Wells College and was a bioethicist at the University of Toronto. She is the author of *Reproducing Persons* and has written on the history of "just war" theory

Joyce E. Salisbury is a historian and social theorist who teaches at the University of Wisconsin, Green Bay. She is the author of a number of important works on the role of gender in world religions, including *Blood of the Martyrs: Unintended Consequences of Ancient Violence*.

Regina M. Schwartz is professor of religion at Northwestern University and director of the Chicago Institute for Religion, Ethics, and Violence. She is the author of *The Curse of Cain: The Violent Legacy of Monotheism* and many other titles.

Robert B. Tapp, professor emeritus of humanities, religious studies, and South Asian studies at the University of Minnesota, is faculty chair of the Humanist Institute in New York. He is the editor of the distinguished series Humanism Today.